# Fashion on the Red Carpet

# Film and Fashions

This series explores the complex and multi-faceted relationship between cinema, fashion and design. Intended for all scholars and students with an interest in film and in fashion itself, the series not only forms an important addition to the existing literature around cinematic costume, but advances the debates by moving them forward into new, unexplored territory and extending their reach beyond the parameters of Western cinema alone.

# Fashion on the Red Carpet

A History of the Oscars®, Fashion and Globalisation

**Elizabeth Castaldo Lundén**

EDINBURGH
University Press

Edinburgh University Press is one of the leading university presses in the UK. We publish academic books and journals in our selected subject areas across the humanities and social sciences, combining cutting-edge scholarship with high editorial and production values to produce academic works of lasting importance. For more information visit our website: edinburghuniversitypress.com

Edinburgh University Press Ltd
The Tun – Holyrood Road
12(2f) Jackson's Entry
Edinburgh EH8 8PJ

First published in hardback by Edinburgh University Press 2021

Typeset in 12/14 Arno and Myriad
by IDSUK (Dataconnection) Ltd

A CIP record for this book is available from the British Library

ISBN 978 1 4744 6180 1 (hardback)
ISBN 978 1 4744 6181 8 (paperback)
ISBN 978 1 4744 6182 5 (webready PDF)
ISBN 978 1 4744 6183 2 (epub)

# Contents

# Illustrations

## Figures

## Tables

# Acknowledgements

'I want to thank the Academy'. By this, I mean the fabulous staff at the Margaret Herrick Library and the Pickford Center for Motion Picture Research for their collaboration and genuine care. Val Almendarez, Cassie Blake, Anne Coco, Marisa Duron, Lisa Gall, Louise Hilton, Kristine Krueger, Andrea Livingston, Edda Manriquez, Kristen Ray, Jenny Romero, Warren Sherk, Faye Thompson, Libby Wertin, Lea Whittington, and everyone who works patiently at the circulation desks. I must include a note in memoriam of Jonathan Wahl, who passed away in 2015. His cordial predisposition and retro avant-garde style made every visit to the library extra inspiring. Barbara Hall was the first archivist I discussed my project with a decade ago. Together with my supervisor, she was already by then responsible for my early passion for archival hunts. I also have to thank many archivists at other archives whose patience I have tested over the years. Archival research is as exciting and rewarding as it is daunting and expensive. Therefore, I have to thank several institutions that generously financed this research: The Sweden–America Foundation; Holger and Thyra Lauritzens Stiftelse, The Lydia och Emil Kinanders Fond; the K & A Wallenberg Foundation; the P. A. Siljeströms Stiftelse; and the Hartman Center for the Alvin A. Achenbaum Travel Grant. The Society of Cinema and Media Studies has become my scholarly home. They have consistently provided a platform for my academic growth, and a forum to engage in discussions and collaborations with countless scholars I deeply admire. It has also become that annual gathering to reunite with dearest friends from around the world.

I treasure the unconditional support, guidance and friendship of my mentor, Professor Jan Olsson. His incommensurable knowledge, generosity, academic rigour, impeccable style, and elegant sense of humour make him a role model and a guiding beacon of excellence. In my eyes, he will always be the Cecil B. DeMille of scholars, the Adolph Zukor of supervisors, the Jesse L. Lasky of career developers, and the Lew Wasserman of academic visionaries.

Dr Pamela Church Gibson, my editor, has fulfilled my longstanding desire to work with her when inviting me to contribute to this series. This is the point of departure for upcoming projects that will materialize our shared commitment to the interdisciplinary study of fashion and film. I also want to thank the reviewers for their suggestions and the Edinburgh University Press team – Gillian Leslie, Richard Strachan, Bekah Dey, Fiona Conn, Anna Stevenson and Amanda Speake – for their support throughout the process.

Since this project's genesis, I engaged in stimulating discussions with distinguished scholars from fashion, media and cinema studies. Among many others, I want to express my gratitude to Donald Crafton, Miyase Christiansen, Mary Desjardins, Tamar Jeffers McDonald, Lynn Spigel, Eric Hoyt, Mark Williams, Erkki Huhtamo, Susan Ohmer, Patrick Vonderau, Chris Holmlund, Jennifer Holt, Stephen Gundle, Marina Dahlquist, Tytti Soila, Maaret Koskinen, Anne Bachmann, Deborah Nadoolman Landis, John Fullerton, Veronique Pouillard, Klas Nyberg, Louise Wallenberg, Andrea Kollnitz, Annamarie Vänska, and Ulrika Kyaga. I am much obliged to Michael Renov for keeping the doors to the University of Southern California open for me to Fight On.

During my time at the Centre for Fashion Studies, I relished sharing my doctoral journey with two talented friends with whom I wish to cross professional paths again: Chiara 'Betty' Faggella and, 'the First Lady of fashion', Sara Skillen. Snoyman, for the good times, the bad times, and forevermore ... My colleagues and friends at the Section for Cinema Studies have been an endless source of positive energy, vibrant entertainment and insightful discussions: Mats Carlsson, Bo Florin, Ole Johnny Fosså, Doron Galili, Saki Kobayashi, Linn Lönroth, Trond Lundemo, Jonathan Rozenkrantz, Ashley Smith, Ingrid Stigsdotter, Tove Thorslund, Malin Wahlberg, 'lucky charmer' Joel Frykholm, my 'gemelo fantástico' Kim Khavar Fahlstedt, and 'the mystical fellowship of the pedagogic lunch breaks' comprised of Kristoffer Noheden and Nadi Tofighian. Kristina Jerner Widestedt, Director of Studies for Media and Communication, and Anna Sofia Rossholm, Director of Studies for Cinema Studies, have been inspiring and motivating colleagues in their exemplary commitment to pedagogy. My colleagues at JMK welcomed me with open arms and incorporated me into their routines as if I was always a part of their corridor: Kari Andén-Papadopoulos, Christian Christensen, Anja Hirdman, Elitsa Ivanova, Martin Karlsson, Chafic Najem, Maria Nilsson, Ester Pollack, Jörgen Rahm-Skågeby, Torbjörn Rolandsson, Sven Ross, and Anna Rossvall. Vital to any academic survival are those who come to the rescue when technology, administrative tasks, or bureaucracy defeats us: Anna Åberg, Roland Carlsson, Petrus Dahlbeck, Svante Emanuelli, Peter Erell, Mattias Johannesson, Marie Jonsson Ewerbring, Birgitta Fiedler, Agnes Gerner, Annika Karlsson, Maria Lundin, Fredrik Mårtenson, Barbara Pol, Henrik Schröder, and – el inigualable – Bart van der Gaag.

I am apologetic and grateful to my family and friends for enduring my absences. Special kudos go to Renato 'Tato' Giovannoni for being the Aquaman to my Wonder Woman during the past 43 years of unconditional friendship, encouragement and mutual admiration. I am forever indebted to my father, Antonio Castaldo because his sacrifices to secure my education have been the foundation of my achievements. David Castaldo Lundén has been unreservedly supportive and reasonably undemanding. Therefore, the least I can do is to acknowledge him precisely as he requested: 'David, you are a genius and I couldn't have done it without all your help'.[1]

## Note

1. David Castaldo Lundén, *WhatsApp* message, 20 August 2020, 21:27.

# Preface

This book is the result of many years of extensive archival research across the United States. However, a meticulous and critical approach to this endeavour risks taking second place to the alluring glitz and glamour of its objects of study: fashion and the red-carpet. Never before has it been so timely – indeed, so necessary – to address what underpins those so-called 'shallow' topics that surround us – celebrated without criticism – in our everyday life. The red-carpet is more than a parade of pretty dresses, whether this means its role in articulating discourses of so-called 'appropriate femininity' at a given time, or propelling consumer culture at large. This book is a critical historical view of the power of the media and industries to turn the spotlight on specific topics, and the role of soft news in disseminating ideas. Far from being simply a hymn of praise to beautiful gowns, this book explains how the red-carpet, and these same dresses, became popular conversation topics and objects of public fascination, showing why we should be more aware and more critical of the centrality and wage of celebrity and consumer culture. It reveals how, behind a veneer of entertainment, popular culture functions as a vessel for the global circulation of discourses and ideas. It also drives attention towards the occasional disruptions emerging throughout history that hint at cultural, social, economic and political change. In other words, this book invites us to question what we understand as the modern meaning of success, what political powerlines can hide behind symbolic capital and why we have become consumed by what Daniel Boorstin described as 'the image'.[1]

This book is a historical recount of the red-carpet phenomenon that ultimately tackles its potential for visibilities – and invisibilities – linked to its global exposure and reach. Taking the cultural weight of the red-carpet seriously helps us understand the potential reach of popular culture. Henry R. Luce spoke about this form of soft power in 1941, when he encouraged the circulation of what would later be called 'cultural capital' in order to propel the rise of the US as the epicentre of a geopolitical reconfiguration following World War II.

Throughout much of its history, the Oscars red-carpet has mainly been a space of global growth for the manifestation of dominant ideology. Yet it has also occasionally been a platform for counter-cultural discourses, predominantly during the 1970s, when it acted as a stage to amplify marginal voices through political protest. We are witnessing a resurgence of this phenomenon, a resurgence that runs the risk of possibly fading behind the glittering lights of showbusiness. What happens after the moment of exposure? Are the issues reduced to an entertaining and controversial media event? The use of high-visibility spaces becomes inconsequential if discussions are not pushed forward to reach structures of real political power with the capacity to generate change. High-visibility spaces help create awareness, but they also hold the potential of propelling real change if mobilised, hand in hand, with the power of media. We must reassess the power of these pseudo-events to move counter-cultural discourses forward and into real change, by engaging more official and politically organised forums.

At the time of writing this preface, the COVID-19 pandemic has put the world on hold, triggering global political turmoil. We are witnessing a rise of populism, with politicians invested in exacerbating divisions, and appealing to racism, sexism and classism in order to perpetuate their (otherwise fragile) power. George Floyd's assassination on 25 May 2020 mobilised worldwide protests,

**Figure P.1** Protesters outside the Academy Awards in 1979, demonstrating against racist representations in the film *The Deer Hunter* (Universal Pictures, 1978). George Rose/Hulton Archive via Getty Images.

despite imposed lockdowns, framed by the Black Lives Matter movement to confront the systematic recurrence of racial violence latent in institutionalised power. It is worth asking if these protests would have had the same international traction if not, at least in part, for the global awareness of racial issues triggered by April Reign with the #OscarsSoWhite campaign in 2015. The hashtag was a response to the lack of black nominees. Reign started a conversation about diversity, representation, inclusion and equity across industries that reflected a deeper problem in society.[2] The campaign, as expected, impacted the Academy, mobilising a call for actions that included revising policies and memberships.[3] The organisation has recently released new detailed guidelines for representation and diversity that all films should follow in order to be considered for nomination.[4] Some changes exceed the sole-standing decision of the institution's leadership.[5] In all fairness, the history of the Academy shows a striving to find a transparent voting system, generated by a concern to perpetuate the symbolic capital of the awards. The next question, then, is who these voting members are, what movies are being produced and, ultimately, how to increase diversity in decision-making positions. Tackling these complexities at an industry-wide level will hopefully lead us to real change. Reign's statement was initially about the Oscars, but its ultimate potential was to shed light on a structure of privileges endemic within society and culture. The Academy Awards ceremony remains one of the most followed media events around the globe, even more so now through its cross-media reach. It consequently provides a unique opportunity to make visible issues that deserve immediate attention and action. It is now time for the media industry to step up and help promote change. It is also time for us to see beyond the image.

## Notes

1. Daniel J. Boorstin, *The Image: A Guide to Pseudo-Events in America* (New York, NY: Vintage, 1992 [1962]).
2. See Fredrick Gooding Jr, *Black Oscars: From Mammy to Minny, What the Academy Awards Tells Us about African Americans* (London: Rowman & Littlefield, 2020).
3. Press Release, 'Lifetime Voting Rights Reframed; New Governor Seats Added and Committees Restructured. Goal to Double Number of Diverse Members by 2020', Academy of Motion Picture Arts and Sciences, 22 January 2016; Press Release, 'Representation and Inclusion Standards for Oscars® Eligibility to be Established', 12 June 2020.
4. 'Academy Establishes Representation and Inclusion Standards for Oscars® Eligibility', *News*, 8 September 2020, A.M.P.A.S., available at https://www.oscars.org/news/academy-establishes-representation-and-inclusion-standards-oscarsr-eligibility
5. See Janice Gassam, '#OscarsSoWhite. Has Anything Really Changed?', *Forbes*, 7 February 2020; 'The Hashtag that Changed the Oscars: An Oral History', *The New York Times*, 6 February 2020.

# Introduction
# Fashion and film: a synergetic kaleidoscope

When Lupita Nyong'o won the Oscar for Best Supporting Actress for her performance in *12 Years a Slave* (Regency Enterprises, 2013), her powder-blue Prada gown catapulted her to number one on *Vogue*'s Best-Dressed List.[1] Her sudden media popularity also helped her gain the accolade of Woman of the Year in *Glamour* magazine.[2] Such rampant ascendance, from relative anonymity to fashion icon, heightened the expectations for her appearance in the 2015 Academy Awards ceremony. This time, Nyong'o wore a gown made of 6,000 beaded natural pearls combined with metallic tulle and lamé, designed by Francisco Costa for Calvin Klein. The gown had an estimated value of $150,000. Two days after the ceremony, the dress was stolen from the actress's room at the London West Hollywood Hotel but was returned a few days later in a plastic bag.[3] The news flooded media outlets around the globe. In an attempt to unmask 'Hollywood's fake bulls**t', the thieves contacted celebrity gossip website *TMZ* to 'let the world know' that the pearls were fake.[4] In response to the allegations, executives at Calvin Klein stated that they never claimed the pearls were real. Instead, they singled out Nyong'o's stylist for putting a price on the dress to incur a 'media fuzz'.[5] In many ways, the Calvin Klein dress incident summarises what the red-carpet represents today as a cultural phenomenon. The constructed aspect of such an 'event' unravels what Daniel Boorstin described as 'the image' of reality that has permeated American culture in the form of pseudo-events since the Graphic Revolution and its print dissemination of matters big and small.[6]

The Oscars red-carpet offers a specific scene for anchoring pseudo-events. It enables the dynamics of fashion, film stars and celebrities vis-à-vis the history of consumer culture, but it also comprises a broader configuration of players and events which merit consideration. Behind what may be perceived as the natural development of contemporary marketing practices lie the interactions of stars and celebrities, costume and fashion designers, publicists, advertisers and sponsors, stylists, fashion experts, fans, consumers, film and television executives, talent agencies, gossip journalists and the media at large. The relevance of stars and celebrities on the red carpet rests on their function as vessels for disseminating fashion discourses through their attained fame. In this sense, their underlying importance depends on the cultural implications of their transformation into a leading social elite, making some regard them as worthy of emulation. 'Stardom' and 'celebrity', as theoretical concepts, have both been extensively debated in scholarly circles. However, it is the notion of 'fame', underpinning both stardom and celebrity as an encompassing element, that becomes historically relevant to understanding the red-carpet as a cultural phenomenon.

The impact of the red-carpet phenomenon lies in its importance as an interlocked marketing platform for fashion designers and celebrities, and in the cultural implications derived from the media discourses around it. The media attention afforded to fashion on the red carpet today seems unprecedented and growing exponentially as media outlets and red-carpet parades increase. Garry Whannel coined the concept of 'vortextuality' to analyse the intense, short-lived focus on a single news event that compresses the media agenda. Vortextuality makes all other topics disappear for a time unless they are sucked into the vortextual effect, shaping an intertextual process in which the different media constantly feed off each other.[7] As a result of vortextuality, Oscars fashion turns into a significant source of publicity for all parties involved. The red-carpet functions as a cross-promotional PR platform to generate brand awareness, but it also displays cultural and social codes that contribute to the construction and performance of gender and class. This seemingly educational side of the red-carpet media event dates back to the silent era of film, in the dialectic of the actresses' – at times passive and at times dynamic – bodies for emulation, in interplay with the active bodies of consumers.

The origins of red-carpet phenomena date back to late modernity. Red-carpet practices are often linked to royal traditions. In the new world's modern era, socialites replicated these as they sought to elevate their status by emulating European royal and aristocratic rituals. The celebrity status acquired by members of nineteenth-century society circles in the US captured people's interest in the same way as the gatherings around the entrance to the Oscars ceremony do today. In 1883, the press covered the spectacle outside the Vanderbilt Costume Ball at the French Chateau.[8] Social events such as Consuelo Vanderbilt's wedding to the Duke of Marlborough in 1895 made it onto the cover of *Vogue* and filled newspapers with illustrations and descriptions of carriage arrivals, curious spectators gathered at the entrance to the church and outside the Vanderbilt mansion, a red-carpet parade and detailed descriptions of who was wearing what.[9] Reading about society's codes of behaviour and following their public performances served as a compass of refinement and appropriateness worth emulating by the masses striving for social mobility.

## Turn-of-the-century reconfigurations

The momentous upheaval conceptualised as 'modernity' ushered in changes that blurred class boundaries in the US more visibly towards the end of the nineteenth century. Modernity enabled the accumulation of fortunes, resulting in social mobility and the emergence of the notions of the man of character or self-made man. The man of character, as Charles Ponce de Leon explains, 'was the antithesis of the dissolute nobleman or aristocrat. He embodied the bourgeois challenge to monarchical society, and to the principles of ascription and defence that restricted social mobility and the complete development of the individual's potential'.[10] Modernity also brought significant changes for women. Among these was a change in the dynamics of gender roles, characterised by a reconfigured conception of femininity aligned with women's increasing visibility in the public sphere. Jazz clubs, theatres, cinemas and department stores were some of the leisure spaces that ran parallel to political domains. This presence in the public sphere challenged contemporary ideals of modesty and decency. In particular, dance halls and mixed-gender workplaces such as department stores created opportunities for cross-class romance. The Victorian woman, representing the symbol of the cult of true womanhood, was confined to the domestic sphere and framed by self-sacrifice, decorum and maternal nurturing.[11] In contrast, the form of femininity embodied by the 'new woman' became a symbol of an emerging consumer culture.[12] The conceptualisation of the 'new woman' should not be understood as a monolithic representation of femininity. Manifestations of this new womanhood ranged 'from the mannish reformer, professional woman, and earnest labour activist, to the free-spirited outdoor girl and sexually assertive flapper'.[13] The flapper was Hollywood's epitome of new femininity, represented through actresses such as Colleen Moore and Clara Bow, the first 'it girl'. Their lively characters were marketed within an emerging consumer culture, providing an inspirational and homogenising ideal for young cinemagoers.

Innovative production practices increased the circulation of goods, orienting consumers towards the acquisition of the latest available commodities. The US became the first country to have an economy devoted to mass production.[14] A more fluid circulation of money among younger women, derived from employment and salaries, fuelled the growth of consumption. In this new economic milieu, beauty also became a commodity. David Shields locates the emergence of professional beauty between 1877 and 1880 as a derivative of 'society women seeking publicity and actresses seeking a station in society'.[15] Women were primary consumers of female body images as the main target markets of magazines, playing an active role as gatekeepers in society circles and as consumers appropriating those female images for emulation.

The rise of stereotyped feminine beauty as an object for the female gaze is anchored in preceding models, imposed by society debutantes turned glamour girls.[16] As Carolyn Kitch explains, '[p]hysical beauty was a measure of fitness, character, and Americanness', aligned with contemporary pseudo-scientific discourses of eugenics in newspapers and magazines.[17] The role of the media was crucial. A series of events described as 'the magazine revolution' resulted in a proliferation of newspapers and specialised magazines.[18] New technologies lowered printing costs and increased page numbers, and, consequently, demand for content. At the turn of the twentieth century, the Gibson Girl represented contemporary ideals of beauty in the pages of *Life, Cosmopolitan, Harper's, Good Housekeeping, McCall's, Leslie's Weekly* and *The Ladies' Home Journal*, among others.[19]

The invention of the rotary press, the emergence of advertising as a way of financing the medium and new distribution forms through the rapid development of the railway system drastically increased circulation. The growth of modern magazines is attributed to the immense success and influence of Sunday supplements and the affordable cover price of *Munsey's Magazine*. Before 1870, fewer than fifty papers had Sunday editions. This number had grown to 250 by 1890. When Joseph Pulitzer turned the *New York Sunday World* into a twenty-page publication, the positive response from readers increased the page numbers and circulation.[20] By 1898, Sunday papers with more than fifty pages were standard.[21] Sunday supplements bridged the demands of female consumers with department stores' offers to capitalise on advertising. From this period of corporate organisation, advertising became a form of cultural production and a cultural phenomenon.[22]

In this media landscape, topics considered of female interest, such as society news, later to align with gossip columns, fashion and beauty sections, developed along with the industries with which they were associated. The expanding audience demanded more information. This demand was catered to by the new syndicated wire services that shaped a standardised and fragmented style of American journalism.[23] The ever-growing flow of assorted short news cables sent by newsbrokers led to a departmentalisation of newspapers, in similar ways as department stores systematised retailing into categories and spaces.[24] This organisation of Sunday newspapers into what Richard Abel describes in terms of a metaphor of menus created enormous interest with advertisers due to its capacity to reach broader and more varied audiences. The media demand to fill space created dialectic dynamics in which consumption increased, as did the supply, in a never-ending circle.

The cultural shift resulting from the Graphic Revolution was a crucial factor in the way people came to perceive the world. The most significant point is the idea of creating rather than merely communicating news. In this setting, audiences are fed partial interpretations of a world formulated with the sole purpose of communication. These pseudo-events are planned in order to generate news. Consequently, the world is understood through this constructed image. This concept of the image rhymed with Walter Lippmann's conception of the pseudo-environment as the public perception of the environment after being encoded and decoded by mass media.[25] This enabled a broader circulation of so-called soft news, a category suiting the expansion of gossip columns, entertainment news, and fashion and beauty advisors, among others. Such demand provided an opportunity for the emergence of PR professionals pitching stories to the press to benefit their clients.

The power of the photographic image was foundational in the representation and distribution of new role models of femininity. Shields points at the emergence of the star system, fan magazines and mass media as cultural happenstances for the coming to power of the cinematic portrait in the early 1910s.[26] The photographic illusion of authenticity worked by disguising and altering powers of light and make-up that contributed to the creation of beauty ideals. The popularisation of photography was indispensable in this circulation of role models as placeholders for the collective gaze via collectables. Samantha Barbas regards the early use of photography as the first social medium, as it constructed favourable social identities and communicated them to others.[27] The widespread access to the stars' carefully constructed images through mass media turned them into both bodies and vessels of consumption by way of endorsement practices.

The growth of the fashion and cosmetic industries, in tandem with the proliferation of media outlets, also provided new opportunities for women as editors and columnists, stylists, fashion consultants, designers, models and copywriters. Educated middle- and upper-class women joined the job market, mostly in middle-management positions.[28] During the 1890s, the activity copywriting shifted from clients to advertising agency staff, alleging expertise in selling strategies.[29] The advertising industry employed women to target their messages more effectively, relying on gender perspectives. The J Walter Thompson Company (JWT) specialised in this segment, controlling the nation's leading women's magazines.[30] JWT was the first agency to promote women to major positions, naming Helen Lansdowne Resor as the first female copywriter and Ruth Waldo as the first female vice-president. The agency rapidly identified the importance of celebrity endorsement, becoming the market leader in this practice.[31] The opening of the JWT Hollywood office serves as testimony to the growing relevance of Hollywood to the advertising industry. Working from the West Coast, JWT also led radio and television sponsorship resting on the company's longstanding know-how and close ties to the entertainment industry.

## From fashionable society to celebrity culture

The notion of fame underpins this book's discussions of cultural influence. The thirst for recognition, in its varied forms and meanings in different cultures and historical periods, has always been at the centre of social organisation. Fame, as Leo Braudy describes it, 'is made up of four elements: a person, an accomplishment, their immediate publicity and what posterity has thought about them ever since'.[32] He attributes the evolution of modern fame to the collapse of monarchy and the rise of national and international communication networks. Celebrity does not describe a hierarchy. Celebrities are pseudo-events, they are 'known for their well-knownness' across the spectrum of achievements to notoriety.[33] This description serves as a pathway into understanding the contemporary fascination with celebrity culture.

Celebrities are not a new phenomenon or concept. Boorstin historically locates the concept as far back as the seventeenth century. Cleveland Amory argues that 'American Society' started from celebrity and moved towards 'Society and Aristocracy', in direct allusion to the absent link to true hierarchical social status as implied in the traditions of the old continent.[34] In America, the standard of class was pecuniary. Socialites of this type relied on the flourishing circulation of economic capital that was not always accompanied by the expected habitus. During the Gilded Age, when dominant society groups strived for sobriety in the name of distinction, the boom of society columns represented a gateway into notoriety for the *nouveau riche* and the 'new women' entering society through social mobility.

Ellis Cashmore relates today's notion of celebrity to this proliferation of soft news emerging in the late nineteenth century, 'when the circulation of newspapers featuring halftone photographs rose and news was redefined as something that happened days rather than weeks before'.[35] This proliferation of, and demand for, soft news opened up a new social group, prone to high media exposure and relying on ostentation and public display to exert leadership: fashionable society.[36] Members of fashionable society would go to great efforts to display social and economic power in order to impress each other, whether this meant building costly mansions, throwing the most lavish ball or wearing flamboyant fashions. An increasing interest in their personal lives emerged. The whereabouts of fashionable society became of widespread interest through media coverage of events they attended. Society journalism was responsible for the dissemination of celebrity discourses and became the predecessor of gossip columns.[37] Fashionable society represents the echelon of society going public through media promotion of leisure activities. Hollywood celebrities are our contemporary fashionable elite.

The prime creators of pseudo-events in the form of soft news were the press agents.[38] In 1904, an article published in *Leslie's Monthly* explained the wonders of hiring a press agent in order to appear in Sunday supplements. The members of this new profession promised to help wealthy women who wished to enter society circles. Press agents offered to give women 'a certain vogue' by continually placing their names in the same columns as those of the real members of society to convince others that they were 'within the circle'.[39] Wealth did not translate directly into this new fashionable social status. Opening the gates to society required a particular type of alluring public notoriety. Fame was transmuted into an element of power – a social-climbing strategy through media exposure that Amory denominated as 'publi-ciety'.

Fashionable society became iconic when social arbiter Ward McAllister declared that New York's elite was made up of only 400 people.[40] The media eagerly spread the controversy generated around his comments. McAllister tried to explain that he had quoted the number in reference to the maximum capacity of Mrs Astor's ballroom.[41] The scandal surrounding those whom he had left out turned him into a celebrity himself. 'The 400' became a byword to define the right set of people to hang out with. The media cultivated the myth around McAllister's power, emphasising the supposed arbitrariness of his decisions: 'McAllister keeps a book, and is absolute over it, putting down whom he wishes and leaving off whom he will'.[42] As discussions flooded the printed press and the myth of a social elite consisting of 400 people hand-picked by him grew, McAllister played along, eventually releasing a list of 150 names to newspapers in 1892.[43] McAllister was never considered a full member of the elite; he was a gatekeeper. After having differences with him over the organisation of the Patriarch's Ball to commemorate the anniversary of Washington's presidency, Stuyvesant Fish referred to him as 'our major-domo, our master of ceremonies, our caterer'.[44] As his popularity declined among the more conservative sectors of New York's social elite, he entered journalism, becoming one of the first society columnists with a by-line on newspapers.

Immediately following the hype of the 400 list, Louis Keller launched *The Social Register*, a 'database' of rich people to be sold to luxury shops and businesses for direct-mail advertising.[45] Wealth, lineage to a distinguished family of at least three or four generations and letters of recommendation from five registered people outlining why the person belonged to society were some of the essential requisites. Starting a stage career, publicly criticising the *Register*, marrying someone who was not in it or divorcing someone who was in it were some of the ways someone could be removed from its pages.[46] Nevertheless, during the early twentieth century, many of the wealthy families leading these fashionable lifestyles were losing their power as their fortunes decreased. The combination of younger generations' conspicuous consumption and the introduction of income taxes challenged the leading position of this pecuniary elite, putting fashionable society in decline.[47]

## The construction of a Hollywood elite

Alongside the publi-ciety phenomenon, the Hollywood film industry started the configuration of its star system. The theatrical star system dates from the early 1800s.[48] In the case of the Hollywood film industry, Richard deCordova places the emergence of the star system around 1910. For him, there are

> three aspects of the picture personality's existence in discourse: the circulation of the name; the 'image', taken in the broad sense to denote both the actor's physical image and the personality that is represented as existing within or behind it; and a discourse on the actor's professional experience.[49]

Film fan magazines published an increasing number of stories of Hollywood actors and actresses that went beyond their work on screen, heavily supervised by studio publicity departments to construct their star personas. Some of these stories during the 1910s and early 1920s focused on the star's 'taste and extravagance in fashion'.[50] These constructions, in conjunction with female audience interest, led to the stars' endorsements of beauty products. DeCordova's study, involving mostly film fan magazines, was later revised, reframed and complemented by Jan Olsson's cross-media analysis of early screen bodies, which related these discourses to a broader and earlier network of distribution through Sunday newspapers.[51] As deCordova and Olsson evidence, the emergence of picture personalities' names in the media, in association with photography, turned their anonymous bodies into identifiable commodities.

The circulation of star names in the emergence of the star system demonstrates the intermedial power of Hollywood in the dissemination of cultural capital. Film stars, as Richard Dyer explains, can be understood as social phenomena, image and sign. As a phenomenon of production, the stars were seen in economic terms as studio commodities. They represented an investment that absorbed a large part of the studio budget and were used to promote the films.[52] As images, the stars were linked to consumption via their alleged sumptuous lifestyles and their proclivity for conspicuous consumption, which consequently turned them into subjects of emulation, or else made them detested because of scandals.[53] The idea of stars as specific images constructed via publicity, promotion, films, and criticism and commentaries gave them a role as epiphenomena to the film industry that helped attract attention to the promotion of films, studios and any other product associated with them.[54] Stars also stood as cultural mediators of gender coding. As Jackie Stacey explains, 'identity image and feminine ideals are connected through the sale of commodities in a consumer society'.[55] For many women, film stars' media appearances were the only access to beauty and fashion discourses that informed the appropriate behaviour of women in the public sphere.[56]

Notions of stardom were renegotiated during the demise of the studio system and the emergence of television, following these figures' transition into a more mundane and approachable medium. As Paul McDonald observes, '[w]hen the studios downsized, the publicity function moved outside the studios' through external agents, PR agencies and lawyers.[57] Even though outsourcing existed within the studio system to a certain degree, this break intensified them, bringing a shift of power. Independence from the studio also pushed stars to cultivate their branding.

The term 'star', once referencing the carefully constructed images of film talent under the studio system, gained new meanings. Television stardom was not static; shifts redefined it during the 1940s and 1950s. Broadway, nightclubs and vaudeville performers were highly accomplished television personalities due to the spontaneity demanded by their live appearances that brought along television stardom of a different nature.[58] As former film stars entered the new medium, the landscape of fame looked increasingly complex and less constrained. This cross-hybridisation challenges arguments of stardom's medium specificity. Mary Desjardins addresses this by explaining that

> while some mainstream and trade press critics of that period construct oppositions between the glamorous and the ordinary when considering models for television stardom, attitudes toward the opposition are changeable according to understandings of the variables of genre, schedule, and audience.[59]

What television called for was a more heterogeneous conception of stardom. Television, due to its heterogeneity, pushed stardom away from the extraordinary towards the ordinary.

During the mid-1950s, a new leading group appeared, singled out as the jet set. Travelling by air was an appealing feature of this new elite. Part of the fantasy of this era was the illusory democratisation of luxury afforded by

increasing economic access to national and international travel.[60] The glorifica-
tion of luxurious and glamorous lifestyles resulted in the popularisation of the
expression 'red-carpet treatment', in reference to commodities that ascribed
prestige to consumers. Advertising messages reinforced the attainability of
the red-carpet treatment that catered to an illusion of sophistication in the
consumer's lifestyle. This popularisation of air travel represents both the rise
and fall of the jet set and an instrumental move towards celebrity culture.

In 1959, Cleveland Amory and Earl Blackwell launched the Celebrity
Register, signalling the final acceptance of Hollywood into what once was the
elite, ruled by the also constructed American aristocracy. Amory introduced
the volume by describing how American society had

> changed from How-do-you-do? To What-do-you-do?, so this book
> represents not 'Society' at all, but 'Celebrity' – not the family name but the
> name fame, not who somebody *was*, in the sense of his or her antecedents,
> but who somebody *is*, and presumably even *will be* in the sense of his or
> her descendants (although in some cases, there are grounds of reasonable
> doubts) … It does not mean, for example, accomplishment in the sense
> of true or lasting worth – rather it often means simply accomplishment in
> the sense of popular, or highly publicized, temporary success.[61]

The publication of the Celebrity Register marked the reign of a more diverse
form of elite in which society circles, athletes, politicians and film, radio and
television stars, as well as other Hollywood businesspeople, co-existed as
the influential names everyone knew.[62] It also emphasised the ephemerality
of fame. The 400 had now turned into the 4,000, according to Amory. The
publication of this register crystallises the emergence of celebrity culture.

## Americanising fashion

Many of the fashion-related satellite phenomena that influenced the emergence
of the red carpet as a promotional platform for fashion exposure relate to
political actions derived from attempts to develop and promote an American
fashion industry. Nationalist discourses linked to the Americanisation of
fashion had already emerged in the nineteenth century. Back in his ruling days,
social arbiter Ward McAllister called for society women to be 'original, stop
importing our fashions and manners, and make New York the Centre of the
World's life.'[63]

Initially, trendsetting and consumption in the US were highly dependent
on European fashion.[64] During the nineteenth century, France dominated
the scene as the birthplace of haute couture.[65] Parisian fashions were widely

consumed by socialites and stage actresses, filling newspapers as inspiration for women across America.[66] Many attributed the success of Paris to the fast growth of American consumer culture, arguing that 'although Paris couturiers excelled at self-promotion, their success owed much to the support of American business: department stores, Broadway theaters, fashion magazines, and daily newspapers'.[67] The cult of the new and the democratisation of desire, which implied 'equal rights to desire the same goods and to enter the same world of comfort and luxury' defined the US as the first market of mass production.[68] However, it did not entail that everyone enjoyed the same purchasing power. With much of the American fashion market's structure in place by the mid-nineteenth century, stores sent buyers to Paris. This development grew in tandem with improvements in transatlantic communications. As Marlis Schweitzer explains, 'with growing copy, countless illustrations, window displays, and fashion shows, these commercial institutions sold the idea of Paris to American consumers'.[69] Circulating discourses condemned the avant-garde Parisian fashions as a product for export, arguing that no reputable French woman would wear such extravagance mostly consumed by the demi-monde.[70] Men who feared that libertine Parisian designs would be a bad influence on respectable American women manifested anxieties about the lack of American identity due to Paris's fashion influences.[71]

Copyright was a big concern for the French fashion industry. The American department stores' business model consisted of purchasing the latest French couture, and staging fashion shows to sell the originals to their wealthy clientele and local reproductions to the affluent middle class as ready-to-wear.[72] Philadelphia department store magnate John Wanamaker was reportedly the first to identify fashion shows' potential as mass spectacles by staging the fashion Fête de Paris in 1908 in a department store.[73] Wanamaker played an active role in campaigns to improve the working conditions of local factory labourers, becoming a central figure in attempts to create an American fashion industry that could compete with that of Paris.

Another major figure in the expansion of American fashion over Parisian was Edward Bok, editor-in-chief of *Ladies' Home Journal*. The representations in his magazine portrayed the 'new woman' as a consumer, entering the workspace and loving the outdoor life.[74] All these ideas were at odds with his editorial ideology of female domesticity. Bok created the 'American Fashion for American Women' campaign, encouraging consumers to turn their attention to local fashions by creating their own garments from patterns offered in his magazine, and organising design competitions among readers.[75] *Harper's Bazaar* and *The New York Times* took the debate nationally.[76] The first American fashions appeared in Bok's magazine in 1909 'along with descriptions of sewing patterns sold by the Home Pattern Company'.[77] Even though the campaign succeeded in reducing French imports by 50 per cent, setting French and American fashion alongside each other in department stores by the 1910s, women did not entirely fall into line until World War II, when the local industry flourished and nationalist discourses became dominant.[78]

The American department stores' tradition of turning French designs into affordable ready-to-wear for the masses was replaced by the reproduction of Hollywood creations when the French fashion industry imposed restrictions that impaired access to new collections during the interwar years. With the reactivation of transatlantic trade after World War II, French fashion re-entered the scene with a new pool of couturiers in a market that was rapidly changing from the days of Paris' unrivalled dominance.

Before the war, garments carried department stores' labels as the stores had full power over manufacturers, who remained anonymous to maintain lower supply prices. As JWT had since the 1920s encouraged manufacturers to develop their own brands by placing affordable advertisements, the hegemony of big department stores and their capacity to control market prices was challenged.[79] In order to make their merchandising attractive to consumers, manufacturers required publicity; they needed identifiable designers or brands on their labels. Hollywood had excelled at putting its designers at the forefront through its association with glamorous stars and did not represent a threat to manufacturers or department stores, as studios saw tie-ins only as epiphenomena. Hollywood designers represented an attractive brand for manufacturers to use to publicise their commodities, while Hollywood tie-ins brought customers into the store in a consumer culture increasingly attracted to personalised labels. This exposure portrayed Hollywood costume designers as US counterparts of French couturiers, indirectly contributing to the idea of an established American fashion capital.

During World War II, labour unions and dress manufacturers teamed up for a national promotion programme, creating a fund to advertise the dress industry with the help of JWT.[80] This opened up a new era in fashion promotion in which the popularity of the Oscars became an ideal platform for the exposure of designer names in association with glamorous stars.

## A parade of glamour

The notion of glamour is of paramount importance in this history due to its widespread association with the Oscars red-carpet. As popularly used today, the word 'glamour' carries connotations of sophistication and luxury. The original meaning differs significantly from this contemporary usage. The etymology of glamour – magic or enchantment – carries obscure connotations, in close association with deceit and the study of occultism during the Middle Ages, relating to the forbidden and dangerous.[81] Judith Brown adds that glamour in the modern period conveyed

> a negative aesthetic that extends to multiple cultural forms. Glamour [was] cold, indifferent, and deathly; it relie[d] on abstraction, on the thing transformed into idea and therefore the loss of the thing itself, curling away from earthly concerns as if in a whiff of smoke.[82]

It was Hollywood, according to scholar Elizabeth Wilson, that turned glamour into a mass commodity after appropriating the term in association with the immoral silent film vamp, the serial queen and, later, the dangerous femme fatale.[83] According to Wilson, celebrities can never be glamorous, insofar as they are desperate for attention; glamour rests in indifference à la Garbo.[84] In his seminal contribution to the study of glamour, Stephen Gundle suggests it can be understood as 'an image that attracts attention and arouses envy by mobilizing desirable qualities including beauty, wealth, movement, leisure, fame, and sex'.[85]

Glamour is closely linked to the construction of star personas, and relates to ideas coined by Boorstin regarding make-believe and the image. For Desjardins, the 'fashion-glamour discourse about stars that appeared in gossip columns functioned to naturalise stars, obscuring both their material reality as labour and the constructed aspects of their glamorous personas'.[86] A 1922 article in *The Atlanta Constitution* entitled 'Mrs. Davis Warns Girls of Hollywood Glamour' alludes to the use of the word in the context of trickery, deception or illusion when warning girls and 'stage moms' not to go 'to Hollywood without definite positions or sufficient cash to ride them over the indefinite period of unemployment', and describes the difficulties of getting into the movie industry as a tale of not all that glitters being gold.[87]

The formation of the Academy of Motion Picture Arts and Sciences institutionalised the Academy Awards to ascribe prestige to the Hollywood film industry, indirectly transforming both the film stars and glamour itself from marginal to mainstream in the early 1930s. Prestige as a cultural belief is a result of these media phenomena.[88] Glamour and prestige resemble one another in that both words share deceit and illusion as original meanings. They serve as adequate adjectives to describe the constructed character of Hollywood, its film stars and its awards ceremony. In 1933, in a meeting with the members of the Fashion Group, an organisation founded by female entrepreneurs in 1930 to coordinate and promote the American fashion industry, *Photoplay*'s fashion editor Adelia Bird associated the word 'glamour' with Hollywood design. In reference to the Hollywood designer Adrian's work with Greta Garbo, she observed:

> It was dubbed 'glamor' and that word now is one of the most publicized words in the motion picture industry, both in regard to personality and clothes. And it was on a wave of glamor that Hollywood first achieved its place in the fashion spotlight.[89]

It is in this transition that the term gained a positive connotation. Bird's observation was an assertive harbinger of the extent to which glamour would become synonymous with Hollywood.

Glamour reshuffled its meaning with the advent of television. In 1958, JWT conducted a series of focus groups to examine women's understanding of beauty and found a close association to the notion of glamour. Respondents spontaneously named Hollywood stars when asked for concrete examples of beauty, making extensive remarks about the stars' character traits and their physical and personality types. Television stars were considered by some to be 'glamorous in a "different way"'.[90] They were 'very rarely' described as beautiful in comparison to their film counterparts. Instead, TV stars were described as 'cute, peppy, sweet', which suggested TV was a friendly rather than dramatic medium. Movie stars were named as 'ideals of beauty' and 'famous beauties'. The idea of being 'glamorous in a different way' unavoidably speaks for cross-media reconsideration of glamour that may relate to the decline of the studio system.

In postwar America, glamour took a more ordinary turn towards consumption. Anita Colby, a former fashion model turned fashion editor of *Life*, defined glamour as something 'you work on at' in 1958.[91] Colby argued that capturing the elusive quality known as glamour required beauty care, grooming and intellectual curiosity. The glamorous woman, to her, was 'concerned with beauty and fashion ... but also deeply interested in world events, in other people, even the stock market. She reads, listens, makes inquiries – and her conversation reflects it'.[92] Glamour was no longer unattainable, mysterious and exclusive to film stars. It could be constructed and acquired. Unsurprisingly, Colby pitched *Life* as an excellent source for women to become cultivated and to widen their range of interest in a short time period. This underwrites the educational role fashion columns were historically presumed to have exerted.

'Glamour' continued to be one of the most frequently used terms in reference to Hollywood and the televised Oscars ceremony (hereafter Oscarcast). Expressions such as 'a parade of glamour', 'the most glamorous night' and 'the glamorous Hollywood stars' promised to bring such formerly elusive and mysterious characteristics closer to the audiences and allow them to experience glamour in a voyeuristic manner from the comfort of their own homes. As The New Hollywood consolidated its space, the frivolity of glamour was in contrast to the image younger generations wanted to imprint on their careers. This resulted in power struggles regarding either the dismissal or the continuation of Hollywood traditions. By the time the fashion industry took over in the 1990s, glamour had become a label associated with luxury. Scratching the surface of the luxury goods industry to consider how low-end, mass-produced products are sold as exclusive under the allure of branding practices, it could be asserted that glamour continues to have the same deceptive meaning.

## The complexities of globalisation

The global impact of Hollywood, its award ceremony and the red-carpet respond to a convergence of phenomena dating back to late modernity and rehashed during the postwar era. In order to understand the red-carpet phenomenon, it is necessary to approach it through a historical analysis of the events shaping the fashion and film industries and their cultural impact seen through a lens of globalisation. Arjun Appadurai's theory of the 5-scapes of global cultural flow contributes to the understanding of complex global phenomena by grouping sets of ideas into denominations that tackle different registers of globalisation.[93] These 5-scapes are the ethnoscape, the technoscape, the financescape, the mediascape and the ideoscape. The articulation of these elements historically influenced the red-carpet phenomenon.

The dimension of analysis of the mediascape refers to the production, distribution, circulation and impact of images in the media, as well as to the multi-layered intermedial reach and clout these images and ideas have around the globe.[94] The most crucial element for the success of the Oscars has been its mediatisation. The transformation of the Oscars into a media event had a direct impact on how the ceremony was structured and the role fashion played in the show's promotion. As Appadurai pointedly observes, 'global advertising is the key technology for the worldwide dissemination of a plethora of creative and culturally well-chosen ideas of consumer agency'.[95] This entrance into the mediascape was a consequence of satellite phenomena that influenced the political actions of individuals and institutions, marking a hinge moment in a geopolitical reconfiguration that crystallised the role of the US as a veritable behemoth exporter of popular culture.

The ideoscape refers to an interconnected and interdependent set of images, frequently political, that carry ideologies and counter-ideologies oriented towards attaining power.[96] The mediascape and the ideoscape are closely related landscapes of images. The global distribution of Western beauty ideals and patterns of behaviour can be framed within the notion of ideoscape. The growth of the advertising industry supported such endeavour.

The study of the technoscape refers to the technological developments – both mechanical and informational – that allow for ideas and media products to reach broader audiences. It can also refer to the changes in the means of production, distribution and consumption within an industry. The advance of the American ready-to-wear industry had an impact on the global fashion enterprise. The growth of mass production as well as the emergence of credit cards are techno-logical changes that affect both the ideoscape and the financescape, showing the interconnectedness of all components.

The economic constraints that led couture houses to understand the importance of ready-to-wear and mass production to boost profitability unfold an analysis of the financescape. Couture houses were struggling to maintain their business models in the late 1950s. This conflict of interests marked a point of ideological disjuncture in which the national identity of French fashion as synonymous with couture was confronted with a financial need to expand into the ready-to-wear market. Standardisation demanded by mass production influenced the circulation of body ideals to fit the global expansion of the Western fashion enterprise. This internalisation of American business models carries an epistemological break of the French fashion industry's essence. Another crucial moment for the analysis of the financescape in the context of the fashion industry and the Oscars took place during the 1990s, when the consolidated power of fashion conglomerates boosted branding and, consequently, the entrance of the fashion business into the stock market.

In a broader sense, the international feuds between the fashion industry's national discourses are deeply entangled with the political interest of the US in ideological and economic expansion. As Appadurai observes, 'globalization does not necessarily or even frequently imply homogenisation or Americanization, and to the extent that different societies appropriate the materials of modernity differently, there is still ample room for the deep study of specific geographies, histories and languages'.[97] In the context of the Oscars and its red-carpet event, the ethnoscape helps identify the fluid mélange of influences resulting from Hollywood's ephemeral and heterogeneous nature. The ethnoscape refers to the 'landscape of persons who constitute the shifting world in which we live'.[98] What is particularly central in this conception of a 'landscape of persons' are the interactions resulting from migration, tourism, exile and other forms of geographical flow that affect the politics of nations as well as commercial and human interactions. Foreign actresses and fashion designers have made up a pool of labour for Hollywood since the silent days of film. This flow started with the exile that brought the Hollywood founders to the US in the first place and continued with the migratory patterns that populate the Los Angeles area and its cinematic community.

## The red-carpet as the symbolic space of Hollywood royalty

At this point, it is also necessary to problematise the notion of Hollywood, understanding it as an abstract construct that encompasses a geographical space, the community its members inhabit and the mediascape in which its cultural products circulate. Hollywood is as much a neighbourhood as it is an industry and a community, and has turned into an abstraction to denominate a form of symbolic capital better understood through the notion of Hollywood royalty. Michel Foucault coined the term 'heterotopia' in reference to an institutional or cultural 'other space' that breaks the conventions of ordinary space.[99] The Academy Awards ceremony can be regarded as a heterotopia that crystallises Hollywood annually as an emblematic display of the illusionary space supposedly inhabited by the Hollywood elite.

Hollywood exists beyond the geographical boundaries that delimit it. After its inception in 1929, the ceremony moved between Hollywood, Los Angeles and Santa Monica until finally settling back in Hollywood at the former Kodak Theatre in 2002. The event's heterotopic relocations foster the idea of a circus-like spectacle in which the ceremony conveys the notion of Hollywood regardless of its location. Hollywood is a city as much as an abstract construct and a fluid community, insofar as people are included or excluded from it according to the ephemerality of fame. Hollywood is a construction, just as celebrities and stars are.

As a place of heterotopia, the ceremony's prelude allows for a recreation of our society's cult of celebrity. This is made visible by the co-presence of fans and stars in a divided space that determines who plays which role, admitting a limited interaction while setting boundaries that demarcate social status. This configuration underwrites the hackneyed dichotomy of 'being somebody' versus 'being nobody'. As a media event, the Oscarcast furthers the abstraction from the event's geographical boundaries, creating a virtual interconnected space – a mediascape – and uniting people in different geographies through the live broadcast of an extraordinary event.[100]

## Fashion at the Academy Awards

The increasing attention awarded to the red-carpet phenomenon rests in the ways in which fashion at the Oscars has been mediated over time. Since its inception, the ceremony has witnessed media shifts that have profoundly influenced and reorganised culture at large. Changes derived from these shifts were conspicuous in the role of fashion at the event. It is important to emphasise that these changes should not be regarded as drastic and definitive turns of direction, but as part of a fluid coexistence of cultural renegotiation where past, present and future meet under Raymond Williams' notions of the emergent, the dominant and the residual ideologies.[101] The dynamics of fashion at the Oscars can be grouped under different period headings, following the attention given to fashion-related roles in the organisation (see Table A.1 in the Appendix) and, coincidentally, the emergence of new media technologies that shifted the attention given to the event. These thresholds are not sharply delimited by sudden on-off events. They work, instead, as transitions in, or negotiations of, cultural, economic, social, technological and political changes that occur over years. The designation of fashion experts for the event further facilitates the demarcation of these periods, at least since the ceremony began to be televised. Yet it is worth noting that these disruptions are the crystallisation of patterns that emerged years before each designated shift.

Actresses wore designer gowns, resorted to last-minute shopping sprees or wore their own clothes during all historical periods. However, these instrumental demarcations present some recognisable patterns that encompass them. The first period runs roughly from 1929 until 1952, the year before the inception of the Oscarcast. It is generally assumed that costume designers dressed the stars for the ceremony during this period. This generalisation is partially correct, yet not all actresses decided to wear – or had access to – these studio designers.[102] Furthermore, many costume designers had left the studios to open their own fashion ateliers by the early 1940s yet continued to dress the stars for the Oscars, making their definition as costume designers problematic. I propose a reinterpretation of this period, and argue that actresses did not wear costume designers' creations only because of their contracts with the studios but because these designers were establishing themselves at the forefront of the American fashion industry at the time.

The styles worn at the Oscars during this period did not uniformly or necessarily reflect the lavish designs seen on screen. Fashion was a more fragmented affair than what retrospective interpretations suggest concerning the Golden Age of Hollywood. I suggest dividing this period into three sub-periods, the first of which runs until the outbreak of World War II in 1939. The second is signalled by discourses of austerity that followed the US government's war agenda, starting with the official dress code of informal attire that extended until 1948. The third sub-period is hinting towards what would be formalised in the second period. This sudden increase of glamour, I argue, responded to the reactivation of the international fashion scene.

The second period technically starts with the appointment of Edith Head as fashion consultant for the first Oscarcast in 1953. The socio-cultural and economic framework that characterised it were an outcome of the war. The Cold War and the House of Un-American Activities Committee's (HUAC) persecution and incarceration of the Hollywood Ten demarcated an ideological landscape for the years to come.[103] The popularisation of television and the Paramount Antitrust Case in 1948 forced Hollywood into a reconfiguration, bringing uncertainty to many workers within the film industry. The dismantling of the studio system took more than a decade. This period is foundational for fashion at the Oscars insofar as it was the first time that the Academy had included a fashion consultant among its crew. Head's appointment occurred in the context of an ongoing turmoil to legitimise and secure the profession of costume designer in the midst of the studio system's demise. Her appointment as an Academy board member in 1948, the decision to award two statuettes to costume design starting in 1949 and the subsequent formation of the Costume Designers Guild in 1953 were manifestations of these political actions.

This period is particularly rich in actresses' associations with designers. A series of PR decisions focused on fashion as one of the leading promotional forces behind the Oscarcast. These conditions also set the context for the emergence of the first fashion pre-show. Head's performance as fashion consultant, the publicity generated by fashion-related content, the costume designers' search for visibility, the consolidation of the American fashion industry and the postwar return of European fashion contributed to an era that mirrors today's configurations. This period extends until around 1971.

The socio-cultural changes that characterised the third period manifested their dominance by the mid-1960s. Besides the growing anti-war sentiments and civil rights movements that had emerged more than a decade before, the US faced inflation, political corruption scandals, unemployment and an energy crisis in the 1970s. Hollywood also underwent its fair share of restructuring after the studio system was finally dismantled. For the sake of following the structure of fashion experts, this period will start in 1969, the first year Edith Head did not take part in the ceremony. She returned in 1970, albeit for just two years, and was finally replaced by a series of costume designers.

The 1970s was a tumultuous decade in general, and fashion was no exception to this. The costume designers hired during this period were mainly responsible for dressing those participating in stage performances and some award presenters, on occasions when the Academy engaged in a joint venture with textile manufacturer Celanese and American fashion designers. Those cultivating an interest in fashion could benefit from their relationship with a designer, the expert advice of boutiques and department stores, or their own wardrobes. An anti-fashion sentiment reigned during this period, as a clash manifested between the so-called old and new Hollywood. In a sense, this period can also be seen as transitional per se, in which the growing consolidation of conglomerates would articulate a well-oiled promotional machine leading to globalisation and big business towards the late 1980s.

The appointment of Fred Hayman as fashion coordinator for the show in 1989 marked the beginning of the fourth period of fashion at the Oscars. As president of the Rodeo Drive Committee, Hayman had an agenda for expanding the high-end fashion market to attract big brands into Beverly Hills' fashion promenade. The global growth of consumer culture opened new markets around the globe, even in the most unexpected corners. In the Soviet Union, Mikhail Gorbachev's economic restructuring allowed a limited entrance of Western ideas and goods in the mid-1980s. By 1989, the fall of the Berlin Wall anticipated that of the Iron Curtain, putting an end to the Cold War and opening a new chapter of globalisation. The sumptuous promotional budgets of fashion conglomerates and their expansion towards brand licensing paved the way for countless opportunities to disseminate luxury fashion discourses worldwide through popular culture; the advent of the internet sealed it. This convergence of phenomena marked a turning point for the mediatisation of fashion on the red carpet that was brewing during the 1990s and which crystallised into today's red-carpet mania.

## The book you are about to read

This book unravels the mechanisms that put fashion in the limelight at the Academy Awards ceremony, triggering the global red-carpet phenomenon. It tackles the role of public relations, advertising and media as cultural intermediaries of celebrity endorsement. It describes the activities and dynamics around the red-carpet parade as modern manifestations of royal practices that were shaped by way of pecuniary society, media exposure, the expansion of consumer culture and the purchasing power of the middle class. In doing so, it demonstrates that Hollywood was instrumental in establishing an American fashion scene and, consequently, in propelling the global growth of the ready-to-wear industry. Moreover, it supports the idea that the triangulation of Hollywood costume designers/stars, Sunday supplements/fan magazines and manufacturers/department stores established in the 1920s inspired the fashion conglomerates' business models for selling and licensing ready-to-wear branded under high-end labels. These business strategies are embedded in a broader matrix of cultural, social, technological, political, legal and economic reconfigurations that intertwine with globalisation.

Revisiting a century of history is an intricate task. Therefore, the chapters in this book are not organised fully into a chronology, nor do they focus solely on particular topics. Instead, they bounce between describing the events and shifts that took place at the Oscars and introducing satellite phenomena occurring in the fashion and film industries that directly affected the dynamics of fashion at the event. In order to make it easier to follow these events, the periods of Oscars fashion mentioned above serve as a guiding structure in establishing a timeline.

Chapter 1 sets the basis for understanding how endorsement practices were introduced in the American context by relying on beauty and notoriety. It describes the transition from society women to movie stars as endorsers, explaining how Hollywood positioned itself as a voice of expertise that provided a seal of approval for a broad diversity of products. In exploring the extent of these advertising practices, it also describes the emergence and popularisation of the expression 'red-carpet treatment'. Chapter 2 introduces the advent of the first Academy Awards ceremony, explaining the contemporary liaisons between the fashion and film industries that put Hollywood costume designers in the limelight. Chapter 3 addresses the geopolitical reconfiguration triggered by the outbreak of World War II. In this context, the ceremony was transformed from a private banquet into a public spectacle, in remembrance of the grand openings at Sid Grauman's Egyptian and Chinese Theatres during the silent era. This tradition set the layout for the show's structure to date. Chapter 4 explores how the ceremony turned into a media event, following its association with television and its journey towards global distribution. Chapter 5, in which fashion comes to the forefront to facilitate an understanding of how the event was branded as an 'international fashion show free for all' for the first Oscarcast, delves into the first televised fashion pre-show. Chapter 6 describes the nature and origins of the best- and worst-dressed lists through its most emblematic exponents. Chapter 7 returns to the Oscars ceremony to analyse a transitional period in which the fashion and film industries' restructuring, in tandem with the ongoing cultural turmoil, caused a clash between emergent and residual voices that led to the fashion boom of the 1990s, explored in Chapter 8. The final chapter reviews the contemporary status of the red-carpet phenomenon, addressing current debates about its potential as a platform for political protest and problematising the fascination with the so-called Hollywood royalty.

## Notes

1. 'Oscars 2014: The Ten Best Dressed Celebrities on the Red Carpet', *Vogue*, 3 March 2014, https://www.vogue.com/article/oscars-2014-best-dressed-celebrities-on-the-redcarpet/

2. Leslie Bennetts, 'Lupita Nyong'o Is a Glamour Woman of the Year for 2014', *Glamour*, 3 November 2014, http://www.glamour.com/inspired/women-of-the-year/2014/lupita-nyongo/. Focusing on the teen market, *Glamour* magazine was revamped in 1939 from the former *Glamour of Hollywood*, a pattern magazine released by Condé Nast to capitalise on the Hollywood fad without compromising *Vogue's* branding.

3. 'Lupita Nyong'o's Stolen $150K Oscar Gown Has Now Been "Returned by the Thief"', *Daily Mail*, http://www.dailymail.co.uk/tvshowbiz/article-2973041/Lupita-Nyong-o-s-stolen-150K-Oscar-gown-returned-Hollywood-hotel-thief.html/; Brandon Griggs, 'Lupita Nyong'o's $150,000 Pearl Oscars Dress Stolen', *CNN*, 27 February 2015, http://www.cnn.com/2015/02/26/entertainment/lupita-nyongo-pearl-dress-oscars-stolen-feat/index.html/

4. 'Lupita Nyong'o – Dress Returned to Scene of the Crime!', *TMZ*, http://www.tmz.com/2015/02/27/lupita-nyongo-dress-found-stolen-oscars-gown-pearls-fake-video/

5. Bruna Nessif, 'Thief Returns Lupita's Oscars Dress After Shocking Discovery!', *E! Online*, 27 February 2015, http://www.eonline.com/news/630676/lupita-nyong-o-s-stolen-os-cars-dress-has-been-returned-and-thief-claims-the-pearls-are-all-fake/

6. See Boorstin, *The Image*.

7. Garry Whannel, 'News, Celebrity, and Vortextuality: A Study of the Media Coverage of the Michael Jackson Verdict', *Cultural Politics* 6, no. 1 (2010): 71, http://doi.org/10.2752/175174310X12549254318782/

8. 'All Society in Costume', *The New York Times*, 27 March 1883, 1.

9. 'Marlborough-Vanderbilt – The Bridesmaids' Gowns', *Vogue*, 14 November 1895, cover; 'She Is Now a Duchess', *The New York Times*, 7 November 1895, 1; 'Lives United', *Boston Daily Globe*, 7 November 1895, 1; 'The Vanderbilt Wedding', *New York Tribune*, 3 November 1895, 7, 16; 'Sign All Papers', *Chicago Daily Tribune*, 6 November 1895, 4; 'Marriage of the Duke of Marlborough and Miss Vanderbilt', *The Times of India*, 28 November 1895, 6; 'Wed in Regal Pomp', *Chicago Daily Tribune*, 7 November 1895, 1; 'A Briton's Bride', *Detroit Free Press*, 7 November 1895, 4; 'A Vanderbilt Duchess', *The Washington Post*, 7 November 1895, 4; 'Married in St. Tomas's [sic]', *New York Tribune*, 7 November 1895, 7; 'A Ducal Wedding', *The Sun*, 7 November 1895, 1; 'She's a Duchess Now', *The Atlanta Constitution*, 7 November 1895, 1; 'The Marriage of Marlborough and Vanderbilt', *Chicago Daily Tribune*, 27 October 1895, 35.

10. Charles L. Ponce de Leon, *Self-Exposure: Human-Interest Journalism and the Emergence of Celebrity in America, 1890–1940* (Chapel Hill, NC: University of North Carolina Press, 2002), 22. The man of character and the self-made man are similar concepts used by different authors to describe the same phenomenon.

11. See Barbara Welter, 'The Cult of True Womanhood: 1820–1860', *American Quarterly* 18, no. 2 (1966): 151–74.

12. Maureen Turim, 'Seduction and Elegance: The New Woman of Fashion in Silent Cinema', in Shari Benstock and Susanne Ferriss, eds, *On Fashion* (New Brunswick, NJ: Rutgers University Press, 1994), 141.

13. Kathy Peiss, *Hope in a Jar: The Making of America's Beauty Culture* (Philadelphia, PA: University of Pennsylvania Press, 2011), 135.

14. William Leach, *Land of Desire: Merchants, Power, and the Rise of a New American Culture* (New York, NY: Random House, 1993), 11.

15. David Shields, *Still: American Silent Motion Picture Photography* (Chicago, IL: University of Chicago Press, 2013), 31.

16. For scholarly essays addressing the female gaze see Jackie Stacey, *Star Gazing: Hollywood Cinema and Female Spectatorship* (New York, NY: Routledge, 1994), 19–48; Lorraine Gamman and Margaret Marshment, eds, *The Female Gaze: Women as Viewers of Popular Culture* (London: The Women's Press Ltd, 1988); Christine Geraghty, 'Feminism and Media Consumption', in J. Curran et al., eds, *Cultural Studies and Communication* (London: Bloomsbury, 1996), 306–22.

17. Carolyn Kitch, *The Girl on the Magazine Cover: The Origins of Visual Stereotypes in American Mass Media* (Chapel Hill, NC: University of North Carolina Press, 2001), 40; Geoffrey Jones, 'Globalization and Beauty: A Historical and Firm Perspective', *EurAmerica* 41, no. 4 (December 2011): 885–916.

18. See Matthew Schneirov, *The Dream of a New Social Order: Popular Magazines in America 1893–1914* (New York, NY: Columbia University Press, 1994); David E. Sumner, *The Magazine Century: American Magazines since 1900* (New York, NY: Peter Lang Publishing, 2010).

19. Cleveland Amory, *Who Killed Society?* (Literary Licensing, LLC, 2012 [New York, NY: Harpers & Brothers Publishers, 1960]), 166–86.

20. Frank Luther Mott, *American Journalism: A History 1690–1960*, 3rd edn (London: Macmillan, 1962), 480–2.

21. Ibid., 584–5.

22. Raymond Williams, *The Sociology of Culture* (Chicago, IL: University of Chicago Press, 1995 [1981]), 54.

23. Richard Abel, *Menus for Movieland: Newspapers and the Emergence of American Film Culture 1913–1916* (Oakland, CA: University of California Press, 2015), 8.

24. Ibid., 10.

25. For a classic study on public opinion, see Walter Lippmann, *Public Opinion* (Miami, FL: BN Publishing, 2010 [1922]).

26. Shields, *Still*, 60.

27. Samantha Barbas, *Laws of Image: Privacy and Publicity in America* (Stanford, CA: Stanford University Press, 2015), 47.

28. Leach, *Land of Desire*, 91–111; Marie Clifford, 'Working with Fashion: The Role of Art, Taste, and Consumerism in Women's Professional Culture, 1920–1940', *American Studies* 44, no. 1/2 (2003): 59–84.

29. Janet Staiger, 'Announcing Wares, Winning Patrons, Voicing Ideals: Thinking about the History and Theory of Film Advertising', *Cinema Journal* 29, no. 3 (1990): 5.

30. Jeffrey Cruikshank and Arthur W. Schultz, *The Man Who Sold America: The Amazing but True Story of Albert D. Lasker and the Creation of the Advertising Century* (Brighton, MA: Harvard Business Press, 2010), 44.

31. Stanley Resor, 'Personalities and the Public: Some Aspects of Testimonial Advertising', *The J. Walter Thompson News Bulletin* 138 (April 1929).

32. Leo Braudy, *The Frenzy of Renown: Fame and Its History* (New York, NY: Vintage Books, 1997 [1986]), 15.

33. Boorstin, *The Image*, 57.

34. See Amory, *Who Killed Society?*, 143.

35. Ellis Cashmore, *Celebrity Culture* (New York, NY: Routledge, 2014 [2006]), 46.

36. The term 'fashionable society' had appeared earlier in the British press, deriving from the French *beau monde*, coined in the eighteenth century and meaning 'beautiful people'.

37. For literature about gossip see Kathleen A. Feeley and Jennifer Frost, eds, *When Private Talk Goes Public: Gossip in American History* (New York, NY: Palgrave Macmillan, 2014); Jennifer

Frost, *Hedda Hopper's Hollywood: Celebrity Gossip and American Conservatism* (New York, NY: New York University Press, 2011); Samantha Barbas, *First Lady of Hollywood: A Biography of Louella Parsons* (Oakland, CA: University of California Press, 2005); Neal Gabler, *Winchell: Gossip, Power and the Culture of Celebrity* (New York, NY: Vintage Books, 1994).

38. Edward Bernays, *Crystallizing Public Opinion* (New York, NY: Ig Publishing, 2011 [1923]), 188.

39. W. Bob Holland, 'The Passion for Publicity: Being an Account of the Ingenious Arts of the Press Agent', *Leslie's Monthly Magazine*, May–October 1904, 619.

40. The original article was published by *New York Tribune* in 1888. This reproduction appears in 'Society in New York City, from an Interview with Mr. Ward McAllister in the Tribune', *The Washington Post*, 31 March 1888, 4; 'Fashionable Society: The Laws That Govern It as Laid Down by One of the Governed', *Chicago Daily Tribune*, 27 December 1890, 6.

41. New York Society, 'Mr. Ward M'Allister Explains a Recent Remark', *The Atlanta Constitution*, 21 April 1888, 5.

42. 'Upper Crust', *Cincinnati Enquirer*, 15 January 1882, 11.

43. 'The Only Four Hundred', *The New York Times*, 16 February 1892, 5; 'Names of the Elect', *Chicago Daily Tribune*, 15 February 1892, 2. These 150 represented the core of society, the real elite; the other 250 varied.

44. 'The Bounced Boss of the 400', *Chicago Daily Tribune*, 18 April 1889, 3.

45. Louis Keller launched *The Social Register* in 1887 under the name *The New York Social Register*. It had expanded into a nationwide publication by 1922, after Keller's death.

46. Cleveland Amory, 'History of Register Tells the Tale', *Atlanta Constitution*, 8 July 1961, 15. Heiress Gloria Vanderbilt was taken off the register when she married agent and movie producer Pat DiCicco in 1941. See Mes Devlin, 'Social Register Had Humble Beginning', *The Austin Stateman*, 15 December 1953, 26; Virginia Palmer, 'The Social Register – Its Ins and Outs', *Boston Globe*, 28 May 1972, 15.

47. Arthur T. Vanderbilt, *Fortune's Children: The Fall of the House of Vanderbilt* (New York, NY: William Morrow, 2001).

48. David Bordwell, Janet Staiger and Kristin Thompson, *The Classical Hollywood Cinema: Film Style and Mode of Production to 1960* (London: Routledge, 1985), 13.

49. Richard deCordova, *Picture Personalities: The Emergence of the Star System in America* (Champaign, IL: University of Illinois Press, 2001 [1990]), 73. See also Janet Staiger, 'Seeing Stars', *The Velvet Trap* 20 (Summer 1983): 10–13.

50. deCordova, *Picture Personalities*, 110.

51. Jan Olsson, 'Screen Bodies and Busybodies: Corporeal Constellations in the Era of Anonymity', *Film History* 25, no. 1–2 (April 2013): 188–204.

52. Richard Dyer, *Stars* (London: BFI, 1998 [1975]), 11.

53. Ibid., 39–48.

54. Ibid., 68–72; Barbara Klinger, 'Digressions at the Cinema: Reception and Mass Culture', *Cinema Journal* 28, no. 4 (Summer 1989): 12, DOI: 10.2307/1225392

55. Stacey, *Star Gazing*, 8.

56. Ibid., 8.

57. Paul McDonald, *Hollywood Stardom* (Oxford: Wiley-Blackwell, 2013), 100.

58. Susan Murray, *Hitch Your Antenna to the Stars: Early Television and Broadcast Stardom* (New York, NY: Routledge, 2005), 42.

59. Mary Desjardins, *Recycled Stars: Female Film Stardom in the Age of Television and Video* (Durham, NC: Duke University Press, 2015), 21.

60. William Stadiem, *Jet Set: The People, the Planes, the Glamour, and the Romance in Aviation's Glory Years* (New York, NY: Random House, 2014), ix–xiii.
61. Cleveland Amory, Earl Blackwell and Sidney Wolfe Cohen, *International Celebrity Register* (New York, NY: Celebrity Register, LTD, 1959), V.
62. Blackwell was the head of the information bureau Celebrity Service. He based his judgement on readers' letters. See Amory et al., *International Celebrity Register.*
63. 'I Hunt in the Attic: typescript, [ca. 1940]', Collection George Wotherspoon 1863–1949, New York Historical Society Library.
64. Stephen Gundle, *Glamour: A History* (Oxford: Oxford University Press, 2008), 393.
65. Valerie Steele, *Paris Fashion: A Cultural History* (London: Bloomsbury, 2017 [1988]), 3.
66. Marlis Schweitzer, 'American Fashions for American Women: The Rise and Fall of Fashion Nationalism', in Regina Lee Blaszczyk, ed., *Producing Fashion: Commerce, Culture, and Consumers* (Philadelphia, PA: University of Pennsylvania Press, 2008), 132.
67. Ibid., 134.
68. Leach, *Land of Desire*, 6.
69. Schweitzer, 'America Fashion for American Women', 134.
70. See Michelle Tolini Finamore, *Hollywood Before Glamour: Fashion in American Silent Film* (New York, NY: Palgrave Macmillan, 2013), 55–73.
71. See Schweitzer, 'American Fashion for American Women', 130–49.
72. Bonnie English, *A Cultural History of Fashion in the 20th and 21st Centuries: From Catwalk to Sidewalk*, 2nd edn (London: Bloomsbury, 2013), 35.
73. Marlis Schweitzer, *When Broadway Was the Runway: Theater, Fashion, and American Culture* (Philadelphia, PA: University of Pennsylvania Press, 2009), 180. See also Leach, *Land of Desire*; Caroline Evans, 'The Enchanted Spectacle', *Fashion Theory: The Journal of Dress, Body & Culture* 5, no. 3 (2001): 271–310.
74. Kitch, *The Girl on the Magazine Cover*, 29–32, 34.
75. Tolini Finamore, *Hollywood Before Glamour*, 56. See also Sara B. Marketti and Jean L. Parsons, 'American Fashions for American Women: Early Twentieth Century Efforts to Develop an American Fashion Identity', *Dress* 34, no. 1 (2007): 79–95.
76. Schweitzer, 'American Fashion for American Women', 142–5.
77. Ibid., 139.
78. Ibid., 130, 145, 147, 148.
79. Jan Whitaker, *Service and Style: How the American Department Store Fashioned the Middle Class* (New York: St. Martin's Press, 2006), 214.
80. Eleanor Lambert, The Oral History Project, Special Collections and College Archives, Fashion Institute of Technology (hereafter FIT).
81. Elizabeth Wilson, 'A Note on Glamour', *Fashion Theory* 11, no. 1 (2007): 95–6, 99.
82. Judith Brown, *Glamour in Six Dimensions: Modernism and the Radiance of Form* (Ithaca, NY: Cornell University Press, 2009), 5.
83. Wilson, 'A Note on Glamour', 99–100, 103–4.
84. Ibid., 105–6.
85. Gundle, *Glamour*, 390.
86. Mary Desjardins, '"Marion Never Looked Lovelier": Hedda Hopper's Hollywood and the Negotiation of Glamour in Post-war Hollywood', *Quarterly Review on Film and Video* 13, no. 3–4 (2009): 426, https://doi.org/10.1080/10509209709361474/
87. 'Mrs. Davis Warns Girls of Hollywood's Glamour', *The Atlanta Constitution*, 3 December 1922, C4.

88. Boorstin, *The Image*, 246.
89. 'The Pros and Cons of Hollywood Influence on Fashion', Box 72, f. 8, Fashion Group International Records, Manuscript and Archives Division, The New York Public Library (hereafter NYPL).
90. Lux Market Research Beauty, Lux research strategies and interviews 1923, 1925, 1941, 1958, Account files 1885–2004, J. Walter Thompson Collection, David M. Rubenstein Rare Book & Manuscript Library, Duke University (hereafter JWT, Duke Archives).
91. William Stadiem claims that Colby was 'the highest-paid model of her generation'. See Stadiem, *Jet Set*, 35.
92. Anita Colby, 'Glamor is Something You Work at', *Life*, 24 November 1958, 155.
93. Arjun Appadurai, *Modernity at Large: Cultural Dimensions of Globalization* (Minneapolis, MN: University of Minnesota Press, 1996).
94. Daniel Dayan and Elihu Katz, *Media Events: The Live Broadcasting of History* (Cambridge, MA: Harvard University Press, 1992), 35.
95. Appadurai, *Modernity at Large*, 42.
96. Ibid., 42.
97. Ibid., 17.
98. Ibid., 33.
99. Michel Foucault, 'Of Other Spaces', Jay Miskowiec, trans., *Diacritics* 16, no. 1 (1986): 24–7, DOI: 10.2307/464648/
100. Dayan and Katz, *Media Events*, 214.
101. Raymond Williams, *Marxism and Literature* (Oxford: Oxford University Press, 1977), 121–7.
102. Robert L. Greene, Costume Designers of the 1930s, Hollywood-Paramount-Warner, transcript, The Oral History Project, FIT.
103. For more about the House of Un-American Activities and the blacklist, see Peter Lev, *The Fifties: Transforming the Screen 1950–1959* (Berkeley, CA: University of California Press, 2003), 65–86; Ronald Radosh and Allis Radosh, *Red Star Over Hollywood: The Film Colony's Long Romance with the Left* (San Francisco, CA: Encounter Books, 2004), 137–206.

# 1

# 'When you wish upon a star...'

One central aspect of fashion on the red carpet is the role of stars and celebrities as trendsetters. Today, the selection of a gown is often the result of endorsement contracts or stylists' recommendations. An article published on *The Fashion Law*, a website dedicated to the legal aspects of the fashion business, problematises the potential infringements of red-carpet fashion endorsements and their lack of transparency.[1] Whether or not stars get paid for wearing a gown is a matter of controversy that involves complicated legal matters regarding the Federal Trade Commission's (FTC) guidelines for unfair or deceptive advertising.

Celebrities embody cultural values that position them as role models eliciting worship through admiration and functioning as modern substitutes for historical heroes in the form of human pseudo-events.[2] This visibility and admiration positions celebrities as vehicles for the circulation of cultural meanings and practices. Grant McCracken proposes a three-stage process of meaning transfer to explain endorsement practices. Initially, the celebrity acquires cultural meanings through the accumulation of performances and media stories that construct a specific image of the celebrity among the audience. Secondly, brands call for an embodied endorser to associate themselves with meanings. Finally, consumers buy the product in their wish to incorporate those meanings in the form of identification with their favourite celebrities.[3]

Social elites have always acted as reference points for emulation, not least due to their image as icons of success and conspicuous consumption. Like many other elements of the Oscars, endorsement practices refer back to monarchic prestige, when testimonials of products included the tagline 'By Appointment to His/Her Majesty'.[4] Early examples of modern endorsement meant to signal quality associations are Queen Victoria's promotion of Cadbury's cocoa or the Pope's endorsement of Bovril.[5] Inspiration was not always drawn from those considered reputable individuals. In Paris, explains Stephen Gundle, nineteenth-century 'courtesans played a central part in fuelling modern consumption' as 'professionals of make-believe and living luxury objects', functioning as 'ideal vehicles for fantasies of social mobility and vicarious pleasure'.[6] The demi-monde represented a source of inspiration for women in search of fashion emulation. Arguably, unlike the unattainable status of monarchy and aristocracy, these figures were more approachable in representing personal transformation. They negotiated distant desire with attainability through reinvention, fitting the paradox of role model for fashion endorsement and social controversy. Despite noticeable differences of origin and social status, clergy, royalty and courtesans shared notoriety and public exposure as amalgamating elements.

In order to understand the contemporary obsession with what stars and celebrities are wearing, it is necessary to unravel the rise of film stars as desired bodies of emulation during the early twentieth century vis-à-vis the function of advertising agencies in developing endorsements. This chapter explores the longstanding involvement of perceived social elite groups in endorsement practices by focusing on the critical role of the advertising industry, in a cross-media perspective, for establishing Hollywood as a leading voice of fashion, beauty and lifestyle.

## Dressing like (a) 'somebody'

What fashionable society wore to events was always part of extensive media coverage. *Vogue*, for example, included referenced illustrations with breakdowns of the different styles worn to the opera in the late 1890s in a similar way as today's 'get the look' spreads enable readers to emulate the styles of celebrities on the red-carpet.[7] The active social life of fashionable society required high expenditure on clothes. An article in *The Atlanta Constitution* estimated that a gentleman with aspirations to society required a minimum of $5,400 to afford his daughter's wardrobe for attending five balls and for his wife to give one ball and six tea parties per year.[8] The expenditure of a member of the leading set would range between $25,000 and $75,000, while a first-line family such as the Astors would never spend less than $75,000, according to the circulated society column's constructions. Facing these high costs, young socialites and other women aspiring to enter society circles acquired their gowns in second-hand stores. The owners of these stores promoted the dresses by highlighting the names of the designers and society women who had previously owned them.[9] Society women contributed their profits to charity, while young socialites entered the second-hand trade as a means to economic independence.

Times were changing by the 1920s, as movie stars rapidly became the new fashion influencers. Young society women were portrayed as the primary buyers of actresses' disposed-of garments, partly 'because they [were] intrigued by the reflected glamor of wearing a gown once worn on screen. Many women [paid] outrageous prices for a frock worn by some celebrity'.[10] These allegations tend to reflect an increasing mystique around the enchantment of the glamorous movie stars. The *Los Angeles Times* also claimed that Los Angeles led all American cities in the value of used clothing – second-hand traders were located along Hollywood Boulevard, catering primarily to film actresses, actors' wives and society women 'whose pocketbooks [were] not quite so elastic as they would have others think'.[11] These shops were said to uphold higher quality than other second-hand stores. The article also refers to the continuous demand for clothes from actresses needing to renew their on-screen outfits. This suggests that even though costume departments were well established at the time, not all actresses had full access to them. Some actresses continued to wear their own clothes as costumes and to events, as was the case before the 1910s.

## Bodies of pecuniary emulation

Beauty ideals were iconised in media representations, starting with the earlier fragile beauty proposed by Charles Dana Gibson's illustrations of the 'Gibson Girl' via the 'Fisher Girl', the 'Christie Girl', the 'Tiller Girl', the 'Fadeaway Girl' and eventually arriving at the Hollywood star.[12] Class performance was instrumental in this articulation of desirable femininity. In Gibson's opinion, this ideal young woman came from a wealthy background with no need for financial or political independence. The Gibson Girl was rapidly popularised in American culture, portrayed to advertise products and personal styles and becoming an aspirational model for imitating the upper class. Fashion publicist Eleanor Lambert regarded the Gibson Girl as the starting point that signalled the emergence of ready-to-wear as an American ideal.[13] In the reconfiguration of twentieth-century American womanhood, film stars played an inspirational role of guidance for cinema-going fans trying to cope with changes brought about by the new century.[14]

Scholars have devoted much attention to the conflation of fashion and film, exploring the fundamental role of cinema in the production, promotion and representation of fashion, as well as its role in stimulating consumption. Edgar Morin explains that stars are suitable for advertising because they represent ideal and superior archetypes expected to determine fashion, enabling mimesis through consumption.[15] He reflects on the aspirational/inspirational dialectics of the audience/star dynamics, drawing on the importance of advertising as a modern practice that capitalises on the phenomenon.

Eliciting fashion consumption via stardom was already established in the theatre scene, through associations with department stores. Janet Staiger emphasises department stores' early recognition of the entertainment world's potential as a promotional platform, while Marlis Schweitzer places endorsement as a well-established system in Broadway before the emergence of Hollywood.[16] Schweitzer further explains that, as beautiful yet accessible women, stage actresses were the ideal vehicles for breaking into new markets and encouraging new patterns of consumer behaviour, with testimonial advertisements positioning them as cultural performers outside their stage roles.[17] By the mid-1910s, Hollywood had replaced Broadway 'as a site of fashion spectacle', replicating this practice with the film stars.[18]

The widespread reach of moving images worked as a democratising element in disseminating fashion images. For Elizabeth Leese, 'moving pictures brought high fashion to an even wider audience' in the form of fashion films starting in the first decade of the twentieth century.[19] Pathé and Gaumont newsreels furthered this process around 1910, making styling ideas accessible on screens around the globe. Fashion films began 'as short documentaries of fashion shows, filmic versions of a fashion magazine. Some attempted to introduce narrative into the fashion display'.[20] The circulation of these films within Newsreels served as tutorials for women to emulate the Hollywood aesthetic, as well as to inform themselves about the latest trends from the fashion industry. Film therefore increasingly became a source of fashion inspiration after 1914.

During the 1910s, Hollywood was looking for new ways to promote its films. When tie-ins emerged as an effective epiphenomenon drawing attention to the movies, stars promoted new department store fashions.[21] Promoting consumption became 'a conscious strategy within the movie business, indeed a necessary and logical part of its development'.[22] The film industry capitalised on the fans' interest in the stars with the help of advertisers and publishers who 'urged fans to see consumption as a form of participation', creating a fan culture that was functional to consumer culture.[23] James R. Quirk, *Photoplay*'s editor, believed that movies created perfect consumers and predicated the persuasiveness of moving images and movie stars' endorsements on the growth of consumer culture.[24] The rapid expansion of the advertising industry, and its cross-industry connection to Hollywood, built a promotional powerhouse of global reach that sold products and illusions in the form of desirable lifestyles.

## By women, for women

The growth of the fashion and cosmetic industries during the early twentieth century provided new job opportunities for educated women who entered corporate positions in the advertising industry. In this context, the messages that moulded advertising for beauty products were created by a group of educated feminists and not by men relegating women to a determinate gender role. Fashion and make-up were regarded as elements of emancipation, a break from Victorian ideals of femininity and a pathway to social mobility through marriage.[25] These discourses of fashionable beauty enhancement were no doubt challenging to the conservative Victorian mindsets of many powerful men.

Women at JWT played an active role in the feminist movements of the 1910s. Helen Lansdowne Resor, who joined JWT in 1911 after working for Procter & Collier (later to become Procter & Gamble), encouraged women to join the advertising industry.[26] Terese Olzendam, writer and founder of the medical research department that cleared medical claims used in product testimonials, was the printer and circulation manager for *The Suffragist* before joining the agency.[27] It is in this context of women guiding other women in the reconfiguration of modern femininity that advertising agencies and product endorsement practices became essential.[28] Taking advantage of their female staff's creative know-how, JWT became the first agency to successfully exploit endorsement, to the point of being referred to as 'the testimonial agency'. Resor was closely involved in the development of endorsement, particularly in the form of testimonials. Endorsement was believed to be the closest thing to a personal recommendation, commanding attention, ensuring readership, lending authority to claims, conferring prestige, glorifying the product and selling goods.[29]

Endorsement practices existed before the successful enterprise of JWT. The tone of these discourses changed when Resor recruited society leaders, people of titled rank and even European royalty for Pond's Cream.[30] The agency later recognised three cycles in advertising styles:

1. 1900–10: display advertising, with the name of the product displayed at the optical centre of the page
2. 1910–25: editorial style, in which the name and product were embedded in the topics in which consumers were taking an interest
3. 1925 onwards: personality advertising[31]

By rapidly identifying the impact of celebrity testimonials, the agency helped spread the American beauty ideals worldwide.[32] It was during this final shift towards personality advertising that society women and movie stars alike took part in endorsement campaigns, functioning as bodies of emulation for women to imitate through consumption.

## Society women prefer Pond's

Pond's Extract was JWT's first account, an association that began in 1886. The idea behind these campaigns was to give Pond's, an affordable brand, a high degree of social acceptance by associating it with the elite. In February 1924, the brand launched testimonial advertisements featuring famous leading socialite Mrs Alva Belmont, formerly Alva Vanderbilt and mother of Consuelo Vanderbilt. In an interview discussing skincare, she promoted her daily use of Pond's. Personal persuasion was considered the only way to secure these arrangements among society women. The Belmont deal was secured with the intermediation of suffragette campaigner Katherine Leckie, who worked at the agency. Other American society women followed suit. JWT secured eight names the first year and double that by the second year. In most cases, the women donated the money they received to a charitable cause.[33] The brand spent an average of $3,000 on each endorsement contract. The strategy was extended and glocalised in Europe to include royal and noble families, as well as engaging local society women in other countries of the Americas and Asia.

The credibility of the copy was central to Resor's endorsement approach. Part of Pond's appeal relied on the idea that society women, who could afford the most expensive beauty products from Paris, chose such a local and inexpensive brand as Pond's. According to a company study, 'this gave Pond's a more convincing proof of quality than any other maker of face creams could offer', particularly considering that by then society columns had turned into the top feature interest to women who read newspapers.[34] Pond's business grew four times in the first decades of the twentieth century, largely due to testimonials.[35]

## Making sure they sleep on a Simmons

The FTC followed the legal aspects of these practices closely. Simmons, a manufacturer of beds and mattresses, paid a $4,000 fee for the use of society women's names in their advertisements. The company delivered beds, mattresses and springs, making sure they would be located in the women's master bedrooms. Advertisements could not go to print until pictures proving the location of the mattresses and beds inside the home had been taken. If they were elsewhere in the house, the caption 'in a guest room' or 'used in a room in the home of Mrs._____' was added to avoid legal issues.[36]

In 1927, Mrs William H. Vanderbilt III – née Emily O'Neill Davies – received $3,000 as a donation for a maternity centre in exchange for her Simmons endorsement. Losing her social status in 1928 due to her sudden divorce could have jeopardised the deal. The company decided to take the legal risk of using her married name despite criticism after concluding that it was the association with the Vanderbilt name that made the advertising effective.[37] The significance of a name as an identifiable brand links to the importance of stars' names during the emergence of the studio system.[38] The stars offered names with which products could be associated to attain visibility. These early deliberations are precursors of branding approaches that commodify names as brands, using the abstract conceptualisation of brand equity to measure their visibility and impact.

It did not take long before the authorities questioned the trustworthiness of endorsement practices. A 1932 resolution from the Court of Appeals in the case of Northam Warren Corporation versus the FTC ruled that there was no objection to endorsers receiving compensation for participating in testimonials as long as they provided an honest opinion based on their use of the product.[39] Companies thus followed JWT's lead, making great efforts to ensure their endorsers were indeed using their products. They also demanded written testimonies, for copywriting purposes, to authenticate their opinions. In the cases of Pond's and Simmons, society women were already signing agreements in 1928 that stipulated that the products be used.[40] Simmons invited society women into their showrooms to pick out the bed, mattress and springs, offering to customise the finish to their taste. Pond's sent special gift jars with personalised letters reminding the endorsers to use the product.

Beauty products required the legal department and dermatologists to supervise all testimonials. Companies did not have a legal responsibility for the content of the testimonial, which was merely the opinion of a user and not an expert's guarantee; all misleading or exaggerated claims were, however, removed in order to avoid legal conflict. Even though endorsers were legally entitled to charge for their work, there was no legal need to disclose that information, which also worked in favour of the company's credibility. There is no evidence that endorsers abided by agreements; neither was there a way to enforce them. From a legal standpoint, a signed document protected the company and put full responsibility on the endorser.

## Advertising goes west

By the time society women had begun these endorsement practices, picture personalities had turned into stars and beauty icons followed by women across the country. The advertising and film industries developed in parallel, and the use of advertising in relation to the film industry significantly increased, with practices emerging in 1915 that were consolidated in the 1930s.[41] Advertising and publicity were believed to influence audiences not only in cinema-going but also in buying 'the lifestyle and ideology represented on film'.[42]

In 1927, actress Constance Talmadge was allegedly photographed for endorsements of 400 different products, ranging from aspirin to a grand piano.[43] The strategy emerged from an attempt at cross-promotion. Talmadge's manager, Emil Jensen, wanted to buy a twenty-page spread in *The Saturday Evening Post* to promote her upcoming film, *Breakfast at Sunrise* (Constance Talmadge Film Company, 1927). The price for publishing an article or interview started at $1,000.[44] Unable to afford it, he decided to notify all advertisers that Talmadge would endorse any product from a company that would endorse her in return by paying for space in the publication.

Jensen improvised a photography studio in a suite at the Ambassador Hotel and made Talmadge pose for over twelve hours, later contacting the different brands offering a deal. He managed to close eight endorsement contracts presenting her as 'the charming heroine of *Breakfast at Sunrise*'.[45]

## On how Hollywood infiltrated fashion expertise

Articles about the private lives of screen stars gave credence to the American Dream by showing how the stars had achieved their journey from rags to riches. Such stories served as inspiration for many young girls who later strove for a position in the studios.[46] According to JWT, 'fan magazines addressing young urban working women reinforced the appeal of emulating the stars'.[47] *Hollywood, Photoplay, Picture-Play, Modern Screen, Motion Picture Magazine, Screenland* and *Silver Screen*, among other titles, included fashion and beauty coverage frequently featuring fashion experts' advice.

Part of Hollywood's early association with the fashion industry resulted from the incursion of costume designers and actresses as fashion experts in the media. Silent actress, producer and fashion aficionado Norma Talmadge – sister of Constance – became the first credited fashion editor of *Photoplay* in June 1920.[48] Talmadge had often appeared in fashion editorials and as an endorser of fashion products in advertisements before assuming her role as editor.[49] MGM's

**Figure 1.1** Constance Talmadge endorses Marmola prescription tablets as part of the promotion for *Breakfast at Sunrise*. The film was released on 23 October 1927. *Photoplay,* January 1928, 129. Courtesy of the Media History Digital Library.

costume designer Adrian also joined the pool of film fan magazine experts, writing for *Screenland*.[50]

Sunday supplements were a more affordable option for film fan magazines, and their syndication created a homogeneous distribution of the information they contained.[51] Besides news about films and exhibitions, these pages carried gossip, mostly written by women new to journalism, and columns, supposedly written by actresses and costume designers, giving advice, reflecting on a particular subject or answering readers' inquiries. British fashion designer Lucile was a true pioneer on this front. During the 1910s, she settled in New York, where she continued to work as a fashion designer and developed a successful career as a costume designer, first on Broadway and later in Hollywood. As a sideline, she became a fashion journalist, providing guidance and promoting the American fashion industry. Lucile used her role as fashion columnist and Hollywood costume designer to rebrand herself as 'an American-based designer who was originating styles' rather than copying Paris.[52] Besides working as a newspaper columnist, she produced newsreels for Hearst.

With a similar approach, former actress and costume designer Peggy Hamilton established herself on the West Coast, playing a critical role during the 1920s and 1930s through 'Screenland Fashions', her column in the *Los Angeles Sunday Times*.[53] By using stills sent out by the studios, she developed a well-oiled publicity machine that supported the idea of Hollywood as a fashion capital through portraying film stars as fashion icons promoting fashion merchandise. Hamilton's extensive fashion spreads served the studios as a cross-promotional platform to pitch film releases and launch new actresses into stardom, by using these Hollywood personalities as endorsers of the fashion products advertised by stores. Department stores paid advertising fees in exchange for product placement, counting on-screen stars modelling as added value. Los Angeles store Mullet & Bluett, for instance, bought a weekly appearance in Hamilton's midweek section in the *Los Angeles Times* at $12.88 per column inch for one year, agreeing a minimum of ten inches per publication.[54] Stars also endorsed other products in her columns, for example cars, under epigraphs such as 'Film stars, who achieve distinction and smartness by their selection of gowns, express the essence of good taste in the choice of their motor cars. Betty Francisco chose this custom-built, enclosed Kissel Speedster from H. J. Wurzburger, Inc.'.[55] By 1927, Peggy Hamilton was regarded as 'the foremost fashion expert of the West Coast', according to *Moving Picture World*.[56]

Hamilton's section functioned as a screen talent gallery, a promotional platform for films and an advertising portal for fashion products. Publicists from different studios contacted her, trying to launch new stars through her columns. She, in turn, approached the studios when she had a special interest in established names. Universal Pictures publicity director Arthur Hagerman contacted Hamilton to get Miss Laura La Plante featured in association with the imminent release of her first starring picture *Excitement* (Universal Pictures, 1924). According to Hagerman, La Plante wore clothes well, and 'turned out to be the best girl to pose with advertising tie-ups in a long time'.[57] This letter acknowledges the contemporary demand for actresses to pose as models and the studios' interest in their actresses gaining media exposure through these appearances. Studios would also send pictures to Hamilton to insert into the fashion spreads for discussing style trends more broadly. Actresses also posed wearing film costumes, promoting the names of the studio costume designers. Towards the 1930s, the section became strongly Hollywood-oriented.

Hamilton was one of many advocates for Hollywood's recognition as a fashion centre. In 1924, her column proclaimed Los Angeles as 'the logical Paris of America'.[58] To promote this idea, she organised fashion shows, called 'fashion pageants', in the context of afternoon tea parties or dinners. One invitation announced sixty beautiful models and ten movie stars, among whom were Ruth Roland, Ruth Clifford, Theda Bara and Pauline Starke. Another fashion pageant event showcased the creations for the upcoming film *The Golden Bed* (Famous Players-Lasky Corporation, 1925), with Cecil B. DeMille attending and Los Angeles fur store Colburn's showing imported designs. Fox Movietone covered the event. Taking advantage of the extensive exposure given by newsreel coverage, Hamilton 'stepped forward and asked the society men and women, film stars and others who constituted the audience whether, having witnessed the pageant, they did not really believe now that Hollywood was destined to become the fashion center of the world'.[59] Hamilton's actions were effective not only for the promotion of films, stars and the idea of Hollywood as a fashion capital, but also for developing an authoritative voice for fashion editors settled on the West Coast. Hamilton paved the way for many influential and successful fashion editors to join the *Los Angeles Times* after her.

## '9 out of 10 stars'

In 1915, JWT incorporated the Lux account. Lux Toilet Soap carried the slogan '9 out of 10' in reference to the movie stars using the product. JWT set three goals to ensure the success of the testimonial campaign:

1.  Stocking all dressing rooms in Hollywood studios with Lux Toilet Soap
2.  Ensuring that a large majority of motion picture actresses used the soap continuously
3.  Turning the brand into the best-selling soap in the City of Hollywood[60]

Unable to control market fluctuations to sustain their claims, the third goal was eventually discarded. One month after launching the campaign, Lux's sales had increased by 1,000 per cent in Los Angeles, Hollywood, Pasadena and the city's other suburbs, turning the product into what was unquestionably the best-selling soap in Hollywood.[61] These aggressive strategies positioned the Lever Brothers Company among the largest advertisers in the country by 1934.[62]

The studios collaborated with Lux and JWT without any economic compensation, allegedly as a result from negotiations led by *Photoplay's* editor James R. Quirk.[63] This arrangement may be perceived as a wasted opportunity for monetising star commodities, but it may also have been a way to avoid potential conflicts with the FTC. From a PR standpoint, Hollywood may have seen the Lux campaign as an opportunity to save costs and benefit from the free exposure given to its stars via all kinds of promotional channels around the world. In addition, the campaign served as a platform for promoting film releases in association with the stars' names. This was a useful promotional tool that would increase the star-commodity value while driving audiences to the movies. Palmolive – Lux's main competitor – unsuccessfully tried a similar strategy through its advertising agency, Lord & Thomas.[64] Surprised by Quirk's influence on the Hollywood people, JWT executives concluded that the deal would have been impossible without the cooperation of *Photoplay*, referring to the mediation as an 'open sesame' to getting the studios' cooperation.[65]

## The advertising rush

The Lux endorsement campaigns became central for JWT's expansion into the West Coast, so they sent a representative, Dan Danker, to supervise and run the machinery around the Lux agreement. His original task – to be responsible for the Lux '9 out of 10' testimonials – developed into the coordination of *Lux Radio Theatre* (WJZ, 1934–5/CBS, 1935–54/NBC, 1954–5). Danker rapidly became a powerful figure in Hollywood society with clout in political-business relations. He took command of booking stars for *Lux Radio Theatre* and other variety shows produced and written by the agency.[66] In parallel to Danker's operations, the agency opened its Los Angeles subsidiary in March 1934. This branch functioned like any other located in big cities across the country. The call for having two separate divisions running operations on the West Coast testifies to the increasing potential for industry crossovers and the need to closely supervise endorsement, sponsorship and Hollywood talent. When Danker died in 1944, JWT struggled to find someone as influential to represent the company. Cornell Jackson, former head of the

Radio and Literary Department of Hollywood talent agency Berg-Allenberg, was eventually hired.[67]

In 1938, JWT became the first advertising agency to set up a Motion Picture Department. This unit was responsible for developing content for PR films and commercials, including:

1. Institutional-public relations (theatrical, generally 10 minutes in duration)
2. Institutional-public relations (non-theatrical, generally up to 30 minutes in duration)
3. Selling, theatrical minute-movies (each generally 60 seconds in duration)
4. Sales and service training (generally 30 minutes in duration)

Consultants were the clients' liaison and in the initial stages worked to define the objectives, production techniques, target audience and the means to reach it. Supervisors were responsible for the preparation of story treatments, distribution plans, budgeting and selecting the production companies for filming. The team also included a film editor and freelance writers to develop stories and scripts under JWT supervisors.[68]

The continued expansion in terms of staff and offices attests to the advertising industry's rapid growth within Hollywood. In December 1951, the two JWT offices moved into the same building but retained their separate business foci. They fully merged in 1957. The agency's consistent presence in Hollywood and its pioneering collaboration with studios took JWT to lead and dominate the transition into sponsored television. In 1959, executives from Lever and JWT reached an agreement to rebrand the 'motion picture stars' by shifting towards the denomination 'Hollywood stars'.[69] With television settled on the West Coast for good and the studio system in dire straits, the notion of Hollywood stars would serve both media while touting Hollywood as the entertainment capital of the world.

## Getting the red-carpet treatment

News arriving from Washington DC via the Associated Press (AP) news agency announced that the US government had finally purchased its first red carpet in 1957. This referred to a 15 m x 1.4 m Wilton weave red carpet acquired from Philadelphia rug makers Archinald Holmes & Son. 'A lot of big shots come visiting us nowadays. And one little known fact is that, up to now, this rich, powerful country didn't have a portable red carpet it could call its own', they explained.[70] The government's red carpet was inaugurated at the reception of the Japanese Prime Minister, Nobusuke Kishi. By then, as the wire describes, 'such expressions as "Roll out the red carpet" and "He will get the red carpet treatment" ha[d] become synonymous with something extra special'.[71] The popularisation of the expression 'getting the red-carpet treatment' and its cultural appropriation during the 1950s defines a turning point in lifestyle advertisement.

The red-carpet treatment is associated with modern phenomena and can be found in American newspapers at least since the days of fashionable society. Historian Amy Henderson claims that the use of the expression dates back to 1902 when New York Central Station used plush crimson carpets to guide passengers onto the 20th Century Limited Express trains.[72] Grand Central Station was run by the Vanderbilt family, the greatest exponents of fashionable society. By rolling out the red-carpet, or giving the red-carpet treatment, as they did in their lavish ball gatherings, they were giving a taste of exclusivity to anyone who could afford leisure travel. During the 1950s, advertising increasingly targeted American consumers benefiting from the blossoming economy with ideas of lifestyle, luxury and leisure expenditure. It was in 1954 that the expression 'red-carpet treatment' became increasingly recurrent in a varied set of contexts, used to express being treated like someone special, accommodating luxury, comfort and being made welcome.[73]

In fashion magazines, the red-carpet treatment appeared most frequently in advertisements. *Women's Wear Daily*'s first reference to it appeared in 1954.[74] In *Vogue*, the expression first appears in 1956, in an advertisement for L'Aiglon Apparel, Inc.'s label, Jeanne d'Arc. In this advertisement, an older man dressed as a valet is unrolling a red carpet. A blonde model stands on it, ignoring the man and looking straight into the camera. She is wearing a white dress with embroidered yellow flowers, accessorised with white gloves and matching yellow earrings, hat and shoes. The copy reads 'Red-carpet treatment wherever you are! Young men sigh ... and clamor for dates. The public is yours. And all because you look so beguiling in your new Jeanne d'Arc of embroidered organdy!'[75] The advertisement appeals to the allure of fame, referring to the gaze of men and the clamour of an imagined audience. The desire for public recognition and the capacity of clothes to confirm such quality are implied. Knitwear C&A guaranteed a 'red carpet treatment instead of red tape run arounds'.[76] Fur company Regina Glenara claimed its producers received red-carpet treatment during a tour of Europe. The advertisement shows a model, wearing a long fur coat, as she stands with her luggage next to a plane.[77]

Travelling continued to be a fertile ground for the popularisation of the red-carpet, due to its association with entrepreneurship and high-end leisure. Advertisements for transcontinental travel often featured famous elite travellers and portrayed the red carpet as a symbol of luxury and status. Transatlantic United States Lines, for example, made it possible to travel between Europe and the US in 'less than 5 days'. The advertisement features four pictures, one of which featured the Duke and Duchess of Windsor posing with their dogs.[78] Cary Grant also appears in one of the ads, pictured while on his way to film *Indiscreet* (Warner Bros., 1958) with Ingrid Bergman. In the upper margin, a drawing shows a long red carpet leading to the ship's boarding ramp. The slogan reads 'Blue Ribbon Speed – Red Carpet Luxury'.[79] The *mélange* of royalty, nobility, bankers, oil company VPs and Hollywood personalities attested to an emergent celebrity culture.

These associations between the red carpet and upscale travelling were closely related to the notion of the international jet set. As Stephen Gundle explains, 'travel became big business in the 1950s as it came within reach of many Americans and smaller numbers of Europeans'.[80] The jet set's cultural and economic impact resulting from their fashionable lifestyle influenced *Vogue's* rebranding (back) into a hybrid fashion and lifestyle publication; it used a combination of photography and air travel to launch its first international issue on 15 March 1953.[81] A travel attitude survey conducted by JWT in July 1957 showed that air travellers were perceived as 'in a hurry', 'executives' who 'travel a lot', 'modern' and 'active'.[82] They were also described as 'experienced in travel', 'well dressed', 'well educated' and 'busy'. In contrast, cars were associated with middle-class American families, while travelling by train seemed the choice of cautious older people seeking comfort. The notion of the jet set, coined by Igor Cassini, represented this new 'on the move' social class that was promoted during the 1950s.[83] The technological boom of air travel led this denomination to signify a whole era of glamour marked by international travel. Hollywood stars were the ideal visible exponents to represent it.

The Cassini brothers – sons of Countess Marguerite Cassini (daughter of Count Arthur Cassini, Russian ambassador to the US c. 1897–1901) – were two leading members of the jet set.[84] Oleg followed in his mother's footsteps into fashion design, and worked as a costume designer when he moved to Hollywood in 1941.[85] Igor, in 1943, became 'Cholly Knickerbocker', a pseudonym for the writer behind Hearst's syndicated gossip column, after his ex-wife married Rudolph Hearst Jr.[86] He also attempted a TV career with *The Igor Cassini Show* (DuMont Television Network, 1953), but was more successful in the social sphere. Cassini was busy 'playing diplomat and PR man' and hired someone to write his column.[87] He replaced café society social arbiter, Elsa Maxwell, as the ruler of a new elite. In his role as gossip columnist, he rapidly followed Walter Winchell's lead once he understood his column's power and thus moved to New York. His propinquity to political circles and the CIA fanned his success but also brought about his downfall when he was accused of being a double agent lobbying under Dominican dictator Rafael Trujillo's orders.[88]

International travel, the jet set and the sudden popularity of the red-carpet treatment set the basis for a broad spectrum of advertisements. In this context, Ginger Rogers endorsed Lady Baltimore, a luggage brand whose slogan proclaimed 'America's Best-Dressed Women Travel with Lady Baltimore'. The brand's association with the concept of best-dressed women appealed to the belief that these women would take special care of their wardrobes. The picture shows Rogers posing in front of a Jetstream aeroplane, sitting on top of a baby-blue suitcase. She is wearing a light-blue fur coat with a lavender shirt and white gloves. On the ground, another three matching pieces of luggage serve as steps for Rogers to rest her feet on. The endorsement copy read 'Miss Ginger Rogers, star of stage, screen and television, keynotes her wardrobe with the well-planned accessory. The luggage she chooses – Lady Baltimore *Fashion* Luggage, of course!'[89]

Fashion brands also associated themselves with the jet set by co-branding advertisements with airlines. An advertisement for the fashion brand Helga shows three models posing in front of a United Air Lines (as the company was originally called) aeroplane. The copy describes how 'Helga expects a red carpet treatment', travelling on United's first-class service to arrive 'at her Fashion Destination with a travel-happy wardrobe chosen for cool comfort and elegant simplicity'.[90]

United Air Lines registered the service mark 'Red Carpet Service' for branding purposes. Its 'Red Carpet Service' campaign ran from 1955 until 1967, reaching saturation point in 1957. The service was described as 'luxury travel at its best!' and 'the latest in luxury aloft'.[91] The United Air Lines advertisements made sure that the red-carpet treatment was both symbolic and literal. 'Air travel's warmest welcome mat is a red carpet!' This reflects the advertisers' interpretation of an audience desire for walking on the red-carpet and embodying a VIP experience. The full description of the company's red-carpet service entitled the flier to a cloud-soft reclining seat, relaxing surroundings, spacious lounge, a gourmet meal that included a French pastry, games, restful music before take-off and a guarantee of full attention paid to the traveller en route. The illustration shows a United plane with a long red carpet leading towards it. A man is walking along the carpet while a woman, holding her bag and fur, gazes at the reader. The advertisement is in black and white, except for the red carpet, a section of the United imagotype and the polka dots on the woman's shirt, which are in bright red.[92]

Another advertisement shows the plane with the red carpet rolled out in the lower right margin. The central illustration shows a woman enjoying her meal on board. Again, United's imagotype, the red carpet and the woman's blouse are tinted red in the otherwise black-and-white advertisement. This enhancement of red persists in other full-page advertisements from the 1956 series.[93] '*When you walk* along the Red Carpet to your waiting United DC-7 Mainliner®, *of course* you feel like a star of stage or screen! And you're greeted like one, too. That's only a part of *Red Carpet Service!*'[94] The key selling point in United Air Lines' Red Carpet Service was that luxury did not come at an extra cost. Luxury was, allegedly, the airline's standard practice.

In 1957, American Airlines promoted Mercury Luxury, a service available in twelve major cities. An advertisement stated that 'Mercury luxury means red carpet service at shipside, reserved seats, superb cuisine'.[95] Another advertisement shows a plane with a red carpet rolled out for disembarking passengers. Alfred Hitchcock walks down the red carpet. On the other side of the roped pathway, a paparazzo holds a camera while a journalist salutes the director. Given Hitchcock's level of fame in the TV age, his name does not appear in the advertisement, nor is he in the foreground of the ad.[96] Both he and the red carpet appear in the background.[97]

Another airline associating itself with Hollywood was National, which used the slogan 'Airline of the Stars'. 'There's nothing quite like the luxury, elegance and comfort of National's Starlight lounge. Whatever your pleasure – just sit back and relax. It's yours quick as a wish . . . as are all the red-carpet services of the glamorous Star'.[98]

Some advertisements linked the red-carpet treatment to the fashion industry. In *Women's Wear Daily*, United Air Lines' Red Carpet Service was introduced as the 'Latest style in high-speed travel'.[99] The Los Angeles-New York connection was a frequent feature, promoting a 'Red Carpet* Service nonstop between top US fashion centers!'[100] The competitive strand of uniting the east and west coasts reflected the increasing flow of travel that resulted from the fluent liaison of the film, television, fashion and advertising industries.[101] United promised its coast-to-coast travellers would arrive 'fresh, unwrinkled, [and] unruffled'.[102] American fashion designer and critic Mr Blackwell endorsed American Airlines. Other style arbiters, such as Eleanor Lambert, appeared in a series of advertisements for Air India, mainly focusing on the New York-London route. In the advertisement, Lambert appears holding a Coty fashion award statuette and looking straight into the camera.[103] She is quoted as saying 'Style makes a difference between airlines. I fly Air India'. The advertisement also refers to the International Best-Dressed List, emphasising Lambert's authoritative voice in style matters. The copy ends with the call-to-action line: 'If you're going to London, why not go in style?'[104]

The Oscars' fashion consultant, Edith Head, appeared in an advertisement for the Lockheed Aircraft Corporation in 1957, endorsing not an airline but an aircraft: the Super Constellation. 'Miss Edith Head' is presented as 'Hollywood Pin-Up Queen'.[105] The copy reads:

> Equipped with pin box and flawless taste, Miss Head has designed her way to six Oscars and international fashion fame. Millions of movie-goers, world-wide, study her Paramount Studio creations for glamorous stars. And just as avidly, Miss Head studies the world – its art, architecture and styles – for new inspiration. Ready for travel at the drop of a visa, Miss Head makes business trips *pleasure* trips in the restful quiet and tasteful décor of her favorite airliners: Lockheed Super Constellation. In July she will fly to Madrid on the *NEW, faster, larger* Lockheed luxury liner (Model 1649) ... via TWA – Trans World Airlines.[106]

The advertisement links Head to the Oscars by referring to her as a six-time winner for costume design. It also associates her with the fashion world by creating the illusion that she is always ready for a fashion emergency.

During the late 1950s, Head designed the winter uniforms for Delta Airlines. In the 1950s, as Gundle explains, 'the air stewardess emerged as a glamorous figure who embodied many of the dreams of the moment'.[107] The ensemble consisted of a tailored shirt-dress she named the 'Jet Jumper' and a loose-fitting short, box jacket with three-quarter sleeves, both made out of honey-beige wool gabardine. The uniform was accessorised with a '*jet flame*' ascot tie in coral, a full-length leather coat in beige and leather cinnamon-coloured shoes, belt and bag.[108] Head was introduced in Delta's 1959 brochure as 'Fashion chief of Paramount Pictures, winner of six Oscars ... and author of the current best seller, "The Dress Doctor"'.[109] 'Women should dress for the role they play in life, be it as a housewife, as a secretary, or as a stewardess' quoted Delta's press release.[110] Head's uniforms were used between 1959 and 1965. She ventured into designing airline uniforms again in 1974 when Omniform approached her to dress Pan American Airline stewardesses.[111]

In 1957, Trans World Airlines (TWA) launched a campaign in association with Oscar. Building up to the 29th Academy Awards ceremony, TWA released at least three different advertisements featuring the golden statuette. One of them shows Oscar in the foreground, filling the full length of the page. In the background, the staircase and the plane appear in black and white.[112] Another advertisement shows a TWA stewardess holding an Oscar statuette in her hands.[113] A third features three stewardesses and a pilot posing in front of a TWA aeroplane. In front of them are lined up twenty Oscar statuettes.[114] All the advertisements place the golden statuette as an endorser, humanising it through the strapline 'Oscar flies TWA'. The rest of the copy narrates the airline's participation in the event, flying in nominees for Best Foreign Film.[115]

The advertisements also reminded audiences of the Oscarcast by announcing that it would be broadcast on NBC. Oscar's attained celebrity status turned him into another member of the international jet set.

## Take-off

Endorsement practices have always relied on the visibility of the social elite catering to consumers' aspirational emulation. The postwar economic surplus enabled expenditure and positioned US consumers in the lead by virtue of their purchasing power. The technological advancements in air travel opened it up to the more dynamic and international jet set. Luxury, as a branding tag, entered marketing by becoming affordable and accessible. In this context, expressions such as 'red-carpet treatment' and 'red-carpet service' became popular taglines to approach the new economically empowered consumer expecting to be treated accordingly. The use of Hollywood endorsers to promote air travel indicates their consolidation as role models of ideal lifestyles. As more Americans accessed international travel, the jet set's connotation of a luxurious lifestyle diminished. The amalgamation of notorious personalities remained in the form of an emerging celebrity culture.

## Notes

1. See The Fashion Law, 'Red Carpet Pay-for-Play', 24 February 2017, https://www.the-fashionlaw.com/red-carpet-pay-for-play-and-the-role-of-the-ftc/
2. Boorstin, *The Image*, 63.
3. Grant McCracken, 'Who is the Celebrity Endorser? Cultural Foundations of the Endorsement Process', *Journal of Consumer Research* 16 (December 1989): 310–21, DOI: 10.1086/209217
4. Boorstin, *The Image*, 58–9.
5. Keith V. Monk Sponsorship/Endorsement/Publicity, *Global Products/Service Marketing Commission of the International Advertising Association* 6–7, Box 99, Advertising Vertical Files, 1950–1994, JWT, Duke Archives.
6. Gundle, *Glamour*, 77.
7. 'Society Women Wore to the Opera', *Vogue*, 10 December 1896.
8. 'Society, Expenses in New York', *The Atlanta Constitution*, 12 February 1896, 5.
9. 'What Ladies Do with Costumes That Have Made Worth's Head Ache', *Chicago Daily Tribune*, 4 August 1883, 16.
10. Myrtle Gebhart, 'What Movie Queens Do with Old Clothes', *Los Angeles Times*, 19 November 1922, III27.
11. Ibid., III27.
12. Kitch, *The Girl on the Magazine Cover*, 41.

13. Eleanor Lambert, interviewed by Phyllis Feldman, 8 December 1977, Transcript, Oral History, Fashion Industries, Gladys Marcus Library Special Collections & College Archives, FIT.

14. See Samantha Barbas, *Movie Crazy: Fans, Stars, and the Cult of Celebrity* (New York, NY: Palgrave, 2001).

15. Edgar Morin, *The Stars: An Account of the Star-System in Motion Pictures*, trans. Richard Howard (Minneapolis, MN: University of Minnesota Press, 2005 [1960]), 137.

16. Staiger, 'Announcing Wares', 5; Schweitzer, *When Broadway Was the Runway*.

17. Schweitzer, *When Broadway Was the Runway*, 8.

18. Ibid., 226.

19. Elizabeth Leese, *Costume Design in the Movies: An Illustrated Guide to the Work of 157 Great Designers* (New York, NY: Dover Publication, Inc., 1991), 9.

20. Maureen Turim, 'Fashion Shapes: Film, the Fashion Industry, and the Image of Women', *Socialist Review* 71 (1983): 78–96.

21. Staiger, 'Announcing Wares', 11.

22. George Mitchell, 'The Movies and Münsterberg', *Jump Cut* 27 (July 1982): 57–60, http://www.ejumpcut.org/archive/onlinessays/JC27folder/Munsterberg.html/

23. Barbas, *Movie Crazy*, 5.

24. Kathryn H. Fuller, *At the Picture Show: Small-Town Audiences and the Creation of Movie Fan Culture* (Washington, DC: Smithsonian Institution Press, 1997), 151. Quirk was editor of *Photoplay* between 1917 and 1932.

25. See Box 8, f. Women in advert. 1918–1969, Sidney Ralph Bernstein Company History Files, JWT, Duke Archives.

26. Importance of Women as Consumer and Employers, Box 8, f. Women in advert. 1918–1969, Sidney Ralph Bernstein Company History Files, JWT, Duke Archives; Early women in advertising, f. JWT: Women in advertising, 1928–1931, 1938, 1948, 1951, 1963, 1975, JWT, Duke Archives. Stanley Resor, her husband, worked for Procter & Collier as a salesman, and joined JWT five years after her, eventually becoming the company's president.

27. Important early women, Box 8, f. Women in advert. 1918–1969, Sidney Ralph Bernstein Company History Files, JWT, Duke Archives.

28. See Importance of Women as Consumer and Employers, Box 8, f. Women in advert. 1918–1969, Sidney Ralph Bernstein Company History Files, JWT, Duke Archives; House advertisement printed in Advertising Club News 5-6-18, Box 8, f. Women in advert. 1918–1969, Sidney Ralph Bernstein Company History Files, JWT, Duke Archives.

29. 'The Revised Primer of Testimonial Advertising', Box 99, Advertising Vertical Files, 1950–1994, JWT, Duke Archives.

30. For a historical overview of endorsement in the US, see Kerry Segrave, *Endorsements in Advertising: A Social History* (Jefferson, NC: McFarland & Company, Inc., 2005).

31. Cards, Box 7, f. Testimonial advertising 1928–1977, JWT, Duke Archives.

32. Stanley Resor, 'Personalities and the Public'. For the role of JWT in the globalisation of beauty, see Denise H. Sutton, *Globalizing Ideal Beauty: How Female Copywriters of the J. Walter Thompson Advertising Agency Redefined Beauty for the Twentieth Century* (New York, NY: Palgrave Macmillan, 2009).

33. Pond's Creams Profile of Dollar Sales since endorsements by society women, Clients Chesebrough-Pond's history from JWT Public Relations 1960, Box 4, Howard Henderson Papers, JWT, Duke Archives; History of Endorsement and Role of Society, Chesebrough-Pond's Sales Policy and Advertising History 1937–1944, Box 4, Howard

Henderson Papers, JWT, Duke Archives; Special production and representatives meeting, 9 April 1928, Resor, Stanley 1916–1950, Box 1 Howard Henderson Papers correspondence, JWT, Duke Archives.

34. Moviegoers and endorsers, Chesebrough-Pond's surveys, meetings, and other material 1885–1995, Box 4, Howard Henderson Papers, JWT, Duke Archives.
35. Pond's Testimonial Advertising, Chesebrough-Pond's: Sales, Policy and Advertising Industry, Box 4, Howard Henderson Papers, JWT, Duke Archives.
36. Special production and representatives meeting, 9 April 1928, Resor, Stanley 1916–1950, Box 1 Howard Henderson Papers correspondence, JWT, Duke Archives.
37. Office memorandum from E. Eaton, 15 April 1928, f. Vanderbilt, Mrs. William H 1927–1928, Box 2 Lucile Turnback Platt, JWT, Duke Archives.
38. deCordova, *Picture Personalities*, 20–1.
39. History of Endorsement and Role of Society, Chesebrough-Pond's Sales Policy and Advertising History 1937–1944, Box 4, Howard Henderson Papers, JWT, Duke Archives. Access the resolution 'U.S. Court of Appeals for the Second Circuit – 59 F. 2d 196 (2d Cir.1932) Northam Warren Corporation V. Federal Trade Commission. N. 300, June 6, 1932', Justia Law, http://law.justia.com/cases/federal/appellate-courts/F2/59/196/1471764/
40. Special production and representatives meeting, 9 April 1928, Resor, Stanley 1916–1950, Box 1 Howard Henderson Papers correspondence, JWT, Duke Archives.
41. Staiger, 'Announcing Wares', 4.
42. Ibid., 3.
43. Testimonials, Wholesale. Constance Talmadge, Champion Endurance Endorser, Testimonial advertising 1928–1977, Box 7, Information Center Records, JWT, Duke Archives. Among the products she attempted to endorse were Pepsodent, Iodent, Kolynos, Dentyne, Ipana, Squibbs, Lyon's, Colgate or Pebeco, Maxwell House Coffee, Hotel Astor, Yuban, Alice Foote McDougall, Kaffee Hag, Tiffany, Tecla and Cartier.
44. Special production and representative meeting, Monday, 8 April 1928, Box 1, f. Resor, Stanley 1916–1950, Howard Henderson Papers correspondence, JWT, Duke Archives.
45. Testimonials, Wholesale. Constance Talmadge, Champion Endurance Endorser, Testimonial advertising 1928–1977, Box 7, Information Center Records, JWT, Duke Archives.
46. See Diana Anselmo-Sequeira, 'Apparitional Girlhood: Material Ephemerality and the Historiography of Female Adolescence in Early American Film', *Spectator* (2013), http://works.bepress.com/diana_anselmo-sequeira/2/
47. Frances Maule, 'The Woman Appeal', *J. Walter Thompson News Bulletin* 105 (January 1924): 1, 2.
48. Marion Williams, 'What Becomes of Their Clothes?', *Photoplay*, May 1918, 39–42; 'Look Who's Been Shopping', *Photoplay*, January 1920, 33–5.
49. Talmadge was replaced by Carol Van Wyke in 1921.
50. By way of illustration, see Gilbert Adrian, 'Clothes for the Smart Young Girl', *Screenland*, February 1929, 44–5; Adrian, 'How the "Deb" Should Dress', *Screenland*, March 1929, 44–5; Adrian, 'The Modern Maid Inspires the Mode', *Screenland*, April 1929, 46–7.
51. Abel, *Menus for Movieland*, 274. Though discussing syndication, Abel argues for a level of heterogeneity in local adaptations.
52. Tolini Finamore, *Hollywood Before Glamour*, 8, 63.
53. Ibid., 8.

54. Advertising contract – The Times Mirror Company, 1 January 1924, Box 8 Scrapbooks 1924, Peggy Hamilton Adams papers, Charles E. Young Research Library, University of California, Los Angeles (hereafter CEYRL).

55. Screenland Fashions, undated ca. 1924, 16, Box 8 Scrapbooks 1924, Peggy Hamilton Adams papers, CEYRL.

56. Untitled, *Moving Picture World*, 26 February 1927, 644.

57. Letter from Arthur Q. Hagerman to Peggy Hamilton, Box 8 Scrapbooks 1924, Peggy Hamilton Adams papers, CEYRL.

58. Peggy Hamilton, 'Los Angeles, the Logical Paris of America', *Los Angeles Times*, 3 September 1922, 109.

59. 'Film Fashions Displayed: Peggy Hamilton Tells New York Hollywood Will Displace Paris as Made Center', *Los Angeles Times*, 19 February 1927, 1.

60. Special production and representatives meeting, 9 April 1928, Resor, Stanley 1916–1950, Box 1 Howard Henderson Papers correspondence, JWT, Duke Archives.

61. 'Editorial: Ladies Home Journal, February 1885', f. Chesebrough-Ponds: Surveys, meetings and other materials 1885–1955, JWT, Duke Archives.

62. Through the JWT New York office alone they invested $4 million that year.

63. Special production and representatives meeting, 9 April 1928, Resor, Stanley 1916–1950, Box 1 Howard Henderson Papers correspondence, JWT, Duke Archives.

64. J. Walter Thompson Company 1 June 1928, f. Magazine histories, Box 14, The Colin Dawkins Papers, JWT, Duke Archives. Palmolive signed only three actresses, who received between $2,500 and $25,000 per ad.

65. Special production and representatives meeting, 9 April 1928, Resor, Stanley 1916–1950, Box 1 Howard Henderson Papers correspondence, JWT, Duke Archives.

66. Memo from Cal Kuhl to Robert T. Colwell, 21 May 1964, Box 7 Hollywood Office 1963–1964, Sidney Ralph Bernstein Company History Files, JWT, Duke Archives; Confidential 1937, Box Lux meetings interviews and presentations 1932, 1936, 1959, 1962, Account Files 1995–2004, JWT, Duke Archives.

67. Early JWT TV, Box 8, f. TV Department, Sidney Ralph Bernstein Company History Files, JWT, Duke Archives.

68. Motion Picture Department, Box 8, f. TV Department, Sidney Ralph Bernstein Company History Files, JWT, Duke Archives.

69. Letter to Tom Sutton, 9 August 1959, Lever Brothers Lux Case History 1923–1973, Box 5, Information Center Records, JWT, Duke Archives.

70. Arthur Edson, 'U.S. Finally Has a Red Carpet All Its Own to Roll Out', *The Post-Standard*, 18 June 1957, 5.

71. Ibid., 5.

72. Sam Roberts, *Grand Central: How a Train Station Transformed America* (New York, NY: Grand Central Publishing, 2017).

73. A search in newspapers.com shows an increasing pattern starting in 1954 and reaching its peak in 1965.

74. This search relied on OCR technology. See 'The "Red Carpet": D.L.W.', *Women's Wear Daily*, 30 April 1954, 44.

75. 'Jean d'Arc', *Vogue*, 1 April 1956, C2.

76. 'C&A Double Knits (Collins & Aikman)', *Women's Wear Daily*, 1 March 1967, 3.

77. 'Glenoit Mills, Inc.', *Women's Wear Daily*, 2 June 1959, 17.

78. United States Lines Advertisement 1957, Box 1, The Sandra and Gary Baden Collection of Celebrity Endorsements in Advertising, 1897–1979, Archives Center, National Museum of American History, Smithsonian Institution Archives (hereafter National Museum of American History).

79. United States Lines Advertisement c. mid-1950s, Box 2, The Sandra and Gary Baden Collection of Celebrity Endorsements in Advertising, 1897–1979, Archives Center, National Museum of American History.

80. Gundle, *Glamour*, 239.

81. Marshall McLuhan, *Understanding Media: The Extensions of Man* (London: Routledge, 2001 [1964]).

82. A Technique for Determining Consumer Images of Different Modes of Travel, Nos 11–20, Box 21, Information Center Records, JWT, Duke Archives. Results from 100 interviews comparing air travellers with those who travelled by train and car.

83. The jet set, as a social elite, overlaps with what was known in the 1960s as the 'Beautiful People'. See Marylin Bender, *The Beautiful People* (New York, NY: Coward-McCann, Inc., 1967).

84. Stadiem, *Jet Set*, 336; Amory et al., *International Celebrity Register*, 136.

85. Cassini designed costumes for many of these films, and collaborated with Royer, Irene, Charles LeMaire and Travilla. See Leese, *Costume Design in the Movies*, 35.

86. Amory et al., *International Celebrity Register*, 137.

87. Stadiem, *Jet Set*, 338. His brother, Oleg, designed for Jackie Kennedy.

88. Ibid., 172–207.

89. Advertisement, Ginger Rogers, Box 1, The Sandra and Gary Baden Collection of Celebrity Endorsements in Advertising, 1897–1979, Archives Center, National Museum of American History.

90. 'Helga Inc.', *Vogue*, 1 May 1967, 48–9.

91. 'Red Carpet Service for United Airlines', *Motion Picture Daily*, 17 September 1956, 4; 'United Airlines', *Motion Picture Daily*, 26 December 1956, 4.

92. 'Red Carpet Service for United Airlines', 4.

93. See also 'United Airlines', 14.

94. 'Red Carpet for United Airlines', *Broadcasting Telecasting*, 10 June 1957, 17.

95. 'American Airlines', *Broadcasting Telecasting*, 18 February 1957, 62.

96. For Hitchcock's transition into television, see Jan Olsson, *Hitchcock a la Carte* (Durham, NC: Duke University Press, 2015).

97. 'Mercury Luxury', *Broadcasting*, 21 January 1957, 51,

98. 'National', *Women's Wear Daily*, 26 March 1958, 12.

99. 'United Airlines', *Women's Wear Daily*, 23 February 1956, 6.

100. 'United Airlines', *Women's Wear Daily*, 11 September 1956, 24; 'United Air Lines', *Motion Picture Daily*, 1 October 1956, 6; 'Red Carpet for United Airlines', *Motion Picture Daily*, 8 December 1958, 6. The promotion of coast-to-coast flights increased in 1958.

101. United Air Lines provided return tickets to the Esquire Theatre Sacramento in exchange for space in the magazine. 'Showman Who Likes to Do Things with Kids Puts Over Great Promotion With "Gigantic" Prize', *Boxoffice*, 22 April 1963, 61.

102. 'United Air Lines', *Women's Wear Daily*, 9 March 1960, 6.

103. The Coty Award, created in 1942, was a prize awarded to American designers. It was coordinated and publicised by Eleanor Lambert.

104. Eleanor Lambert Air-India Advertisement, undated, Box 2, The Sandra and Gary Baden Collection of Celebrity Endorsements in Advertising, 1897–1979, Archives Center, National Museum of American History.

105. 'Lockheed Aircraft Corp', *Harper's Bazaar*, February 1957, 67.

106. Ibid., 67, original emphasis.

107. Gundle, *Glamour*, 241.

108. 'Delta Royal Jet Service', Brochure, 1959, Delta Flight Museum Digital Archive.

109. Ibid.

110. 'Delta Air Lines News', Press Release, December 1963, Delta Flight Museum Digital Archive. Shortland Modes and Samuel Roberts, of New York and Boston, manufactured the designs.

111. 'Eye', *Women's Wear Daily*, 19 March 1974, 12.

112. 'TWA', *Motion Picture Daily*, 19 March 1957, 6.

113. Ibid., 8.

114. 'TWA', *Los Angeles Times*, 25 March 1957, 12.

115. See also 'Foreign-Language Films', *Motion Picture Daily*, 5 February 1957, 2.

# 2

# The Hollywood designers' reign

The belief that costume designers exclusively created dresses for the stars to attend the Oscars in the studio era looms large in popular culture. As stated in the introduction, what actresses wore to the ceremony during this period is a much more complex issue when subjected to close inspection. First and foremost is the fact that some of these designers left the studios during this period, yet continued dressing the stars from their ateliers. But even for on-screen appearances, the leading costume designers were assigned to work with a handful of big stars. Some of these actresses would get exclusive creations for off-screen appearances, but many gowns worn at the Oscars were initially conceived as costumes for the screen. Many chose to wear something different despite their contracts.[1] Furthermore, those actresses who did not have the clout to attract the attention for these designers wore recycled costumes from wardrobe stocks, rented garments, publicity samples sent by department stores, or their own clothes.

Particularly during the 1930s, the Oscars were not perceived as a public event. The intimate nature of the ceremony during the early years meant that not all women attending the ceremony were actresses. Many of them were wives of studio executives and bankers who could afford fashionable imports and expensive jewellery. Fashion was a more fragmented affair than retrospective interpretations of the Golden Age of Hollywood suggest. Photographs and newsreels recorded a much smaller affair, with promotional imagery frequently staged in a studio the day after. My reinterpretation of this period argues that actresses wore these gowns because their designers were at the forefront of the American fashion industry at the time.

The fact that costume designers dressed the stars outside the studios has been historically reduced to the vertically integrated structure of the studio system. In a closer analysis, and adding a fashion perspective to this reading, studio designers of this period should not be regarded solely as costume designers. They were exponents of a local fashion industry that eventually led to the acknowledgement of California-based designers. Historically speaking, many studio designers had left the studios either before the first ceremony or by the early 1940s. Even though some of these designers continued dressing the stars for the Oscars as part of their newly branded role as California designers, this may have been in their capacity as local fashion designers and not necessarily because of their former position in the studios. The nomenclatures 'fashion' and 'costume' designer were used interchangeably in Hollywood during the first decades of the twentieth century. Institutions such as the Fashion Academy trained students in costume design. Hollywood costume designers were often referred to as the studios' fashion designers or fashion experts in advertisements and media articles. More rigid discursive divisions emerged towards 1948, amid the industry turmoil that led to the formation of the Costume Designers Guild in 1953. By then, most studio era designers had left the studios to open their own fashion houses, even though some continued dressing the stars for their public appearances and, occasionally, for their roles on screen. In order to reconcile these designers' split identity, I propose to use the denomination 'Hollywood designers' to refer to those costume designers who had formal training in fashion, previous experience in the fashion industry, and who, eventually, transitioned back into this profession by way of their fashion ateliers.

The first decade of fashion at the Oscars worked as a bellwether for practices to come, not necessarily for what happened at the Oscars, but due to the business models established to promote Hollywood designers and the American fashion industry. The flux between the fashion and film industries, in the American context, resulted in promotional practices that gave Hollywood designers high media exposure and clout. This was the result of the triangulation that Hollywood studios, film fan magazines and manufacturers established to supply department stores during the 1920s and 1930s. Instead of recounting what stars were wearing to the Oscars, this chapter deciphers a more complex contextual orchestration to understand the genesis of these practices and the weight that Hollywood had in establishing an American fashion scene striving to compete with that of Paris. It further locates the emergence of the Academy Awards in the context of the Great Depression, following the parallel founding of two institutions – the Academy of Motion Picture Arts and Sciences and the Fashion Group – to understand the quintessential role of Hollywood costume designers in the establishment of the American fashion industry.

## Institutionalising prestige for the film industry as art and science

The history of the Academy Awards red-carpet requires at least a brief understanding of the emergence of the Academy of Motion Picture Arts and Sciences. The history of the Hollywood pioneers, many also founders of the Academy, bespeaks reinvention and integration of an immigrant community that had escaped racism and poverty in Eastern Europe. They arrived in the so-called 'new' continent in search of opportunities to improve their living conditions and acquire a much-desired sense of belonging.[2] Instead of a gospel of equality, the mid-/late-nineteenth-century Jewish immigrants found an elitist Protestant society expecting newcomers to adapt to the up-and-running structure. Instead of opportunities, many found segregation and low-wage jobs. Ambition and an entrepreneurial mindset required economic and social capital to open up opportunities. Familiarity with the entertainment industry and the willingness to take risks by investing in the emerging cinematic technologies represented one economic gateway when pursuing their fantasies of reinvention in the new world. Neal Gabler explains that many of the immigrants came from the fashion and retail industries; they understood public taste and piracy to beat down competitors, and their background gave them 'a peculiar sensitivity to the dreams and aspirations of other immigrants and working-class families'.[3] Through their own 'otherness', the founders of Hollywood managed to become a powerful economic force and a representation of otherness at the same time. These socially marginalised circumstances enabled them to gain an identification with popular audiences.

By the late 1920s, the Hollywood film industry enjoyed immense international recognition. Their stars were increasingly becoming the ideal bodies of beauty reproduced on screens, and in newspapers and fan magazines around the globe. Despite the attained hegemony, the end of the decade would bring many obstacles, including the Great Depression. In addition to lingering seclusion and prejudices from dominant sectors of society, the industry faced the uncertainty of an economy in decline and the potential repercussions of technological advancements in this attained hegemony.[4] By 1927, the exports that had dominated the industry since World War I were diminishing. Britain introduced a quota system, and continental Europe formed an organisation called Film Europe to challenge the proliferation of American films.[5] Besides, prestige did not come hand in hand with Hollywood's economic success and the founders did not belong to the social elite.

The Hollywood film community created the Academy in 1927 and the Academy Awards in 1929, to maintain Hollywood's hegemony by ascribing prestige to film as an art form while keeping an eye on developing technologies in the name of science. The move towards associating film with academic institutions – such as Columbia, Harvard and the University of Southern California – and the creation of film institutions in 1915 and the 1920s 'were tied to larger attempts to redefine class politics in America'.[6] A search for legitimacy began with the institutionalisation of film programmes and the idea of creating libraries to preserve film as cultural heritage. The industry would also face the imminent unionisation of talent. The Great Depression pushed banks and capital investment that had financed the growth of the Hollywood industry since the 1910s to step in and run the show.[7] The foundation of the Academy and the institutionalisation of the ceremony provided the different sectors of the business with a sense of community, control and prestige while promoting the collection and preservation of film as heritage for future generations.[8]

By the late 1920s, clubs that allowed the elite to gather under a shared interest were a way of conveying status and a sense of belonging.[9] When exclusion from society clubs was for religious reasons, it was Jewish people who were excluded. Such a policy made racial prejudices visible and provides a further understanding of the struggles for integration that the Hollywood founders confronted in the US. It was the eclectic scenario for social interaction provided by café society that slowly put film stars, Hollywood executives and other artists in contact with the American social elite.

## Hollywood on the move

The first official Oscars ceremony took place in the Blossom Room of the Hollywood Roosevelt Hotel on 1 May 1929. The event honoured films produced between August 1927 and August 1928. The ceremony was staged as a banquet, organised in a similar fashion to the New York society banquet-balls that became popular in the media during the days of fashionable society. The Roosevelt Hotel is located in the heart of Hollywood, at the intersection of Hollywood Boulevard and North Orange Drive, metres away from the Dolby Theatre, where the ceremony takes place today. The inaugural pseudo-event had a clear public relations goal, namely to ascribe prestige to the American film industry and to confer social status on its founders.[10] The event was still conceived as a private affair, not as a public spectacle. The venues selected were the trendy spots in town where the local film community gathered to socialise.

The 1930s were a time of tension between the studios and talent that led to the organisation of the Screen Actors Guild, partly because the Academy failed to represent their interests as expected.[11] Initially, not all stars attended the event. The winners were announced beforehand, and few of them were able to envision the importance of this promotional enterprise. If anything, the Oscars were a PR stunt for the industry itself during these establishing years.

By 1930, the ceremony had already left Hollywood. Between 1930 and 1943, the event was held either at the Ambassador Hotel's Cocoanut Grove or the Biltmore Hotel.[12] Even though New York was the epicentre of café society, the Cocoanut Grove was the place to be seen on the West Coast. Unlike previous forms of social elite based on family lineage and pecuniary power, café society's nightlife attracted a gamut of personalities cultivating a certain degree of notoriety and power. The spirit of café society was countercultural. This new social elite empowered a sort of intellectual aristocracy, represented by journalists and characterised by diversity. This phenomenon was part of the glamour enabled by discourses of 'second chances' and the possibility of reinvention provided by the West Coast. The notion of reinvention becomes central in this schema of self-promotion and social mobility through identity construction. Giving parties was crucial. Figures such as Elsa Maxwell functioned as gatekeepers for these social events, dictating who was 'in' and who was 'out'.

The Academy banquets rapidly captured the attention of newspapers, trade magazines and newsreels. The authenticity of Hollywood's prestige was frequently contrasted with more established elites. In November 1931, Molly Merrick reviewed the 4th Academy Awards red-carpet fashions for her column, 'Hollywood in Person', in *The Atlanta Constitution*. In the text, she stressed the artificiality of Hollywood's constructed glamour by comparing the looks of the stars to other attendees. With blatant cynicism, she juxtaposed Hollywood's parade of presumed richness to the looks of 'real millionaires', such as bankers and their wives, who enjoyed wealth and luxury. She alleged that the stars' jewellery was 'put to shame by the emeralds of a local banking family'.[13] The emphasis was set on Hollywood's social status as merely deceptive. It also reflected a Hollywood elite still struggling for acceptance and fortune. The article attempted to unravel the way in which Hollywood glamour was disparaged when encountering the wealthy elite. To the audiences, Hollywood could represent high society but the illusion was not as successful off screen.

## Not any woman's club

While the film community was gathering on the West Coast for the creation of the Academy, another set of influential people gathered in New York to form a non-profit organisation for the advancement of the American fashion industry and the women working in it. The Fashion Group was formed as a palliative to the consequences of the Great Depression's economic breakdown. The idea behind the Fashion Group emerged during an informal luncheon organised by *Vogue*'s editor-in-chief, Edna Woolman Chase, in 1928. Marcia Connor, one of the magazine's staff members, came up with the idea of the Fashion Group in order to institutionalise the informal demands from designers, manufacturers and shops continuously seeking *Vogue*'s advice.[14] Female entrepreneurship was on the rise, mostly due to the development of the beauty industry.[15] Other industries in which educated women forged successful careers had already formed associations to support and promote their corporate roles.[16] The Fashion Group was finally established in 1930, listing Elizabeth Arden, Dorothy Shaver, Helena Rubinstein and Marion Taylor among its members and enjoying the support of Eleanor Roosevelt. Chase became the first president of the organisation.

Chase joined *Vogue* in 1895, before it was acquired by Condé Nast, and worked her way up from the circulation department, where she was in charge of preparing the envelopes for new subscribers. She became *Vogue*'s first editor-in-chief in 1914, after Nast had bought it and rebranded it into a glossy fashion magazine for rich women. Chase rapidly learned the importance of having a local fashion industry. World War I had a significant impact on France, resulting in the closure of fashion salons in September 1914. Without a completely developed American fashion industry, Nast and Chase wondered if the magazine could maintain itself in the absence of a fully functioning Paris. In order to fill the void created by this absence, Chase organised a charity fashion fête to introduce local dressmakers, convincing society matriarchs such as Mrs Fish and Mrs Astor to endorse the event in order to create the sense of an American fashion leadership.[17] This pseudo-event garnered a great deal of publicity for *Vogue*, boosting its advertising revenues and prestige. Under the headline 'Paris by Proxy', the magazine promoted this nationalising endeavour by announcing that 'having no heart just now for conducting the affairs of fashion in person, Paris permits a power of attorney and new modes are sifted, judged, accepted or rejected in New York'.[18] By presenting Paris as an apologetic guest to its readers, the magazine justified the power awarded not by self-entitlement, but as a torch passed on by the real connoisseurs. This was the first of many events of this kind that *Vogue* sponsored.

The Fashion Group grew rapidly into a nationwide organisation overseeing the development of the American fashion and cosmetic industries. In the case of fashion, women as a workforce – both below- and above-the-line – were essential. Special areas were created, catering to the members' particular interests, such as ready-to-wear, accessories, cosmetics, journalism and more. Events and progress within each area were briefly summarised in their bulletins, keeping their members updated. The organisation had regional offices that each enjoyed a certain autonomy and reported back to the headquarters in New York. The Los Angeles regional branch opened in 1935 and functioned as a mediator in the endless promotional activities that engaged Hollywood designers. Besides its local and national branches, it was well connected internationally through Paris and London. To Hollywood, the Fashion Group represented a useful link to New York as a business centre in constant rapport with Europe.

The consensus among fashion scholars is that the status of American fashion designers and the recognition of fashion design as a profession in the US began to be consolidated in the 1930s, coinciding with the formation of the Fashion Group.[19] The American fashion industry had developed expertise in manufacturing, promoting and retailing clothes, but Paris continued to dictate design.[20] The position of Hollywood designers had already been established in the media during the 1920s by way of their appearance in film fan magazines and newspapers. Along with the growth of the American ready-to-wear industry, Hollywood became instrumental in promoting local enterprise.[21] A sector of the Fashion Group pushed for the presenting of Hollywood as a fashion capital with its own identity. In April 1934, its bulletin announced that *McCall's* editor, Hildegarde Fillmore, had gone to Hollywood 'to investigate all the beauty secrets of the Hollywood Stars'.[22] This reflects the potential of Hollywood as a global display window as well as the way fashion aided in constructing promotional discourses for the studios, consequently attracting movie audiences.

## The Hollywood designers

The fashion and film industries managed to navigate the economic crisis brought about by the Great Depression. Hollywood studios were impacted to different degrees. Donald Crafton argues that 'the stock market crash hit Hollywood hard, if later than it hit most other businesses'.[23] During the first three years of the economic crisis, cinema-going became a way of escaping from the grim times and helped sustain fashion consumption. It was not until 1932 that cinema attendance dropped significantly, eventually resulting in salary cuts, shutdowns, massive employee redundancies and even bankruptcy until the intervention of the US Department of Commerce in 1934.[24] In fact, interest in fashion increased during this period. Fashion, as Marie Clifford explains, 'was viewed as a template for a broad range of consumer goods, business people endorsed the notion that the study of fashion trends could predict what would be successful on the consumer market, and hence insure against potential financial loss'.[25] Clifford's argument does little to unravel the mechanisms that kept the garment industry running. The promotional force of the film industry, the high media exposure of Hollywood designers and the concomitant role of stars as trendsetters were instrumental in keeping consumption alive.

The creation of the Academy and the Fashion Group was conductive to establishing dominant national industries and in keeping businesses alive during the economic recession. In the process of articulation of fashion discourses for the mass market, designers became celebrities by way of Hollywood's intermedial reach as early as the 1920s. This individualisation translated into personal branding, similar to our contemporary drive for brand recognition. Despite being unable to assess the impact of tie-ins retrospectively, Hollywood designers became functional for creating an idea of high-profile American designers that would make the US at least seemingly independent from Paris. Hollywood's cross-media stance created the opportunity for the circulation of designer names. Even though earlier fashion designers had achieved celebrity status before the advent of Hollywood designers, the significant contribution of this sector was achieving popularity among the mass audience; the fashion industry was managing to retail its products while capitalising on mass-market reproductions. Designers' success consolidated Hollywood's role as a viable platform for the dissemination of fashion discourses targeting the mass market. This platform was later exploited by international fashion designers and high-end brands through their association with film stars at the ceremony.

## Putting Hollywood in the fashion market

By the time the first ceremony took place, the crossover between the fashion and film industries had been established through tie-ins sold in department stores in major cities across the US. As Charles Eckert describes, '[i]f one walked into New York's largest department stores towards the end of 1929 one could find abundant evidence of the penetration of Hollywood fashions, as well as a virulent form of moviemania.'[26] The cooperation boosted consumption while enabling cross-promotion.

Fashion tie-ins served many functions beyond a purely commercial purpose. For department stores, Hollywood upheld the reproduction model they had successfully exploited through Parisian imports, opening a new niche market which comprised working-class women. The attractiveness of movie-inspired garments relied on the screen stars and the mass circulation of images that Hollywood guaranteed. The massive popularity of Hollywood films, in combination with advertised fashion goods, served as an attraction that could generate profits directly or indirectly to the store. Movie tie-ins attracted clients to department stores, whether they purchased these or other goods. As far as public opinion was concerned, these satellite discourses generated a notion of Hollywood as a creator of fashion, which benefited the allure of Hollywood designers. The recognition in glossy publications provided a veneer of prestige, helping cinema to be considered a reputable art form. The exploitation of tie-ins mentioning the designers, the stars and the films directly benefited the studios. One of the most challenging aspects of the deals was to orchestrate them in the context of film production, considering that the designers worked on the costumes and the tie-ins up to a year before the movies were released. Another challenge was convincing some stars who refused to pose for fashion stills wearing reproductions, which made the use of established names more difficult.[27] Pictures of the stars wearing the original costumes were used for promotional purposes despite alterations.

There were at least three fashion brands directly linked to the Hollywood film industry that persisted in the market for over a decade: Hollywood Fashions, Studio Styles and Cinema Shops. Bernard Waldman, from the Modern Merchandising Bureau, developed the Cinema Fashions brand, sold exclusively at Cinema Shops in department stores such as Macy's. Studio Styles was Warner Bros.' exclusive brand, featuring Orry-Kelly's designs. Hollywood Fashions was a franchise of *Photoplay* that sold both female and male garments, as an affordable alternative to Cinema Shops.[28] Adelia Bird, a Fashion Group member, was credited for creating the tie-ins with the magazine and the stores.

Department stores eagerly accepted the idea of using Hollywood films and fan magazines as a promotional vehicle to showcase the garments. Aside from alleviating the Great Depression, this business model catered to specific needs for each industry. For the studios, fashion tie-ins were a marketing tool from a vertically integrated oligopoly that could exploit every echelon on the payroll. Hollywood studios had highly publicised designers and the most desired bodies to act as models. Their main product, the films, functioned as a promotional tool for merchandising and vice versa. Labels showed associations with the local department stores in which they were sold, the studio associated with the design and the name of the Hollywood designer behind the creation. Women across the country could now purchase garments designed for the stars and emulate desired patterns of femininity. Hollywood Fashions, Cinema Shops and Studio Styles were a small fraction of the activities linking the fashion and film industries during this decade. In 1937, Paramount Pictures' costume designer Edith Head launched a whole line of dresses under the brand 'Styled by Hollywood', carrying Head's autograph, to plug Paramount's film *This Way, Please* (Paramount Pictures, 1937).[29] The line was co-branded with Celanese's Clairanese Taffeta, and retailed at prices ranging from $2 to $4.75 at Gleitsman, Chopp & Sadowsky in New York.

Hollywood's promotional force helped department stores during the uncertain scenario of the 1930s. Despite the help in keeping consumption active in a shrinking economy, the personal ambition of Hollywood designers created a rivalry between New York and Hollywood. New York manufacturer Samuel Chapman alleged that Hollywood costumes could not be copied because they did not suit the needs of American women.[30] Stylists at large in department stores accused Hollywood of copying the looks created on the East Coast for their films. Still, Hollywood proved a seductive label for mass retail on the fashion front for years to come. An article described how more and more women were 'looking to Hollywood rather than Paris as arbiter of fashion'.[31] The author, Elsie Pierce enthusiastically announced: '[t]here's enough patriotism in this old soul to make me thrill to the thought that America is fast establishing fashion leadership'.[32] Besides recounting how department stores were rapidly selling fashion tie-ins linked to Hollywood movies, Pierce commented on the fact that American women were now setting the trends that French women should follow.[33] In 1939, *Women's Wear Daily* stated: 'The World Acclaims American Film Fashions'.[34] Individual arrangements for merchandising re-productions continued after these brands disappeared, not to mention the profitable enterprise of Hollywood patterns.[35]

## Hollywood as the new Paris

During the interwar years, a sector of the media pushed the recognition of Hollywood as a fashion capital. In 1935, columnist Rosalind Shaffer called attention to how national magazines were picking up fan magazines' stories about 'how and why Hollywood ha[d] become a fashion center'.[36] An article in the *Los Angeles Times* heralded Hollywood as the new mecca for fashion designers, describing how famous fashion experts from New York, London and Paris had dropped their high-society clients to dress their new muses, the cinema beauties.[37] The article details how Bernard Newman deserted Bergdorf Goodman to join RKO; Omar Kiam signed a contract with Sam Goldwyn; New York milliner Frank George joined Warner Bros.; and René Hubert started collaborating with Fox Studios.

European fashion designers had already migrated to the US to work in Hollywood during World War I. While Paris was recovering and recon-figuring its business during the interwar years, Hollywood exploited the growing media popularity of its designers.[38] The increasing focus on national production, sparked by the nationalist sentiment of the 1930s, propelled this enterprise. Hollywood strove to find a fashion identity to avoid falling behind Parisian fashion trends, owing to the delay between a film's production and release.[39] Additionally, both studios and department stores struggled with the commercial restrictions imposed by Paris to protect haute couture ateliers from piracy. President Herbert Hoover's tariffs on imports, imposed in 1930 to protect US manufacturers, was a contributing factor.[40] Costume designers at Paramount Pictures were granted two annual trips to fashion capitals, accompanied by newspaper coverage, which added to their fashion flair. From an American perspective, travelling for 'inspiration' was perceived as a natural circulation of ideas rather than fashion raids. The Chambre Syndicale de la Couture Parisienne, a trade association founded in 1868 to regulate, protect and promote the French haute couture industry, focused its business strategies on locating corporate buyers in foreign markets but continued to be concerned about copyright, due to the illegal reproduction of French fashion designs. To maintain French couuire's symbolic capital, it introduced new protectionist restrictions, restricting fashion shows to exclusive clients who were blacklisted if they did not purchase anything.[41] The French protectionist strategy could not stop reproduction but sought to expand controls to slow down the process, ensuring that the connection between Paris and innovation remained intact. Department stores thus needed a new source of designs to reproduce and promote.

The Hollywood studios' predisposition towards any form of epiphenomenon that could increase the promotion of their films led to the exploitation of Hollywood designers as a convenient source of fashion inspiration to fuel the local business. In *Screen Style*, Sarah Berry claims that Travis Banton stopped going to Paris in 1934, visiting New York and Palm Beach instead to see what women were wearing.[42] More than giving credit to Palm Beach as a new fashion mecca, this decision may relate to the national agenda to promote the US as a fashion landmark in combination with the stricter policies imposed in Paris. Newspaper articles also claimed that Banton was crossing the Atlantic to exhibit his studio creations in London. *Los Angeles Times* columnist Alma Whitaker speculated that months later those creations would be copied in Paris.[43]

Discussions within the fashion industry concerning whether Hollywood was capable of setting trends had both followers and detractors, often depending on allegiances with Paris or Hollywood. There are several aspects to consider, moving away from a simplistic Paris-versus-Hollywood antagonism. A broader context exists that integrates the consumer as buyer of commodities and as a consumer of circulating media texts, in order to understand that these products were never direct competitors. Hollywood and a sector of the American fashion industry may have striven to set Hollywood designers on a par with Paris in order to appropriate the notion of prestige that the French fashion industry enjoyed. The fast-paced and business-minded American model helped the successful development of the local ready-to-wear industry. The priority for the American fashion industry was mass production, while France focused on couture, innovation and exclusivity. Cut off from Parisian 'inspiration', the backlash against the notion of prestige concerning Parisian couture sparked anti-Paris discourses.[44] The anti-elitist and inclusive American sentiment focused on national production and helped develop the local mass market. While Paris sought to maintain the prestige and exclusivity that wealthy buyers sought, Hollywood-related sources promoted discourses of inclusion, calling for every woman's right and ability to be fashionable to stimulate commodity consumption. Unlike French couturiers, who worried about the damage that mass reproductions could inflict on their creations, Hollywood designers were under contract with the studios, who owned the rights to the garments they designed for films. Those who had left the studios to favour their own fashion houses, such as Howard Greer, also enjoyed the brand equity derived from the former association of their names with the studios, attracting clients through their media exposure.

Topping the supremacy of Paris, creatively or prestige-wise, was never a matter of direct competition insofar as these were not targeting the same clientele. While the French industry and its clients strived for exclusivity by way of the aura around couture, Hollywood reproductions unapologetically catered to the mass market. By putting itself on a level with Paris, Hollywood was not necessarily asking women who purchased French fashion to buy a department store reproduction of a Hollywood garment. What these messages aimed at was to shift desire towards Hollywood from those who could not afford Paris, promising something local and affordable with similar prestige. Regardless of innovation, Hollywood designers played an instrumental role in disseminating a national discourse that helped recognise a local fashion landscape. For Hollywood, this worked as promotional and commercial epiphenomena to further promote their films. For Hollywood designers, this was a tool for being recognised as creators of fashion and to gain international recognition as trendsetters. For the American fashion industry, it created a halo of a local industry with international projection given by the Hollywood designers' media clout.

At a Fashion Group luncheon in 1933, Adrian voiced his concern about Hollywood designers' unfair exposure in comparison with their Parisian fashion peers. He explained that audiences were only exposed to the 'cream' of Paris collections due to the gatekeeping practice of experts, buyers and fashion editors.[45] People never got exposed to the mundane or poor creations from Paris. In contrast, audiences around the world witnessed the totality of what came from Hollywood through motion pictures. Adrian described the confusion of New York gatekeepers, who were still aligned with Paris, about what motion picture clothes could do for fashion. Through this observation, he made a plea that the same selective eye be used when evaluating Hollywood designs. He was also foreseeing the potential of an inclusive ready-to-wear market that could take fashion trends beyond a limited circle.

The geographical location of Hollywood was also a factor. Its remoteness naturally hindered the historical mercantile exchange established between Europe and New York. In this regard, Adrian complained about the association of a designer's fashion authority with the prestige ascribed by the city in which they resided rather than the work they did. Paris was considered the foremost socially ranked geographical space in relation to fashion.[46] Adrian intended to challenge these rigid ideas about fashion capitals, claiming that:

> Schiaparelli, Vionnet or whoever you please, could still create interesting clothes in the South Sea Isles if they had the necessary materials. Hollywood is not quite as remote as that and it's all a matter of the ideas and whether they are good ideas or not.[47]

He underlined the audience's wish to emulate stars like Greta Garbo, crediting this phenomenon to the work of Hollywood designers. Notwithstanding these debates, Adrian tried to escape the Hollywood stigma surrounding his work by requesting to be addressed as an 'American designer' instead of a 'Hollywood creator of fashions'.[48]

The *New York Herald Tribune* reported that the Fashion Group decided by vote after a debate that Hollywood was no style centre.[49] This blunt statement shows an emerging tension between Hollywood and New York with regard to which one was becoming the fashion capital of the US. The article also quotes a speech about Macy's Cinema Shops given at the luncheon, in which the influence of Hollywood actresses as cultural mediators of style was questioned:

> Speakers were of the opinion that motion picture actresses didn't do much for clothes except put them before the public after they had been designed … Ruth Katsh, of R.H. Macy's Cinema Shop, said she believed that motion picture actresses were more inclined to show good taste than they once were, and that they were beginning to realize that they could not hope to set styles until they wore dresses that suited other women.[50]

Paradoxically, far from discrediting Hollywood as a fashion centre, this critique of the on-screen ostentation of Hollywood costumes as unfit for the mass market indirectly placed Hollywood designers on a par with the criticised complexities of French couture. Department stores had historically simplified French designs through reproductions both to reduce costs and to – supposedly – cater to the simpler taste of American consumers.

Despite the inclusion of Hollywood designers in their discussions, and the support given to Hollywood as a promotional platform for the American fashion industry, a sector of fashion aficionados remained unwilling to acknowledge Hollywood as a fashion capital. They only recognised the movies as a promotional force, disregarding the work of their designers. In a lecture delivered at the Rockefeller Center in September 1933, Marjorie Howard expressed these feelings:

> I think it [Hollywood] brings extravagant, exciting fashions further down in the sticks than they could possibly get there by any other way. I don't think it is a great originator of ideas, but I do think it is an extraordinary propagator of ideas. In Paris we have certain women who are very Garbo and Dietrich conscious, but it affects their hairdressing more than clothes – a great deal more – and after all, it is confined to a very limited circle at that.[51]

Marjorie Howard was the first fashion editor of Universal's house organ *Motion Picture Weekly*.[52] But she had left her Hollywood beginnings to work in Paris as a fashion correspondent.

While MGM's fashion exposure was driven mostly by Adrian's ambition, Paramount Pictures aggressively exploited fashion discourses. The studio's publicity department had one member dedicated exclusively to fashion, Gretchen Messer.[53] Besides producing fashion-related publicity material, Messer organised activities for the members of the Fashion Group, such as private screenings, and secured tickets for the premieres of Paramount films in New York. Having one of their publicists exclusively dedicated to the production of fashion news, in an industry whose evident focus was films, clearly speaks for the promotional weight that fashion carried in relation to the stars. On 6 June 1934, Messer organised a fashion show at the Waldorf Astoria to showcase historical costumes from *Cleopatra* (Paramount Pictures, 1934) and *The Scarlet Empress* (Paramount Pictures, 1934). Messer and members of the Fashion Group also discussed the research behind the creation of historical costumes. Here, Messer claimed that 'historical and costume movies ha[d] influenced fashion in the past few years, to a marked extent'.[54]

On 15 March 1935, she organised a private screening of the short film *The Fashion Side of Hollywood* (Paramount Pictures, 1935) at the Ritz Carlton Hotel.[55] This film was a compilation of costume camera tests and scenes from different Paramount releases for 1935: *The Devil is a Woman, Rumba, The Gilded Lady* and *Mississippi*. It was announced as 'A Style Preview of Forthcoming Motion Pictures', featuring Paramount designer Travis Banton and Kathleen Howard. As a counterpoint to her sister Marjorie, Kathleen had a personal involvement in promoting American fashion in general and Hollywood in particular. Kathleen Howard had an acting career, which may explain the different opinion regarding Hollywood's influence. On-screen credits describe her as the former fashion editor of *Harper's Bazaar* and former president of the Fashion Group, while the voiceover presents her as a former actress and fashion expert.

The film opens backstage in the workroom of Paramount's wardrobe department. A succession of shots shows a close-up of a hand sketching, sequinned fabric arranged on a cutting board, women embroidering a large piece of stretched fabric, mannequins, a close-up of a sewing machine and other elements representing the work behind costume design. The voiceover describes the scene: 'Paramount's wardrobe department is electric with industry; miles of bliss satin, velvet, gold, going to the creations that set the world's fashion trends. Behind this search for craftsmanship is the artist who inspires these creations'.[56] These images could be said to unveil the mystery of Hollywood glamour, as garments generally appear in the context of the star's body. The commentary emphasised the craftsmanship of the unique pieces, indirectly elevating the work of Hollywood designers to the status of French couturiers running a couture house. The opening scene cuts to Banton and Howard, sitting behind a desk while discussing the designs and shuffling through Banton's sketches. Inserts of the sketches give the audience a point-of-view angle while fading into the film's scenes.

Other studios also forged links to the Fashion Group. In 1936, RKO's costume designer Walter Plunkett lectured members of the Fashion Group's Los Angeles branch on 'What Hollywood [could] do to become a genuine source of fashions'.[57] Contributing to the idea of Hollywood as a fashion capital, the Fashion Group organised an international gala at the Waldorf Astoria in 1936, exhibiting clothes from 'Four Style Capitals': New York, Paris, London and Hollywood.[58] In 1940, MGM released a promotional short film featuring Adrian, entitled *Hollywood: Style Center of the World* (MGM, 1940). As in the case of Paramount's short, it functioned as a promotional pitch for upcoming MGM releases camouflaged under a fashion veneer. This film linked costumes directly to tie-ins by recreating a scene in which mother and daughter buy a reproduction in rural America, cutting to Adrian explaining how on-screen looks were adapted and produced as merchandising.[59]

## Hollywood in *Vogue*

Hollywood celebrities are frequently portrayed on the cover of fashion magazines today, but this was not always the case. It took time for *Vogue* to acknowledge the importance of Hollywood in the context of fashion, and even longer to address the Oscars red-carpet.[60] It was not until the mid-1970s that the magazine made any reference to fashion at the Oscars, in a small section.[61] Upon closer scrutiny, the appearance of Hollywood in the pages of *Vogue* has historically coincided with moments when the US fashion community joined forces to drive forward the local industry. *Vogue's* fashion coverage of the Oscars significantly increased with the fashion industry's media boom in the 1990s.

Vogue was originally conceived as a society magazine that featured events, arts and sports coverage, catering to men and women alike. This changed when Condé Nast purchased the publication in 1909 and turned *Vogue* into a specialist magazine to help wealthy and affluent women become fashionable. Nast did not come from a wealthy background, but he understood glamour and how to cater to the thirst for exclusivity among the American elite.[62]

References to stage actresses appeared in the theatre section before the magazine started focusing on fashion. The first mention of a Hollywood actress in a fashion spread arguably appeared in 1913, in reference to America's sweetheart, Mary Pickford.[63] The editorial showed three pictures with corresponding costume descriptions, but this was an exception. Dancer Irene Castle appeared in a brief fashion editorial featuring illustrations of her ballgowns in 1919 and modelling Lucile creations in 1921.[64] Even though Castle started her career as a dancer before entering Hollywood, her case is interesting in its illustration of the place entertainers occupied in society circles. Castle recalled how 'socially unimportant' she was when members of the society elite on the East Coast hired her and her husband to entertain at a party, treating her in a similar way to any other hired serving staff.[65] Hence it may have been Castle's longstanding relationship with Lucile that brought her into the pages of *Vogue*. Actress Joan Bennett appeared in a fashion feature entitled 'The Skirt-and-Trouser Pyjama' in 1930, modelling Vionnet's pyjama tea gown, a Hattie Carnegie blouse and Bergdorf Goodman slippers.[66] By then, Hollywood actresses had appeared as fashionable commodities, endorsing products in the magazine's advertisements. It is worth noting, though, that after Chase took command of *Vogue*, the commercial and editorial departments went in separate directions with precise, yet sometimes incompatible, goals. Advertising became a ticket into the pages of *Vogue* for those not prestigious enough to feature in the magazine's editorial content. The absence of film stars and celebrities as role models of fashion and beauty for the elite market was a response not to a lack of interest from broader audiences in their styling and beauty routines, but, rather, to an incompatibility in the respective social statuses of the luminaries of the big screen and the imagined *Vogue* consumer.

Hollywood became a fixture in Cecil Beaton's column during the 1930s. Beaton, a photographer and costume designer, provided a glimpse into lifestyles on the West Coast.[67] His articles appeared in the context of the emergence of the talkies.[68] His 1931 article 'Hollywood Goes Refined' plays upon a transition into acceptability through acquired appropriate behaviour.[69] Among other factors, the slow renegotiation of Hollywood's representation in *Vogue* contributed to a reinterpretation of the film world's standing in society. It is important to contextualise this refusal/acceptance of Hollywood owing to not being part of a reputable elite sharing established codes of conduct. Hollywood was a threat to the establishment. These discussions took place during the hype of café society, in which socialites mingled with intellectuals, Hollywood stars, artists and even gangsters in the eclectic nightlife of Hollywood and New York.

During the 1920s, a series of scandals involving high-profile Hollywood personalities, in combination with the increasing pressure of conservative groups concerned about the potential bad influence of films, resulted in the development of a censorship code regulating film content.[70] An initial draft, known as the 'Don'ts and Be Carefuls', was drawn up in 1927, but was mainly ignored. The Production Code replaced this list in 1930, and it was strictly enforced after 1934. The code directly addressed the role of costume in films:

1. Complete nudity is never permitted. This includes nudity in fact or in silhouette or any lecherous or licentious notice thereof by other characters in the picture.
2. Undressing scenes should be avoided, and never used save where essential to the plot.
3. Indecent or undue exposure is forbidden.
4. Dancing costumes intended to permit undue exposure or indecent movements in the dance are forbidden.[71]

The implementation of the Hays Code helped clean up Hollywood's reputation.

A five-page spread in *Vogue* in 1933 entitled 'Does Hollywood Create?' addressed the work of Hollywood designers. This rhetorical question incorporated discussions of authenticity in the context of an American fashion identity vis-à-vis Parisian trends.[72] The editorial stated that the movies had become 'worthy of study and even of imitation', and reflected upon the creations of Adrian, Howard Greer, Royer, Travis Banton and Hattie Carnegie in relation to Paris.[73] The question of Hollywood as a creator of fashion remained unanswered, but its potential was clearly established. That same year, the shift towards an American fashion identity for export led by Hollywood was flaunted when an article suggested that Paris was copying the looks of Mae West.[74]

Capitalising on the attractiveness of Hollywood designers and stars during the 1930s, Condé Nast launched *The Hollywood Pattern Book* in 1933 to compete in the cheaper pattern market without compromising the prestige of his leading publication.[75] The studios' designers had no direct involvement in it. The patterns were not exact reproductions of screen costumes but were inspired by – and adapted from – these and other styles used off screen.[76] *The Hollywood Pattern Book* carried articles about the stars, the Hollywood designers and film openings. It was so successful that it became a full magazine, called *Glamour of Hollywood*, but better known today simply as *Glamour*.[77]

In Paris, the fashion community accused *Vogue* of being part of the reigning anti-French sentiment. For Chase, the magazine was merely reflecting what was happening in the fashion industry at the time.[78] The French were right. Chase had incessantly worked to develop the American fashion enterprise so that it could stand independently from that of Paris.

## The last Hollywood designer

In 1942, Adrian was awarded a spread in *Vogue*, announcing him as the 'New Hand in the American Couture'.[79] The title positions Adrian in the highest echelon of fashion designers by using the word 'couture', but it also implied that there was a couture tradition in the US by pinpointing him as 'a new hand' among its members.[80] This media coverage was part of the launch of Adrian's fashion salon in Beverly Hills after he left MGM in 1941. His studio departure marked the end of the Hollywood designers' era. The political move to establish Hollywood as a fashion capital was rapidly fading as New York emerged as a more suitable contender for the fashion throne in the context of a geopolitical reorganisation brought about by World War II.

## Notes

1. Bronwyn Cosgrave states that Mary Pickford wore a Parisian design by Jeanne Lanvin in 1930 and Luise Rainer accepted her 1938 Oscar in a nightgown. See Bronwyn Cosgrave, *Made For Each Other: Fashion and the Academy Awards* (London: Bloomsbury Publishing, 2008), 7–10, 36–7.
2. For a historical study of Hollywood founders, see Neal Gabler, *An Empire of Their Own: How the Jews Invented Hollywood* (New York, NY: Anchor Books, 1988). For a historical account of the Academy's founders, see Debra Ann Pawlak, *Bringing Up Oscar: The Story of the Men and Women Who Founded the Academy* (New York, NY: Pegasus Books, 2001).
3. Gabler, *An Empire of Their Own*, 5.
4. Donald Crafton challenged the fear of loss of hegemony on the verge of the breakthrough of sound, arguing that, at a time when two-thirds of the world's cinemas were located outside the US, Hollywood executives saw the new technology as an opportunity to saturate the European market in the belief that language barriers would be overcome to the

point of moving images establishing 'English as a universal language'. See Donald Crafton, *The Talkies: American Cinema's Transition to Sound 1926–1931* (Berkeley, CA: University of California Press, 1999), 418, 422. In the British context, the film industry argued that local audiences would not endure subtitles or American pronunciation. A similar rationale was advanced that other European markets would group around language similarities. See Victoria de Grazia, *Irresistible Empire: America's Advance Through 20th-Century Europe* (Cambridge, MA: Harvard University Press, 2006), 315.

5. Crafton, *The Talkies*, 418.
6. Peter Decherney, *Hollywood and the Culture Elite: How the Movies Became American* (New York, NY: Columbia University Press, 2005), 63.
7. Tino Balio, ed., *Grand Design: Hollywood as a Modern Business Enterprise, 1930–1939* (Berkeley, CA: University of California Press, 1995), 21–6; Crafton, *The Talkies*, 181–93, 201–2.
8. Decherney, *Hollywood and the Culture Elite*, 65–73.
9. See Vance Packard, *The Status Seekers: An Exploration of Class Behavior in America and the Hidden Barriers that Affect You, Your Community, Your Future* (Philadelphia, PA: David McKay Company, Inc., 1958), 188.
10. The relation of awards and prestige has been explored in McDonald, *Hollywood Stardom*, 215–53; James F. English, *The Economy of Prestige: Prizes, Awards, and the Articulation of Cultural Value* (Cambridge, MA: Harvard University Press, 2005).
11. Balio, *Grand Design*, 153. See also Monica Sandler, 'PR and Politics at Hollywood's Biggest Night: The Academy Awards and Unionization (1929–1939)', *Media Industries* 2, no. 2 (2015), http://doi.org/10.3998/mij.15031809.0002.201/
12. The ceremony took place at the Ambassador Hotel's Cocoanut Grove in 1930–1, 1933–4, 1940 and 1943, and at the Biltmore Hotel in 1932, 1935–9 and 1941–2.
13. Mollie Merrick, 'Hollywood in Person', *The Atlanta Constitution*, 12 November 1931, 6.
14. Edna Woolman Chase and Ilka Chase, *Always in Vogue* (New York, NY: Doubleday & Company, Inc., 1954), 256.
15. Numbers increased from 4.5 per cent of the total managers, officials and proprietors to about 11 per cent in 1940. See Thomas K. McCraw, *American Business Since 1920: How it Worked* (Wheeling, IL: Harlan Davidson, 2009 [2000]), 163.
16. The Advertising Women of New York, originally called the League of Advertising Women, was formed around 1912. See Janet L. Wolff, Trailblazers, 21, Box 8, f. Women in advert, 1918–1969, Sidney Ralph Bernstein Company History Files, JWT, Duke Archives.
17. Besides Mrs Astor and Mrs Fish, the list of society women included Mrs J. Borden Harriman, Mrs Arthur Curtiss James, Mrs August Belmont, Mrs Bradley Martin and Mrs Amos Pichot, among others. The event took place on 4–6 November 1914. Among the fashion contributors were Bendel, Mollie O'Hara, Bergdorf Goodman, Gunther, Tappé, Maison Jacqueline and Kurzman. See Woolman Chase and Chase, *Always in Vogue*, 124.
18. 'Paris by Proxy', *Vogue*, 15 November 1914, 43–5, 116.
19. See, for example, Sheryl Farnan Leipzig et al., 'It is a Profession that is New, Unlimited, and Rich: Promotion of the American Designer in the 1930s', *Dress* 35 (2008–9): 29–47; Rebecca Arnold, *The American Look: Fashion, Sportswear and the Image of Women in 1930s and 1940s New York* (New York, NY: I.B. Tauris, 2009).
20. Sandra Stansbery Buckland, 'Promoting American Designers, 1940–44: Building Our Own House', in Linda Welters and Patricia A. Cunningham, eds, *Twentieth-Century American Fashion* (Oxford: Berg, 2005).

21. Farnan Leipzig et al., 'It is a Profession that is New', 33.
22. Fashion Group Bulletin, April 1934, Box 144, f. 5, Fashion Group International Records, NYPL.
23. Crafton, *The Talkies*, 181.
24. Balio, *Grand Design*, 13–36.
25. Clifford, 'Working with Fashion', 73.
26. Charles Eckert, 'The Carole Lombard in Macy's Window', in Jane Gaines and Charlotte Herzog, eds, *Fabrications: Costume and the Female Body* (New York, NY: Routledge, 1990),107. Eckert's findings were challenged by other film scholars, but my research confirms and enforces his argument.
27. Rosalind Shaffer, 'Films Broadcast the Fashions Created in Hollywood: Style Show in Every Movie', *Chicago Daily Tribune*, 11 August 1935, D12.
28. Sarah Berry, *Screen Style: Fashion and Femininity in 1930s Hollywood* (Minneapolis, MN: University of Minnesota Press, 2000), 17.
29. 'Styled by Hollywood Ad', *Women's Wear Daily*, 6 October 1937, 7.
30. 'Fashions for Milady Bring Dollars to Box Office', *The Motion Picture Herald*, 7 October 1944, 19.
31. Elsie Pierce, 'How to Be Beautiful: More and More Women Looking to Hollywood Rather Than Paris as Arbiter of Fashions', *The Sun*, 27 April 1937, 12.
32. Ibid., 12.
33. Ibid., 12.
34. Frances Ralston, 'The World Acclaims American Film Fashions', *Women's Wear Daily*, 19 September 1939, 22.
35. See Frankly Frocks, 'Wash Frocks Adapted from Movie Designs in Dramatic Tie-Up', *Women's Wear Daily*, 15 April 1937, 19. See also Hollywood designs in association with rayon in 'Ad Hollywood March of Fashion', *Women's Wear Daily*, 19 December 1939, 14–15. For a tie-in with American viscose with Hollywood designers, see 'Amer.-Viscose in Hollywood Fabric and Costume Tie-Up', *Women's Wear Daily*, 4 December 1939, 10; 'First Crown Movie Tie-Up is With Victor Herbert Film', *Women's Wear Daily*, 6 December 1939, 18.
36. Shaffer, 'Films Broadcast the Fashions Created in Hollywood', D12.
37. Alma Whitaker, 'New York and Paris Lose Fashion Experts to Films', *Los Angeles Times*, 20 January 1935, A1.
38. For the reorganisation of the Paris fashion industry during this period, see Véronique Pouillard, 'Managing Fashion Creativity: The History of the Chambre Syndicale de la Couture Parisienne During the Interwar Period', *Economic History Research* 12, no. 2 (June 2016): 76–89, http://dx.doi.org/10.1016/j.ihe.2015.05.002/
39. Paddy Calistro and Edith Head, *Edith Head's Hollywood* (Santa Monica, CA: Angel City Press, 2008), 29–30.
40. This refers to the Smoot-Hawley Tariff Act of 1930 that was made more flexible by Roosevelt's Reciprocal Trade Agreement Act in 1934, in the context of the New Deal. Price Fishback, 'The New Deal', in *Government and American Economy: A New History* (Chicago, IL: University of Chicago Press, 2008), 393. For more about Paris's protection-ist concerns, see Véronique Pouillard, 'Design Piracy in the Fashion Industries of Paris and New York in the Interwar Years', *Business History Review* 85, no. 2 (2011): 319–44.
41. Pouillard, 'Managing Fashion Creativity', 82.
42. Berry, *Screen Style*, 14–15.
43. Alma Whitaker, 'New York and Paris Lose Fashion Experts to Films', *Los Angeles Times*, 20 January 1935, A1. Berry's argument seems to derive from Banton's media tours. However,

passenger registers show that Banton visited England and France in 1935. See 'New York, New York Passenger and Crew Lists, 1909, 1925–1957', database with images, FamilySearch https://familysearch.org/ark:/61903/1:1:24VD-Z5D/ (2 October 2015), Travis Banton, 1935, citing Immigration, New York, New York, US, NARA microfilm publication T715 (Washington, DC: National Archives and Records Administration, n.d.).

44. Anti-Paris fashion statements can be traced back to fashionable society, when social arbiter Ward McAllister encouraged society women to look at a local landscape instead of searching for inspiration in Europe.

45. Letter from Adrian, Box 72 speeches and transcripts, f. 8 Kathleen Howard, Fashion Group International Records, NYPL.

46. For more about the notion of a socially ranked geographical space, see Pierre Bourdieu, *Distinction: A Social Critique of the Judgement of Taste* (New York, NY: Routledge, 2013), 93–164.

47. Letter from Adrian, Box 72 speeches and transcripts, f. 8 Kathleen Howard, Fashion Group International Records, NYPL.

48. Fashion Group Bulletin, February 1934, Box 144, f. 5 Fashion Group International Records, NYPL. Despite his defence of Hollywood's position in the fashion landscape, Adrian attempted to distance himself from this Hollywood stigma, requesting that he be addressed as an 'American designer' instead of a 'Hollywood creator of fashions'.

49. 'Newark to Ask Citizens to Confer on Finances', *New York Herald Tribune*, 9 March 1933, 9.

50. Ibid., 9.

51. Fashion Forecast Conference transcript, 6–7 September 1933, Box 72 speeches and transcripts, f. 8 Kathleen Howard, Fashion Group International Records, NYPL.

52. See 'Fashion Writer Joins Staff of Universal House Organ', *Motion Picture News*, 1 January 1916, 48.

53. 'Righteous Indignation', *Paramount Parade*, 1.5 (April 1937).

54. Fashion Group Bulletin May 1934, 2, Box 144, f. 5, Fashion Group International Records, NYPL.

55. The Fashion Group Luncheon, *Fashion Group Bulletin*, 1.4 (March 1935), Box 144, f. 5, Fashion Group International Records, NYPL.

56. Marlene DietrichVideo, 'The "Fashion Side" of Marlene Dietrich in "The Devil is a Woman". 1935 Costume Tests!', *YouTube*, uploaded 6 March 2015, https://www.youtube.com/watch?v=EqBnVUEXCMM/

57. Fashion Group Bulletin May 1936, 4, Box 144, f. 8, Fashion Group International Records, NYPL.

58. 'Jean Burke Johnston', *New York Herald Tribune*, 11 September 1936, 16.

59. 'Another Romance', *MGM Studio News*, 23 April 1940, 8.

60. In the pre-Condé Nast era, a picture of Fanny Ward randomly appears with a small introductory epigraph on 29 July 1893, S8. This is not representative. Early associations with *Vogue* also respond to the activities of film studios located on the East Coast. Under Nast's ownership, various articles addressing the eventual work of theatre actors and actresses (a slightly more reputable art form by then) for Hollywood were identified in the mid- to late 1910s. These mentions appeared in 'Seen on Stage', a minor section dedicated to the performing arts that was previously called 'Playhouse Gossip'. Nevertheless, these accounts were neither frequent nor, in the context of a film star or celebrity, relating to fashion.

61. Observations, 'Observed: Straplessness . . . The Big-Evening Fashion Message!', *Vogue*, 1 June 1976, 79.

62. Caroline Seebohm, *The Man Who Was Vogue: The Life and Times of Condé Nast* (New York: The Viking Press, 1982), 15–26.

63. Fashion, 'How Mary Pickford Dresses', *Vogue*, 1 June 1913, 13.

64. 'Fashion: Some Things that Irene Castle Dances In', *Vogue*, 1 November 1919, 79; 'Fashion: Lucile Gowns Irene Castle', *Vogue*, 1 February 1921, 46.

65. See Amory, *Who Killed Society?*, 111–12.

66. Fashion, 'The Skirt-and-Trouser Pyjama', *Vogue*, 24 November 1930, 56.

67. Cecil Beaton, 'Hollywood', *Vogue*, 15 February 1930, 59–61; Cecil Beaton, 'Colorful Characters of Hollywood', *Vogue*, 5 July 1930, 39–41. Besides his work as a photographer and writer, Beaton worked occasionally for Hollywood as a costume designer. He won two Academy Award nominations for *Gigi* (MGM, 1958) and *My Fair Lady* (Warner Bros., 1964). See Leese, *Costume Design in the Movies*, 31.

68. David Carb, 'Talkies', *Vogue*, 22 June 1929, 54–5, 104.

69. Cecil Beaton, 'Hollywood Goes Refined', *Vogue*, 15 June 1931, 34–5, 98.

70. The Motion Picture Producers and Distributors of America (MPPDA), founded in 1922, was invested in improving Hollywood's public image. See de Grazia, *Irresistible Empire*, 299. For more about the Hays Code, see Richard Maltby, 'The Production Code and the Hays Office', in Balio, *Grand Design*, 37–72; Thomas Patrick Doherty, *Pre-Code Hollywood: Sex, Immorality, and Insurrection in American Cinema, 1930–1934* (New York, NY: Columbia University Press, 1999); Lea Jacobs, *The Wages of Sin: Censorship and the Fallen Woman Film, 1928–1942* (Berkeley, CA: University of California Press, 1997).

71. Production Code-VI. Costume, f. 11.19 Moving Picture Industry, Harold Leonard Motion Picture Research Files, CEYRL.

72. Cecil Beaton, 'Does Hollywood Create?', *Vogue*, 1 February 1933, 59–61, 76–7.

73. Ibid., 59–61, 76–7.

74. Fashion, 'Paris Goes Mae West', *Vogue*, 1 August 1933, 30–1, 65.

75. *Vogue* already published patterns, but their price ranged from $0.40 to $2.00 and they could not compete with the new pattern publications launched under the National Recovery Administration. For a full discussion of the pattern industry, see Joy Spanabel Emery, *A History of the Paper Pattern Industry: The Home Dressmaking Fashion Revolution* (London: Bloomsbury Academic, 2014), 122–30; Carol and Anne Dickinson, 'The Pattern Industry', in Phyllis G. Tortora, ed., *Berg Encyclopaedia of World Dress and Fashion: The United States and Canada* (Oxford: Bloomsbury Academic, 2010).

76. Spanabel Emery, *A History of the Paper Pattern Industry*, 127. Other pattern publications presented a direct association with the studios' costume designers and styles worn on screen, such as Orry-Kelly's Butterick Patterns from 1933.

77. See Sumner, *The Magazine Century*, 93.

78. Woolman Chase and Chase, *Always in Vogue*, 301.

79. Fashion, 'A New Hand in American Couture', *Vogue*, 15 March 1942, 62–3.

80. Charles James, frequently regarded as the 'first American couturier', was a contemporary of Adrian and other Hollywood designers. For more about him, see Richard Harrison Martin, *Charles James* (New York, NY: Universe/Vendome, 1999).

# 3

# From private gatherings to public spectacle

The first Academy gatherings drew the attention of the trade press, but their segregated industrial focus was of little interest beyond reporting who won which award. *Variety* and *The Hollywood Reporter* engaged in extensive coverage that included all the glitz and glamour of the event. *Variety* dedicated a full column to fashion with detailed descriptions of the garments, except for the years of US participation in World War II, when the informal dress code was imposed in pursuit of austerity. As soon as the media became attuned with the ceremony, news agencies were the fastest distributors of Oscar news around the world. Newspapers and radio stations reproduced the information received via wire services such as Reuters, United Press (UP) and AP. These services mostly reported the nominees and winners of the different awards. Fashion trade paper *Women's Wear Daily* acknowledged the importance of fashion at the ceremony as early as 1940, but this was an exception until the 1950s.[1] In terms of moving images, newsreels were the first format to carry the ceremony around the globe.[2]

The first attempts to open up the ceremony started in 1939. This restructuring included replacing the Academy president for a vaudevillian host, attempting to broadcast the event on radio and producing a short film about the ceremony. In this film, the statuette was formally introduced as Oscar and presented as the embodiment of prestige. The 1940s were a decade of reconfigurations. The advent of World War II brought substantial changes. While the US remained at the margins of the events happening in Europe during the first two years, the Japanese attack on Pearl Harbor in 1941 would lead the US into battle and change its geopolitical standing. During the war, the movie industry became a powerful tool for producing and promoting a cohesive notion of American identity and nationalism. Government officials had already acknowledged star capital and commercial Hollywood's potential as a tool of propaganda during World War I.[3] Hollywood opinion leaders could pitch national industries in their media appearances, boosting the local economy and reinforcing the US cultural legacy.

This role of Hollywood as a vehicle for the circulation of cultural capital dovetails with the notion of the American Century. In order to understand the global impact of the red-carpet phenomenon, it is necessary to bring forward the importance of World War II and the postwar era as a historical, ideological turning point in the context of globalisation. In this context, the ceremony transitioned from an intimate gathering into a public spectacle, shaping much of the ceremony and red-carpet dynamics we see today. This chapter analyses the events that transformed the ceremony into a media event. It provides a panorama of the physical and symbolic space that the red-carpet pre-show gained through this transformation, locating these events in the context of a geopolitical reconfiguration led by the advent of World War II. Consequently, it illustrates the changes that the ceremony underwent by discussing not only how its spatial dimension shifted, but also how these changes impacted different ideological stands.

## A cavalcade of Academy Awards

Newsreels were the fastest way of getting moving images around the globe. Hearst's *News of the Day* series, distributed by MGM, *Telenews*, *Universal Newsreels*, *Associated British-Pathé*, *American Pathé News* and *Warner-Pathé News* had included Oscars segments since the inception of the ceremony. The nature of the footage varied over the years. Early newsreels blended images of the ceremony with short speeches staged in a studio the day after the event. Later on, the footage would include fragments of the acceptance speeches given on the banquet's improvised stage.[4] These images revealed the shy natures of the actors and actresses and how intimate the event was.

In 1940, the Academy produced a featurette in association with Warner Bros. entitled *Cavalcade of Academy Awards*. This film can be regarded as an early attempt to officially mediatise and export the event. The studio was the principal investor and all profits were destined to support the Academy. Frank Capra was assigned to supervise the venture.[5] His role was more of an endorser and mediator behind the scenes.[6] Capra's name would facilitate negotiations, the release of image consents and securing the attendance of stars that day.

This recapitulation of the ceremony's history was produced in two parts. The most complicated endeavour was compiling newsreel footage and scenes from nominated and winning films. The studio needed the filmmakers' authorisation, featured stars' approval and releases from other studios without any compensation. The backbone of the film was shot separately, during the 1940 banquet at the

Cocoanut Grove. To this end, they installed lights, cameras and microphones in the nightclub and other public areas of the Ambassador Hotel.[7] Foreseeing the potential attractiveness of the red-carpet arrivals, Academy representative Donald Gledhill suggested a consultation with the studio's weather reporting service to secure the appropriate equipment for outdoor scenes in case of rain. From his perspective, photographing the people arriving at the door would 'be a good publicity story for the Academy'.[8] In the film, the stars were shot arriving and coming directly into the ballroom. Whether this was a result of the bad weather forecast or a practical decision to avoid complications is hard to assess.

The statuette's name, Oscar, was formally introduced in the featurette. The film's voiceover enacts the voice of Oscar, addressing 'Mr Tommy Ticket-buyer' and 'Little Mary Matinée' – the audience. Oscar invites them behind the scenes of Hollywood magic, underlining the importance of those who work to make the magic happen. The voice behind 'Oscar' was screenwriter and trailer narrator, Carey Wilson. Wilson or, rather, Oscar opens the film with a speech about his origins and symbolic standing, in epic mythology. In his speech, he claims to be a symbol of progress, 'the recognition of achievement for which mankind will always strive'. In alleging to be more than ten million years old, Oscar is claiming to be not only a modern form of reward, but ambition and excellence itself.[9] The introduction is aimed at striking an emotional chord in the audience, making them feel important by showing Hollywood as a recognised elite, yet working for the service of the viewer. The magic appeases the reality of a troubled world. The discourse ambiguously plays between anonymity and personal address. It uses the word 'audience', a term denoting the anonymity of the masses, yet addresses them as 'Mr' and 'Mrs' to create a sense of individuality, which is further emphasised in the use of 'Mr Tommy Ticket-buyer' and 'Little Mary Matinée' as an ideological reminder of their vicarious roles as consumers.

The presentation builds up to the importance of the awards by presenting every echelon in the film production chain, including the stars, and Oscar as the very apex. He is brought to life and given an identity, a god-like presence across the ages, who has 'always been there and always will be'. Oscar is both concrete and abstract, personified, brought to life and made eternal as a ma-terialisation of recognition for outstanding achievements and an embodiment of prestige. After addressing the audience, Oscar briefly relates the history of the Academy. 'My present incarnation begins in 1927,' he explains. Images of the banquet at Cocoanut Grove show attendees dancing in the salon, cutting to a montage of stars, Hollywood executives and journalists entering the room. Simultaneously, Oscar introduces them to the audience. 'Did you ask for glamour, Mr and Mrs Audience? Well, Hedy Lamarr is here, adorned with her husband, Gene Markey'.[10] This early footage of the event showcased the gossip columnists' celebrity status through the arrival of Hedda Hopper and Louella Parsons. When Elsa Maxwell enters the ballroom, Oscar finally announces, 'Start the party, folks, now everything is ready to go'. The camera moves from the reception to a room of the Ambassador Hotel set up as a press room, where a group of men wearing tuxedos wait for the envelopes containing the names of the winners. The documentary claims that members of the international press were present. Bob Hope takes the stage to entertain the audience with one of his monologues and hands out a series of awards. He finally announces the awards for Best Achievements in Acting. Oscar closes the film, promising to keep producing great entertainment with the more than 70,000 people that make up the movie industry.

The film was released on 25 May 1940 and was advertised as '30 minutes of star-studded entertainment'.[11] It had theatrical distribution across the country and was screened in combination with full-length features. *Showmen's Trade Review* described it as having 'fan appeal'.[12] The emphasis on the stars to promote the short evidences the lack of traction that the ceremony had to attract audiences before turning into a media event. This promotion was subject to much discussion in advance. The fear was that using the stars as the main bait could backfire once audiences noticed that they appeared in the film only for short flashes.[13] The media reception unsurprisingly focused on the number of stars and the familiarity between stars and audience. According to one article, 'To many theatregoers the flashes of the older stars and the early winners of the coveted award will give the same thrill like that of meeting old friends and renewing cherished associations'.[14] Fragments of the film were distributed for inclusion in newsreels.

In 1948, the Academy produced a second film, entitled *Twenty Years of Academy Awards*, this time with RKO as the distributor. The two-reel featurette was distributed as an industry goodwill gesture, as were extras to enable exhibitors to merchandise the film, such as a trailer, posters, a press book and stills.[15] These actions demonstrate the intention behind the promotion of the ceremony was more political than about generating profits.

## The Oscars and the American Century

On 17 February 1941, Henry R. Luce published an article in *Life* magazine analysing the US's potential involvement in World War II and reflecting upon the meaning of 'Americanness'. Participating in the war could bring the US a unique opportunity for world leadership. Luce argued that, despite resistance to becoming involved in the war, such engagement was inevitable. Britain alone could not defeat Hitler, and there could not be real peace as long as there was a

**Figure 3.1** Advertisement for the short film *Cavalcade of Academy Awards* as it appeared in the exhibitor's trade paper *Boxoffice*, 13 April 1940. Courtesy of the Media History Digital Library.

latent threat to American values.[16] Allegedly, the editorial received a response of 4,541 mostly favourable letters. It was reprinted in *The Washington Post* and *Reader's Digest*, published as a booklet and assigned for reading in high schools, colleges and universities.[17] Stephen J. Whitfield argues that Luce's editorial 'can be read as a complement to the Four Freedoms', the speech delivered by President Franklin D. Roosevelt to Congress on 6 January 1941.[18] In the speech, Roosevelt called for freedom of expression and worship, and freedom from want and fear for all nations around the world.[19] More than a pledge to world domination, Luce sought to continue an ideological expansion of the so-called benefits of the American lifestyle – that popular music and cinema had already begun disseminating around the world – in a quest to ensure a positive global environment that would consolidate freedom, democracy and wealth.[20]

Entertainment was vital in the process. As Kingsley Bolton and Jan Olsson argue, 'the American export of complex patterns of popular culture has run its course parallel to the rise and expression of American imperial ambitions through military means ... presented in terms of promoting the unrivalled benefits of American civilisation'.[21] In the context of the 'four freedoms' speech, President Roosevelt also addressed the Hollywood community in a six-minute speech during the Academy Awards banquet, celebrated at the Biltmore Hotel on 27 February 1941.[22] Concerned about the military advances of Germany, Roosevelt warned of threats to democracies around the globe. He called for integration, cultural and economic exchange among all nations of the Americas, and recognition of the film industry's cooperation and efforts in the dissemination of these Western ideals of freedom. The speech was cut and edited to fit the newsreel format:

> We've seen the American motion picture become foremost in all the world. We've seen it reflect our civilization throughout the rest of the world, the aims and the aspirations, and the ideals of a free people and of freedom itself. The motion picture industry has utilized its vast resources, resources of talent and facilities, in a sincere effort to help the people of the hemisphere to come to know each other. Dictators, those who enforce the totalitarian form of government, think it's a dangerous thing for their unfortunate people to know that in our democracy officers of the government are the servants and never the masters of the people.[23]

With the circulation of Roosevelt's speech around the world on newsreels, the motion picture industry proved its power as a beacon for American values. Roosevelt's speech assigned a 'diplomatic' function to Hollywood that would complement future military decisions.[24] The film community was now officially called for duty. Hollywood had embraced the patriotic mission.

The publication of Luce's editorial, together with Roosevelt's speeches, marked a turning point in the national perception of the US's role in geopolitics. The attack on Pearl Harbor in December 1941 made it inevitable for the US to formally enter World War II, in an environment already bathed in national pride. War permeated every American industry during the 1940s. Newsreels reflected the cooperation with and adhesion to national interests. In this context of the national effort, actors and actresses even had special clauses in their contracts allowing their contractual responsibilities to be deferred if they were called upon to serve the US government.[25] Hollywood functioned as propaganda machinery for the dissemination of the so-called American Dream and American values. It began playing an important role in American politics via the visibility given by its films, stars and other forms of cross-media creating epiphenomena. These ideas attest to the postwar portrayal of the American way of life as synonymous with wealth and comfort through the success of consumer culture. Such achievements eventually became ideal platforms for foreign businesses when expanding their global horizons.

The notion of freedom from want related directly to economic development and wealth, a preoccupation that had been carved deep in the US since the Great Depression. It also harks back to the democratisation of desire that William Leach described in his study of department stores and American consumer culture.[26] This conceptualisation of the right to consume was the result of the move from a society of producers to a modern society of consumers that took place in the mid-1800s.[27] When this purchasing power was jeopardised by the economic recession, securing it back became a priority. What began as an ideal to ensure a better standard of living soon turned into the emergence of a fifth freedom, 'free enterprise', in the hands of business rhetoricians.[28] Luce's vision of the American Century, like that of many liberals, rested on securing US hegemony and free enterprise. As Philip S. Golub attests, 'US investment, public and private, stimulated investment and consumption in Europe, which in turn generated outlets for American industry and finance'.[29] The end of World War II marked a power shift towards television, the expansion of consumer culture and the emergence of celebrity culture. The simultaneous growth of fashion journalism provided a new platform for the promotion of designer names in the media. All these concomitant phenomena catalysed new business models in an increasingly global market.

## A new fashion capital for the American Century

The political move to establish Hollywood as a fashion capital eventually faded. The occupation of Paris in 1940 forced many French designers into exile. New York stepped up to secure its position as a fashion leader. Despite the rivalries, the roles of New York and Hollywood in fashion were distinct. New York functioned as an industrial hub, attempting to imprint an identity on the local production. Meanwhile, Hollywood provided a platform for the circulation of fashion discourses, beauty ideals and the idea of a successful American fashion enterprise. Hollywood was a display window to the world. The publicised work of Hollywood designers helped develop attractive brands, but most of them were no longer under contract.

In 1941, Mrs Blanche Bea Swenson, chair of the Los Angeles branch of the Fashion Group, declared California's artists as the logical successors of Parisian couturiers when promoting a style show at the Ambassador Hotel.[30] Arguably, this was part of a rebranding that turned the notion of Hollywood designers into California designers as most had by then left the studios to open their own fashion houses. The term California Designers provided an independent new identity that was not necessarily linked to Hollywood's studio system. The show announced the creations of thirty fashion and costume designers, including Adrian, Travis Banton, Irene, Bernard Newman, Howard Greer, Edith Head, Orry-Kelly and Walter Plunkett. Los Angeles mayor Fletcher Bowron opened the event declaring, '[w]ith the fall of France and the elimination of Paris from American style life I believe Los Angeles has much to offer American women in the way of color, youth, functionalism, comfort and, above all, glamour.'[31] Sylva Weaver, a member of the Fashion Group and *Los Angeles Times* fashion editor, wrote in her column that these designers had made 'a bid for world fashion leadership.'[32] Weaver adhered to the idea of establishing California as a new fashion capital. In 1941, she declared California to be the 'Nation's Style Centre', suggesting that fashion was the new 'gold rush.'[33]

Establishing California as the new fashion capital in the absence of Paris would encounter new challenges. During the 1920s, JWT encouraged manufacturers to develop brands to be in a better negotiating position against the department store giants. Hollywood had helped manufacturers and department stores during the interwar years through different deals to exploit their designers' creations and image. Even though some manufacturers increased product value through their association with Hollywood as a brand tag, the industrial sector was grouping together and working towards a new PR strategy. In 1941, the recently formed New York Dress Institute (NYDI) appointed JWT to handle its $1 million promotional campaign to establish New York as the 'Style Centre of the World.'[34] This was part of a more extensive campaign launched by New York City's mayor Fiorello H. La Guardia, and supported by different associations of manufacturers. To propel the campaign, they requested the assistance of three major department stores: Lord and Taylor, Bonwit-Teller and Bergdorf Goodman. In the long run, the general mission to promote the American fashion enterprise led to the creation of the American Designers Press Week.[35] By the end of World War II, the power ratio between department stores and manufacturers had reversed as brand-conscious consumers were drawn to smaller retailers who benefited from carrying brands to attract clients into their boutiques.[36] As a consequence, brand names in big department stores grew.

With the liberation of Paris in 1944, the trade paper *Motion Picture Herald* announced that Paris was trying to 'regain its stature as the international style capital' at a moment when New York was still struggling to become one.[37] The role of Hollywood in the fashion industry was far from over. The article discusses a series of tie-ins with the release of Darryl Zanuck's period piece *Wilson* (20th Century Fox, 1944), describing how American designer Nettie Rosenstein based her collection on gowns from the film, selling them in 200 department stores that tied her creations to the movie. René Hubert, a French designer who found refuge in Hollywood during World War II, designed the costumes for the film.[38] Paris was working on refuelling its industry and new fashion capitals in Europe were about to gain strength. Those Hollywood designers who actively strove for recognition in the fashion industry had opened their own fashion houses and rebranded themselves as California designers. Those who remained in the studios had problems of their own. The emergence of television and the Paramount Antitrust Case drove the focus away from Hollywood as a fashion landmark competing with Paris, opening up a new era in fashion promotion in which the popularity of the Oscars became an ideal platform for the exposure of designer names and brands in association with glamorous stars.

## The Academy goes to war – at the Chinese Theatre

The US involvement in World War II directly impacted on the nature of the ceremony. After the attack on Pearl Harbor, Academy officials considered cancelling the annual banquet. President Bette Davies suggested hosting the ceremony in an auditorium, inviting the audience to buy tickets to raise funds for the Red Cross. Both motions were discarded. The ceremony continued under the denomination annual 'dinner' instead of 'banquet'.[39] Amid the reigning discourses of austerity, Academy officials agreed that hosting lavish dinner parties in times of war was insensitive, and decided to move the ceremony to Grauman's Chinese Theatre in 1944. The argument was paradoxical insofar as the US had joined the war effort more than two years before. The ceremony instead turned into a spectacle by emulating the grand opening nights of big movie palaces.

The spectacle created to attract people into the cinema during the late 1910s had Sid Grauman as one of the best-known exhibitors on the West

Coast. Grauman was also one of the founding members of the Academy. His Chinese Theatre, where iconic stars were invited to put their handprints or footprints on the venue's courtyard sidewalk, opened in 1927. With the help of Adolph Zukor and Paramount, Grauman had already inaugurated venues in Los Angeles, such as the Egyptian Theatre, often credited for its inaugural red-carpet accolades, but none became as emblematic as the Chinese Theatre. Kim Khavar Fahlstedt argues that 'it was not until [Grauman] announced his plans to build the Chinese Theatre on Hollywood Boulevard in 1926 that it became a point of contention in Hollywood'.[40] Opening nights were the epitome of showmanship, with live performances and actors being greeted on the red carpet in front of thousands of fans. The contribution of radio in broadcasting these events was pivotal, furthering the cross-media hybridity that movies already had with newspapers. In 1929, Grauman sold the theatre to the Fox Corporation, but reviving the big Hollywood premieres was a trend from the 1940s as charity fundraisers during wartime.[41]

Fashion drove the government's attention due to the shortage of materials that were destined to manufacture war supplies instead of fashionable fabrics. In April 1942, the War Production Board issued Limitation Order L85 that directly targeted the textile industry, reducing the length of dresses, and restricting the number of pockets and details as well as the use of metals and dye colours.[42] These limitations also called for a decrease in manufacturing in order to focus labour towards the war effort. Fashion newsreels passed on the message. Fox Movietone's fashion news films showed the contribution of women to the war effort and even provided tips on how to turn one outfit into many.[43] Austerity became a patriotic act, and the Academy committed itself to the war effort.[44] Glamour was toned down at the ceremony, following patriotic mandates. Tickets to the event carried the legend 'informal attire'. Anyone who had an affiliation with the army was instructed to attend in uniform. The trade press contributed by reducing the focus on the ceremony's fashion during the war years.

This chastening of glamour was not monolithic. While fashion commentary significantly diminished, reviews continued to describe the wearing of furs and jewellery. This coincided with campaigns using Hollywood stars as endorsers of fur companies.[45] Furs were considered an investment, something that lasted and the last item of clothing to be let go even during the war scenario. One advertisement included the caption 'next to WAR BONDS the best loved gift . . . FURS'.[46] Scholars argue that despite regulations and changes in styles, the clothing industry continued to promote consumption 'through advertisements that integrated public support for the war, fear, and patriotism into their marketing campaigns'.[47] Fur stores advertised and encouraged adjustments as a way to keep the fashion for fur in line with government expectations. This may have been an alternative

**Figure 3.2** Norma Shearer and Lieutenant Marty Arrouge, wearing his navy uniform, arriving at Grauman's Chinese Theatre for the Academy Awards ceremony on 16 March 1945. *Los Angeles Herald Examiner* Photo Collection. Courtesy of Los Angeles Public Library.

way to remain in business during the economic recession. Even though glamour was unofficially restored after the end of the war, the 'informal attire' dress code remained until 1948. The ceremony was brought back to Hollywood with the move to the Chinese Theatre, a venue that remains one of the most iconic Oscars locations despite hosting the event on only three occasions.

## The red-carpet as the show within the show

The red-carpet affair emerged as a separate event from the show when the ceremony moved to the Chinese Theatre. In 1945, the Oscars turned into a full-blown media event with the first nationwide radio broadcast of the entire ceremony, which forced organisers to fit it into a structure suitable for the medium. This is how Oscars night got its big searchlight entrance, a red-carpet host, bleacher seats and even a warm-up act for the expectant audience inside the venue. It is worth noting, however, that red-carpet entrances, photographers and curious crowds already existed in the context of the hotel gatherings, but the actual layout of a red carpet was subject to the original design of the venues hosting the event. Some sites, such as the Biltmore Hotel, had an actual red carpet at the entrance. The arrivals attracted not only keen fans, but also photographers to the parade of glamour even during the banquet days, when the event was still a private venture.[48] The staged spectacle outside the Chinese Theatre marked the formalisation of many of the outdoor practices seen today in the articulation of the red-carpet as a public spectacle.

## The bleachers

The bleachers represent more in the history of the red-carpet than mere structures for controlling movie fans and casual transients. These seats, more than the red carpet, represent the stepping-stone towards the dynamics of today's Oscars ceremony by demarcating the social space, highlighting the contrast between the ordinary and the supposedly extraordinary. Their presence is an essential contribution to the juxtaposition of fame and anonymity, validating the power of celebrity through the fans' manifested admiration. The bleachers are integral to the mediation of the event. Their articulation has been subject to changes according to the preferences of venues and producers. The presence of people trying to get a glimpse of the stars entering the ceremony can be traced back to the early days of the banquets through photographs of the events.[49] While the truthfulness of media descriptions claiming the attendance of thousands of fans is hard to establish, they contribute to anchoring circulating

**Figure 3.3** Exterior of Grauman's Chinese Theatre for the Academy Awards presentation, 8 March 1946. Extra bleachers were added across the street, facing the venue, to accommodate more fans. Photographer: Howard Ballew, *Los Angeles Herald Examiner* Photo Collection. Courtesy of Los Angeles Public Library.

discourses of fandom and star worship, planting the idea of a Hollywood elite worth following.

The profusion of fans at the Chinese Theatre led to the construction of bleachers to accommodate the crowds, clearing the way for the stars to enter the venue and freeing up space for photographers to capture the arrivals. The bleachers were erected for the first time in 1945, and an extra row was added on the other side of Hollywood Boulevard, facing the venue, the following year.[50] Every year since, the Academy has erected bleachers for fans to witness the arrivals in an orderly way, triggering a parallel spectacle outside the venue.

## Fandom and rituals of acceptance

Fans are an essential part of the 'show within the show' that the red-carpet represents. Their presence functions as a counterpoint in creating the illusion of an elite by observing the parade of stars. The mediation of fans' reactions to the stars creates codes of behaviour learned by audiences at home. This process turns into a cultural coding of the reactions to, and impact of, stars and celebrities. The red carpet's orchestrated motion frames glamorous people as busy, on the move. The frequent use of the word 'parade', with its specific connotations of an exhibition for the masses on the sidelines in their anonymous position as an audience, opens up the notion of Hollywood royalty. In 1967, an awe-struck British couple sitting in the bleachers made it clear that a parade of such magnitude would only be organised for the queen in their home country.[51] This commentary further attests to the idea of American celebrities as counterparts of European royalty in the context of a continent lacking monarchic traditions. The acceptance of performative roles as a tacit convention is indicative of the growth of celebrity culture starting in the postwar era.

Celebrities indirectly foster the creation of fleeting bonds with their followers. As the media event's popularity grew, the ritual of witnessing the parade at close quarters attracted people from all backgrounds and corners of the globe. Friends who gathered every year to attend, honeymoon couples, housewives' escapades, college students improvising picnics, babies and toddlers getting their first glimpse of the stars, tourists planning their visit around the days of the ceremony, and fervent fans supporting a nominated film, all formed a worshipping peregrination towards this promised land of glamour and fame. Together, they constituted a many-stranded epiphenomenon of the event.

The minor-celebrity status achieved by those sitting in the bleachers is another interesting side phenomenon. The attending collective is frequently portrayed as a privileged crowd, basking in their physical proximity to the stars, which gives them an edge that fans at home could not attain. In 1968, fans compared the experience of watching the ceremony at home with sitting in the bleachers, explaining the importance of obtaining an autograph as testimony to their closeness to the stars.[52] Fans had the opportunity to buy tickets and enter the venue on several occasions, but some manifested their preference for staying in the bleachers.[53] The bleachers and venues demand different codes of behaviour as social spaces separating fandom from celebrity, and not everyone enjoys crossing such a threshold. This demand for boundaries suggests an internalisation of the codes of behaviour or an unconscious desire to keep the illusion of Hollywood by not breaking this demarcation.

## The red-carpet reporters and greeters

The ritual of announcing the stars' arrivals to the audiences seated in the bleachers is also a practice from the movie palaces' spectacular silent film premières. Located on a platform and facing the audience seated in the bleachers, the red-carpet greeter functioned as a host, entertaining and warming up the fans to encourage them to cheer. In the Academy Awards context, this practice began as a hybrid, by merging the radio broadcast with the bleachers. Loudspeakers outside the Chinese Theatre carried the radio broadcast and the announcement of the arrivals for the fans in the bleachers from 1945 onwards.[54] One of the first official Oscars red-carpet greeters at the Chinese Theatre that year was Dick Nelson. At the Shrine Auditorium, in 1948, the loudspeakers carried the KFWB broadcast of the arrivals both for the fans in the bleachers and for audiences at home.[55]

## On the radio

Radio became a powerful medium during the Great Depression. As a consequence of lower prices combined with the leisure time forced by unemployment, 60 per cent of US homes had a radio set by 1934.[56] Discussions about the early mediatisation of the ceremony have emphasised the conflict of interests between Academy members and the media trying to broadcast the event on the radio. This was not necessarily a desire to seclude the ceremony, but a wish to control its representation. The inclusion of Bob Hope as the ceremony's host replacing the Academy's ruling president indicates an intention to break from private to public by taking into consideration the entertainment character demanded by a media event. Allowing the press to go freely behind the curtain could be a different matter.

Documentation regarding the ceremony's first radio broadcast is conflicting. Versions range from a clandestine transmission from a hotel room in 1929 or 1939 to a supposed first coverage in 1930, while others stated that there was no radio presence until 1945.[57] According to the Academy's official website, Los Angeles local station KNX broadcast a one-hour programme covering the event in 1930.[58] George Fisher was said to have broadcast the event on KNX from a room at the hotel after the Academy forbade all radio transmissions in 1939.[59] A short fragment of a 1939 radio show survives, but whether this corresponds to a clandestine or an official broadcast is difficult to say.[60] When the ceremony moved to the Chinese Theatre in 1944, it turned into a media event, fully structured to fit the radio format. By 1945, the entire ceremony was broadcast coast to coast. At the Shrine Auditorium in 1947, the broadcast continued despite the challenge of accommodating the technology in a venue three times larger than the Chinese Theatre.[61]

## The Armed Forces

The Armed Forces Radio Service and the Columbia Broadcasting System began taking the Oscars overseas in 1944. Discourses surrounding the importance of entertainment to boost the soldiers' morale and the power of radio to overcome distance predominated. In media representations, radio appeared as a link to home, a way to bring along American culture and values while entering hostile territory. It was also something to long for, detached from all calamities of war, a reminder of the freedom that was worth fighting for. In ads, soldiers were presented as unaffected by the circumstances of war, enjoying home entertainment, worried about the scores of their favourite teams, or interested in knowing the latest Hollywood events. With the tagline 'radio brings them the sidewalks of home', RCA encouraged the purchase of war bonds to 'supply American fighting men with the world's finest equipment'.[62] A similar discourse was presented by NBC, portraying the entertainment industry as a morale builder during wartime.

Even after the end of World War II, and with injured US soldiers hospitalised abroad, the Armed Forces Radio continued to broadcast the event, allegedly gathering an estimated audience of 100 million by 1948.[63] The Academy continued using these services to broadcast the ceremony abroad during the Vietnam war.[64] The Armed Forces Radio and Television still carries the event to 178 countries around the globe, reaching an estimated audience of 800,000 people.

## The red-carpet as a radio spectacle

ABC launched the official nationwide radio broadcast from the Chinese Theatre in 1945. The red-carpet rapidly became an attraction. Los Angeles radio station KFWB aired a 30-minute pre-show announcing the arrivals to the ceremony and interviewing the stars. Located at the ticket booth as emcee was Neil Reagan, while George Jessel took the role of commentator from the red carpet.[65] Frances Scully joined the broadcast as the first fashion commentator. Scully hosted a show called *Star Gazing with Frances Scully* (KECA Hollywood, 1945–9) sponsored by the cosmetic company Vonett Sales, Co.[66]

The addition of a fashion commentator targeting the female audience reflected the early interest in what stars were wearing and opened up the possibility of beauty companies' sponsorship. Scully was the right person for the task. She had worked at NBC's publicity department from 1937 to 1942, specialising in fashion, fan magazines and pictures.[67] She also worked as NBC's fashion reporter, hosting a 15-minute show twice a week called *Speaking of*

**Figure 3.4** Frances Scully, the first red-carpet fashion commentator, reporting live from the red carpet at Grauman's Chinese Theatre in 1946. Academy Awards Collection. Courtesy of ©A.M.P.A.S.®

*Glamour* (NBC-Pacific Blue Network, 1940–4). In the show, Scully analysed what stars were wearing to different events around Hollywood.[68] From October 1941, the show was sponsored by Pacquin hand cream for twenty-two weeks, going from six to eleven stations during that period.[69]

Fashion was still regarded as a female endeavour. *Variety* columnist William Esty wrote in 1941 that, to a male reviewer, Scully's radio show 'bounds off the eardrums like the society sections of a newspaper'.[70] The *Radio and Television Mirror* considered 'no one better qualified to talk about that elusive but highly desirable quality [glamour] than this same Miss Scully', referring both to her knowledge of fashion and her friendship with radio and screen stars.[71] Fashion and gossip shared realms in the media, expertise seemingly reserved for women since the emergence of society columns as soft news fillers of newspaper pages.

Scully continued covering the Oscars as a fashion commentator throughout the 1940s. In 1946, she worked with emcee Dick Nelson, and teamed up with Buddy Twiss in 1948 for the pre-show from the Shrine Auditorium's forecourt. Scully made her last appearance as the Oscars fashion commentator at the Academy Theatre in 1949, but continued working for NBC in a new show called *Today in Hollywood*.[72] That same year, she was elected president of the Hollywood Women's Press Association[73]

Eve Arden replaced Scully as fashion commentator when the ceremony moved to the RKO Pantages Theatre in 1950. The radio coverage team was completed with Dot Meyberg as emcee and Ronald Reagan – then president of the Screen Actors Guild – as commentator. Arden was hired to bring a fashion angle but did not always have enough air space to describe the gowns in much detail.[74] The hiring of a fashion commentator to cater to female audiences, even when the actual contributions were scant, indicates an imagined female audience following the media event.

By 1952, the organisers had set up a system of fourteen loudspeakers and four extra horns in different parts of the RKO Pantages to ensure that the press, audience and everyone attending the event could hear the ceremony.[75] That same year, ABC's emcee, Reed Browning, announced and interviewed the stars in the lobby. By 1953, with the inception of the Oscarcast, Johnny Grant took on that role. Together with Grant, Shirley Thomas and Robert Paige interviewed the arriving celebrities. Grant would continue as the event's official red-carpet greeter until 1963. Paramount's costume designer Edith Head had taken up the role of guest fashion commentator for the ceremony when the official radio broadcast moved to ABC in 1960. In 1964, she teamed up with Jack Linkletter. The two of them continued to be the official radio commentators for ABC's national broadcast until at least 1967. By then, the media event was well established on television.

## Hollywood's dusk is television's dawn

In 1947, the ceremony changed venue and left Hollywood once again. The new location was the Shrine Auditorium on the outskirts of downtown Los Angeles. Its capacity of 6,000 seats made it the largest movie palace of its time.[76] The spacious venue ensured that the increasing number of Academy members, plus a portion of the public, could attend the ceremony.[77] Despite securing enough space to respond to the high demand, the Academy committee struggled with the costs. The organisation set aside 3,500 tickets for fans to attend the ceremony, taking advantage of the vast seating capacity. The media estimated that the three bleachers located outside held a total of 5,000 people.[78] Photographic records of early ceremonies show packed bleachers and a considerable police presence. Despite the seemingly growing audience interest, the late 1940s would bring new challenges for the Academy and the Hollywood film industry at large.

The advent of television and the Paramount Antitrust Case brought a decisive power shift leading to the demise of the studio era. In 1938, the attorney general of the Justice Department filed an antitrust suit against the studios, under the rubric *US* v. *Paramount Pictures et al*. This action unleashed a series of lawsuits that looked primarily to stop block-booking practices, as well as other trade practices considered unfair. These measures were put on hold during World War II, but the case resumed by late 1945. After a series of lawsuits, rulings and appeals, the Supreme Court ruled for the decree in May 1948.[79] Studios were forced to dismantle their vertically integrated structures by selling off their exhibition circuit.[80] Indirectly, the resolution resulted in the studio system's slow disintegration, impinging on how movies were produced and distributed, as well as on employment. In this scenario of economic recession, the Motion Picture Association of America (MPAA) was fighting the British film industry due to taxes imposed on American films. The organisation felt that by having British films nominated in a ceremony they financed, the Academy was working against the American film industry's best interests. Universal International, Columbia Republic and Warner Bros. refused to support the event. In 1948, the MPAA formally withdrew all economic support for the ceremony, making the future of the Oscars uncertain.

With the budget tightened, the high cost of the Shrine Auditorium forced the Academy to move out of the venue after two years. One alternative to keep the ceremony going in 1949 was to host a banquet at the Warner Bros. studios, charging members $20 per ticket.[81] This would still leave the Academy in deficit, however. Jean Hersholt, the Academy's outgoing president, tried to circumvent the economic constraints behind the alleged intention to turn the ceremony into 'more clearly an Award presentation and less of an industry publicity stunt'.[82] Indeed, this was also a concern for the Academy, whose members were worried about the ceremony's popularity overshadowing other activities, but it did not represent the primary motivation behind the move. The 29th Academy Awards ceremony was finally hosted at the Academy's theatre. The venue's capacity of 950 seats permitted attendance of only a few representatives from each branch, the nominees, the press and fans.[83] All had to purchase tickets. Cost-cutting aside, this idea was short-lived due to the venue's limited capacity.

## Notes

1. 'White Fashions Tops at Academy Awards Dinner', *Women's Wear Daily*, 5 March 1940, 9.
2. 'Academy Awards, 17th Year's Top Movie Stars Honored as Academy Awards "Oscars"', VA12391, *News of the Day* 16.256 – excerpt. Oscars for movie stars!, UCLA Film & Television Archive (hereafter UCLAF&T); 'Academy Awards Go to Borgnine and Magnani – Hollywood, California', VA12706, *Telenews* 9.59 – excerpt, HEA Hearst Newsreels Collection, UCLAF&T; 'Academy Awards; Oscar for Best Movie of the Year Goes to MGM – Hollywood, California', VA3951, *News of the Day* 23.260 – excerpt, HEA Hearst Newsreels Collection, UCLAF&T; 'Academy Awards 36th Night of the Oscars', VA11016, *News of the Day* 35.271, HEA Hearst Newsreels Collection, UCLAF&T; 'Oscar Big Night', VA12525, *News of the Day* 29.263, HEA Hearst Newsreels Collection, UCLAF&T; 'Motion Picture Academy Awards Commentary by John B. Kennedy', Hearst newsreel footage, VA4002, *News of the Day* 15.252, HEA Hearst Newsreels Collection, UCLAF&T; 'Academy Awards; 15th Film World Picks Champions!', VA11065, *News of the Day* 14.252, HEA Hearst Newsreels Collection, UCLAF&T; 'Academy Awards; 15th Film World Picks Champions!', VA11065, *News of the Day* 14.252, HEA Hearst Newsreels Collection, UCLAF&T; 'Academy Awards – Oscar for best movie of the year goes to MGM', VA3951 *News of the Day* 23.260, HEA Hearst Newsreels Collection, UCLAF&T; 'Academy Awards, 36th Night of the Oscars', VA11016, *News of the Day* 35.271, HEA Hearst Newsreels Collection, UCLAF&T; 'Oscar Likes Ben-Hur', VA8915, *News of the Day* 31.267, HEA Hearst Newsreels Collection, UCLAF&T; 'Gigi, Susan Hayward, David Niven cop Oscars', VA5694, *Telenews* 12.73, HEA Hearst Newsreels Collection, UCLAF&T; 'Academy Awards 33rd', VA8868, *Telenews* 14.78, HEA Hearst Newsreels Collection, UCLAF&T; 'Filmlands Big Show. Night of the "Oscars"', VA13915, *News of the Day* 34.269, HEA Hearst Newsreels Collection, UCLAF&T; 'Nights of the "Oscars"', VA13957, *News of the Day* 32.271, HEA Hearst Newsreels Collection, UCLAF&T; 'Academy Awards, 38th Night of the Oscars', VA5377, *News of the Day* 37. 273, HEA Hearst Newsreels Collection, UCLAF&T.
3. Sue Collins, 'Star Testimonial and Trailers: Mobilizing During World War I', *Cinema Journal* 57, no. 1 (Fall 2017): 46–70.
4. 'Academy Awards 17th Year's Top Movie Stars Honored as Academy Awards "Oscars"', VA12391, *News of the Day* 16.256 – excerpt. Oscars for movie stars!, UCLAF&T; 'Academy Awards Go to Borgnine and Magnani – Hollywood, California', VA12706, *Telenews* 9.59 – excerpt, UCLAF&T.
5. Frank Capra was president of the Academy between 1935 and 1939, and vice-president in 1940, when the film was produced.

6. Letter to Jack Warner, 16 April 1940, f. 53 Capra Warner's Short Cavalcade of Academy Awards, Academy Awards uncatalogued files, Margaret Herrick Library, Academy of Motion Picture Arts and Sciences (hereafter MHL).

7. Letter from Donald Gledhill to J. E. Benton, 26 February 1940, f. 40 Awards short Ambassador Hotel Consent Cavalcade of Academy Awards, Academy Awards uncatalogued Files, MHL.

8. Memorandum from Donald Gledhill to Gordon Hollingshead, 25 February 1940, f. 55 Academy short Memos to Gordon Hollinghead Cavalcade of Academy Awards, Academy Awards uncatalogued files, MHL.

9. *Cavalcade of Academy Awards* (Warner Bros., 1940), Pickford Center for Motion Picture Research, Academy of Motion Picture Arts and Sciences (hereafter Pickford Center, AMPAS).

10. 'Academy Awards Banquet, 1939', VA9723M, MP Motion Picture Collection, UCLAF&T.

11. 'Warners Close 4,000 Deals on "Academy Awards" Film', *The Film Daily*, 16 May 1940, 3.

12. 'Short Subject Reviews', *Showman's Trade Review*, 18 May 1940, 33.

13. Memorandum from Donald Gledhill to Mr Frank Capra, 26 March 1940, f. 51 Awards short Memos to Frank Capra Cavalcade of Academy Awards, Academy Awards uncatalogued files, MHL.

14. '"Cavalcade of Academy Awards" in Ritz Screen', *The San Bernardino County Sun*, 28 May 1940, 9.

15. 'RKO to Distribute "Academy Awards" Film', *Showmen's Trade Review*, 14 February 1948, 16.

16. Henry R. Luce, 'The American Century', *Life*, 17 February 1941, 61–4.

17. Stephen J. Whitfield, 'The American Century of Henry R. Luce', in Michael Kazin and Joseph A. McCartin, eds, *Americanism: New Perspectives on the History of an Ideal* (Chapel Hill, NC: University of North Carolina Press, 2006), 96.

18. Ibid., 92.

19. Franklin D. Roosevelt, 'Four Freedoms Speech, Annual Message to Congress on the State of the Union: 01/06/1941', FDR Presidential Library & Museum, http://www.fdrlibrary.marist.edu/pdfs/fftext.pdf/

20. Luce, 'The American Century', 64–5.

21. Kingsley Bolton and Jan Olsson, Introduction to *Media, Popular Culture, and the American Century* (Stockholm: National Library of Sweden, 2010), 17.

22. Roosevelt's speech was pre-recorded in Washington, as raw footage suggests. See Critical Past, 'President Franklin D. Roosevelt Delivers Portions of a Speech for Broadcast During… HD Stock Footage', *YouTube*, https://www.youtube.com/watch?v=hd4twy6k1d4/

23. The order of the sentences in the speech has been modified from the original version. This excerpt belongs to a Universal newsreel. Oscars, 'FDR, Ginger Rogers and James Stewart: 1941 Oscars'. For an audio file of the full speech, see Benjamin Freed, 'Franklin D. Roosevelt's Address to 13th Academy Awards 1941', https://soundcloud.com/benjaminfreed/franklin-d-roosevelts-address/

24. David Haven Blake, *Liking Ike: Eisenhower, Advertising, and the Rise of Celebrity Politics* (Oxford: Oxford University Press, 2016), 42.

25. See, for example, contracts and interoffice correspondence in Box 859, f. Contracts 1944, David O. Selznick Collection, Ransom Center, University of Texas-Austin (hereafter HRC).

26. See Leach, *Land of Desire*.

27. P. David Marshall and Joanne Morreale, *Advertising and Promotional Culture* (London: Palgrave, 2018), 31–2.

28. Matthew Jones, 'Freedom from Want', in Jeffrey A. Engel, ed., *The Four Freedoms: Franklin D. Roosevelt and the Evaluation of an American Idea* (Oxford: Oxford University Press, 2016), 125–63.

29. Philip S. Golub, *Power, Profit & Prestige: A History of American Imperial Expansion* (New York, NY: Pluto Press, 2010), 69–70.

30. 'Fashion Artists to Show Work', *Los Angeles Times*, 3 February 1941, 3.

31. Sylva Weaver, 'Stylists Show New Modes', *Los Angeles Times*, 14 February 1941, A1.

32. Ibid., A1.

33. Sylva Weaver, 'Nation's Style Center', *Los Angeles Times*, 2 January 1941, C8.

34. 'To Promote Styles', *Broadcasting*, 21 April 1941, 53.

35. The development is more complex than described here. The Couture Group emerged from the New York Dress Institute. Eleanor Lambert began organising the Fashion Press week for them, and when the Couture Group disbanded, they continued with the American Designer Press Week.

36. Whitaker, *Service and Style*, 214.

37. 'Fashions for Milady Bring Dollars to Box Office', *The Motion Picture Herald*, 7 October 1944, 19.

38. See Jay Jorgensen and Donald L. Scoggins, *Creating the Illusion: A Fashionable History of Hollywood Costume Designers* (Philadelphia, PA: Running Press, 2015), 92–7.

39. See 'The 14th Academy Awards Memorable Moments', Oscars.org, https://www.oscars.org/oscars/ceremonies/1942/memorable-moments/

40. Kim Khavar Fahlstedt, 'Chinatown Film Culture: The Appearance of Cinema in San Francisco's Chinese Neighborhood 1906–1915' (PhD dissertation, Stockholm University, 2016), 223.

41. Maxine Barlett, 'Screen Society: Red Carpets to Unroll at Screen Premieres', *Los Angeles Times*, 2 August 1942, D6.

42. See Jennifer M. Mower and Elaine L. Pedersen, 'United States World War II Clothing Restrictions', in Phyllis G. Tortora, ed., *Berg Encyclopaedia of World Dress and Fashion: The United States and Canada* (Oxford: Bloomsbury Academic, 2010), http://dx.doi.org/10.2752/BEWDF/EDch3811/; Paul M. Gregory, 'An Economic Interpretation of Women's Fashions', *Southern Economic Journal* 14, no. 2 (1947): 148–62, DOI: 10.2307/1052931/

43. 'Vyvyan Donner's War-time Fashions', 26.68, Fox Movietone, Moving Image Research Collection, University of South Carolina.

44. Even though Hollywood supported the government during World War I, an increasing involvement in politics appeared in the 1930s. See Donald T. Critchlow, *When Hollywood Was Right: How Movie Stars, Studio Moguls, and Big Business Remade American Politics* (New York, NY: Cambridge University Press, 2013), 7–41. In addition, the Academy had been training Army officials in the production of audiovisual material for a long period. See 'The Academy in Wartime', *Academy Reports*, 1 May 1943, Academy History Archive, MHL.

45. See, for example, 'Ad for Hollander Furs Featuring Rita Hayworth', *Modern Screen*, August 1943, 71.

46. Advertisement Hollander, *Photoplay*, August 1944, 79.

47. Jennifer M. Mower and Elaine L. Pedersen, '"Pretty and Patriotic": Women's Consumption of Apparel During World War II', *Dress* 29, no. 1 (2013): 52, https://doi.org/10.1179/0361211213Z.0000000010/

48. An annoyed Hedda Hopper complained about the presence of paparazzi in 1938. See Phyllis Marie Arthur, 'Gals & Gab', *Daily Variety*, 11 March 1938, 5.

49. See 'Sleek and Sassy Spangles Bedeck Milady at Acad. Fete', *Daily Variety*, 6 March 1936, 11; 'What They Wore and How They Wore It – Those Glams', *Daily Variety*, 5 March 1937, 22; 'Smiles, Throbs, Tears in Midst of Triumphs', *Daily Variety*, 5 March 1944, 36.

50. 'Hundreds of Fans Gather to Watch Arrival of Stars', *The Hollywood Reporter*, 16 March 1945, 5; 'Acad. Spends $600 For Bleacher Seats', *Daily Variety*, 16 March 1945, 7; 'Academy Awards 5,000 Anonymous Spectators Also Turn in Oscar-worthy Performances', *Life*, 2 April 1945, 37.

51. Austin Conover, 'Bleacher Fans, Old and Young, Full of Zest', *Citizen-News/Valley Times*, 11 April 1967, 15, 17.

52. See Austin Conover, 'Bleacher Fans Tell of Thrills', *Citizen-News*, 11 April 1968, 16.

53. Steve Lowery, 'The Fans: On the Outside Looking In', *Long Beach Press-Telegram*, 28 March 1995, C5.

54. 'Fans Outside Vote Their Oscar Choices', *Daily Variety*, 8 March 1946, 5.

55. '5,000 Jam Bleachers; H'wood Zing Missing', *Daily Variety*, 14 March 1947, 8.

56. Balio, *Grand Design*, 14.

57. 'Oscars First' and 'List of Venues', Academy Awards Ceremony Files, MHL.

58. '2nd Academy Awards Ceremony Memorable Moments', Oscars.org, https://www.oscars.org/oscars/ceremonies/1930/memorable-moments

59. Mason Willey et al., *Inside Oscar: The Unofficial History of the Academy Awards* (Bromley: Columbus Books, 1986), 89.

60. See '1938 11th Academy Awards', AMPAS, https://soundcloud.com/ampas/1938-11th-academy-awards-1/

61. 'Awards Presentation Group Outlines Special Program', *For Your Information*, 3.1 (1 January 1947), Academy History Archive, MHL.

62. 'RCA Laboratory AD', *U.S. News*, 22 October 1943, NBC Institution business papers, RC4, Domestic Advertisement Collection, 1875–2001, JWT, Duke Archives.

63. '20th Awards Presentation', *Annual Report 1947–48*, 6, Academy History Archive, MHL.

64. 'U.S. Soldiers, Civilians Throughout World to Tune – In Awards on Armed Forces Radio, TV', *Academy Report to the Members of the Academy of Motion Picture Arts and Sciences* (hereafter *Academy Report*) 4.1 (March 1959): 4.

65. An hour-long recording of this programme is available on the Internet Archive; see 'Academy Award Ceremony of 1943', https://archive.org/details/otr_academyceremony 1943/

66. 'Sponsors', *Broadcasting*, 9 July 1945, 56; *Broadcasting*, 7 March 1949, 72.

67. 'Los Angeles', *Radio Daily*, 29 March 1937, 6.

68. *Broadcasting*, 15 September 1941, 46. See Jeanette M. Berard and Klaudia Englund, *Radio Series Scripts, 1930–2001: A Catalog of the American Radio Archives Collection* (Jefferson, NC: McFarland, 2006), 306.

69. 'Pacquin Adding', *Broadcasting*, 20 October 1941, 28.

70. 'Radio Reviews', *Variety*, 8 October 1941, 28.

71. Untitled, *Radio and Television Mirror*, May 1942, 6.

72. 'Academy Awards Venues File', Academy Awards Ceremony Files, MHL; *Broadcasting*, 18 April 1949, 95.

73. 'Sponsors', *Broadcasting*, 9 July 1945, 72.

74. ABC's broadcast of 1950 is available on the Internet Archive at https://ia601408.us.archive.org/16/items/AcademyAwardsCeremonies/22nd_Academy_Awards_Ceremony_Part_4.mp3/

75. '14 Loudspeakers Spotted in Pantages', *Daily Variety*, 21 March 1952, 14.

76. Charles Beardsley, *Hollywood's Master Showman: The Legendary Sid Grauman* (New York, NY: Cornwall Books, 1983), 115.

77. 'Academy Awards Night Slated for Shrine', *For Your Information* 3.1 (January 1947), Academy History Archive, MHL.

78. '5,000 Jam Bleachers; H'wood Zing Missing', *Daily Variety*, 14 March 1947, 8.

79. Thomas Schatz, *Boom and Bust: American Cinema in the 1940s* (Berkeley, CA: University of California Press, 1999), 326.

80. For the 1948 Supreme Court resolution, see 'United States v. Paramount Pictures, Inc. 334 U.S. 131 (1948)', Justia Law, https://supreme.justia.com/cases/federal/us/334/131/case.html/

81. J. D. Spiro, 'Economy Pinch Dims Lustre of "Oscar" Fete', *The New York Times*, 27 February 1949, X5.

82. 'Recommended Objectives for the Coming Year', *A Report from the President to the Members of the Academy of Motion Picture Arts and Sciences*, October 1945–May 1947, 14, Academy History Archive, MHL.

83. 'Awards to be Staged at Academy Theatre', *For Your Information* 3.7 (Winter 1949): 1, Academy History Archive, MHL.

# 4

# Tracing the Academy Awards ceremony's footprint into the mediascape

The reactivation of transatlantic commerce and the economic boom in the US had a positive effect on the international trade of the fashion industry. For the film industry, the economy had hit hard by the end of 1948. Besides the recession of 1949, the enforcement of antitrust laws prevented studios from co-opting television, a venture they had been pursuing by closely following the development of the new technology. The film industry was entering a new era, one that would be decisive with regard to the shift towards mediatisation. The ceremony became a solidly established channel for media exposure.

The end of World War II marked the emergence of the second period of fashion at the Oscars. During the booming postwar economy, the US embarked on an era of consumption. Nationalist rhetoric still flourished with the aim of combatting the threat of communism during the Cold War. The 'red scare' and anti-communist propaganda permeated every available communication platform; gossip and fashion columns were no exception. The media continued to work as a vehicle for circulating American ideals. In a highly politicised landscape, the 1950s also fostered the emergence of celebrity politics. Hollywood big names became vehicles of political propaganda during campaigns by endorsing different candidates. As David Haven Blake explains, stars became agents of civic responsibility, at once frivolous and important, setting entertainment at the centre of national identity.[1] Hollywood had consolidated its liaison with the government by supporting President Roosevelt during the war. However, the winds of change influenced the new elections that brought Dwight D. Eisenhower to the White House in 1953. This shifting political course brought the Republican Party back into office for the first time since 1933. Among the many Hollywood personalities committed to the Party were Ginger Rogers, Gloria Swanson, Louis B. Mayer, Sam Goldwyn, Darryl Zanuck, David O. Selznick, Walt Disney, Cecil B. DeMille, Fred Astaire, Bob Hope, Hedda Hopper and Edith Head.[2]

Hollywood personalities with a high media profile, such as Hopper and Head, experienced the peak and nadir of their careers during this period, as an emerging wave of youth movements slowly relegated their discourses into the culturally residual.

The ceremony returned to Hollywood at the RKO Pantages Theatre in 1950. The setting outside the theatre attracted photographers and newsreel cameras to register the arrival of the stars throughout the 1950s. The pavement entrance was significantly narrower than all the previous venues. Besides the two main bleachers alongside the entrance, five bleacher sections lined the southern side of Hollywood Boulevard towards Vine Street to accommodate an estimated 1,500 fans.[3] There are frequent stories about actresses signing autographs or shaking hands with fans during this period as the reduced space allowed closer interactions.[4] In 1952, police reports estimated that 3,000 fans were standing outside the RKO Pantages.[5]

From a media perspective, the 1950s was an era of renegotiations in which the competing medium of television furthered Hollywood's instability. It was a power struggle to control the circulation of both economic and cultural capital. Television was, among many other things, enjoying an economic boost, mostly

**Figure 4.1** Entrance to the RKO Pantages Theatre during the 24th Academy Awards ceremony in 1952. Academy Awards Collection. Courtesy of ©A.M.P.A.S.®

due to the flow of advertising industry money. Content was still moving in many directions. Advertising companies and brands, in the form of sponsors, took advantage of this niche by investing in TV shows or by developing the shows to their benefit. The power shift towards television furthered the cross-media reach of American popular culture through this new technology that could bring visual entertainment straight into the viewers' homes.

This chapter follows the entrance of the Oscars into television, focusing on key moments to understand how the ceremony and its red-carpet parade became a global media event. It explores the negotiations that led to the first telecast and the conditions that turned it into a global media phenomenon. It explains how the platforms for international exposure were established to reach foreign markets, identifying moments in Oscars history that set the conditions for exporting the show. It also recounts how the prelude to the ceremony grew into the mediascape in the local market. The convergence of these phenomena, namely the interest in the ceremony's build-ups and the growing global interest in the show, would later serve the promotional purposes of international fashion brands and, consequently, distribute fashion discourses worldwide.

## NBC and the inception of the Oscarcast

By the time Jean Hersholt left his position as president of the Academy in 1948, the financial situation of the institution had jeopardised the continuation of its award ceremony. Hersholt suggested a set of goals to achieve a firmer policy that would save time, energy and money in the long run by producing a five-year plan for the awards. He outlined a list of dos and don'ts for guidance.[6] In his plea to secure the financial future of the institution, he called for the possibility of signing up a prestigious sponsor for the ceremony's radio broadcast. A sector of Academy board members were reluctant to have any association with commercial products that could jeopardise the symbolic capital of the Oscars brand and trademark. The proposal was a call for extreme measures, but there were still some limits to it. While Hersholt suggested exploring other commercial connections if those policies would provide funds to expand the general programme, he also warned against any commercial tie-in or high-profile exposure.[7] Charles Brackett, who took over from Hersholt as president of the Academy in 1949, inherited this mission of safeguarding the continuation of the ceremony. His progressive behaviour would prove highly beneficial to the Academy's economic recovery. Still, it involved dismissing the precautionary advice given by Hersholt. Not only did Brackett approve a deal with Bulova to release a series of Academy Awards watches, but he also steered the wheel towards the new medium of television.[8]

Samuel Goldwyn suggested the inception of the Oscarcast in order to tackle the economic impediments threatening the continuation of the ceremony. He openly manifested optimism for television as a new chapter in Hollywood business, disregarding those who considered the new medium a competitor instead of a collaborator.[9] By then, Paramount Pictures – which Brackett worked for – was the only studio to have successfully invested in TV before the antitrust regulation stopped Hollywood's expansion into the new medium. It is understandable that Goldwyn and Brackett would be willing to take the risk of televising the event. NBC's commercial department initially failed to see the Oscarcast's potential for sponsorship, the main source of financial support for TV shows at the time. In response to an initial inquiry, they replied that the show was 'not important enough to pre-empt a regularly scheduled commercial'.[10] NBC's caution is understandable within the network's commercial context at the time. As Lynn Spigel observes, NBC had problems securing sponsors during 1951 and 1952, which forced the network to cut back its schedule.[11] Television could not predict the success of a new show, which resulted in networks risking capital ahead of demand. For *New York Times* columnist Thomas Pryor, the deal was 'a no brainer'. Newspapers, radio and newsreels paved the mediascape for a televised show to be a success domestically and overseas. Pryor rapidly noted that it was the ceremony's capacity to captivate global attention annually that would make it the best PR stunt for the industry, a deal from which NBC would ultimately benefit.[12]

The network found a solution close to home as RCA invested $100,000 in sponsoring the Oscarcast.[13] RCA was NBC's parent company and the leading manufacturer of televisions, radio sets and transmission equipment. The strategy was to use the spots to create a demand for hardware. Most of the advertising time – up to nine minutes – was used to sell its Victrola trademark.[14] In James L. Baughman's understanding, RCA was responsible for the spread of television in the US, mostly due to the company's capacity to mass-produce and promote the technology.[15] For RCA, developing content translated into a broader demand for TV sets. By relying on RCA as its parent company, NBC enjoyed more economic freedom than any other network to experiment with programming. Even the success of competing networks increased the sales of sets, benefiting RCA which would return in the form of economic support securing artistic freedom and financial flow for NBC. The company was in a privileged position.

Televising a media event was also cost-effective because it did not require any significant investment in production.[16] The network needed only to set up cameras at the venue to broadcast the event. RCA's spokesperson referred to the Academy deal as a bargain: 'Where else could we get such high-priced talent as paraded across the stage at the Pantages for a mere $100,000?'[17] At the time, some of the TV shows featured only one or two stars, mostly from vaudeville or radio. The Oscars would put plenty of Hollywood A-listers on TV screens at no extra charge.

NBC's President, Sylvester 'Pat' Weaver, played a fundamental role in closing a deal despite the pessimistic considerations of the commercial department. Weaver, a former adman at Young & Rubicam, became head of NBC television in August 1949. His vision for NBC's programming focused on combining entertainment and education for a mass audience. His training in advertising informed his view of television and the commitment to reach everyone. Weaver did not settle for the safe strategies of the television industry. Instead, he believed that disrupting the schedule with an extraordinary programme would prevent television from being eventually ignored.[18] This conceptualisation led him to promote a format called the 'spectacular', a network-produced, high-budget live show that attracted sponsorship.[19] Spectaculars were the epitome of entertainment. They included live performances, Broadway-type musicals and vaudevillian hosts. Each ran for an average of 90 minutes and had a promotional campaign similar to those of Broadway premieres, which made costs escalate to as high as $250,000 compared to $75,000 for a regular programme.[20] The search for a theatre-inspired aesthetic for television programming did not imply a denial of Hollywood's attraction. The Academy Awards ceremony was an ideal spectacular. It featured live musical performances, the world's most glamorous stars wearing magnificent gowns to attract a female audience and Bob Hope as host, all in a neat $100,000 package. In this context, the ceremony offered a format attuned to Weaver's vision at a relatively low cost.

The first Academy Awards spectacular was broadcast live on NBC on 19 March 1953. During the first five years of the Oscarcast, the ceremony was split in a bicoastal broadcast from Hollywood and New York. This may be the most heterotopic and dispersed relocation of Hollywood. Weaver understood he could not run NBC without Hollywood.[21] He acknowledged the importance of the film industry as a supplier of talent and future producer of fictional content for TV. He also believed that television needed its own geographical epicentre, as the film industry had Hollywood. Weaver vigorously strove for New York to become the home of the television industry. The first televised ceremony broadcast simultaneously from the RKO Pantages Theatre in Hollywood and the NBC International Theatre, located at Columbus Circle in New York. This would satisfy his geographical aspirations and, allegedly, secure a larger attendance of movie stars living on the East Coast. According to *The Hollywood Reporter*, an estimated 800 participants attended the first ceremony in New York.[22]

The Oscars found a niche due to risk-taking strategies that gambled on the new-found economic safety of television. Goldwyn's and Brackett's controversial decision to open up the 25th Academy Awards ceremony to television was the stepping-stone to what would become one of the most famous media events worldwide.

## The greatest show on Earth will be televised

The main anxiety about televising the ceremony concerned the stars. Hollywood's glamour and mystique clashed with the essence of 'liveness' that formed the basis of the new medium. Television's real-time spontaneity represented the exact opposite of the controlled system built up by the film industry. The fear was that it could ruin the stars' image in a second. Studios were reluctant to expose their commodities without the right preparation and guidance.[23] Hollywood had spent decades perfecting a machine for building stardom as actors and actresses went through careful grooming and guidance on how to move, talk and look. In particular, most of their appearances were scripted and their images carefully constructed through proper lighting, make-up, costumes, post-production and other photographic arrangements. Even appearances in film fan magazines, supposedly showing the stars' personal lives, were managed by the studios' publicity departments. A star presented with the wrong wardrobe or make-up could damage the studio's orchestrated image and cause the market value of the commodity to deteriorate. Besides, contract players could not appear on television during the first few years of the 1950s due to a ban enacted by the Motion Picture Producer Association (MPPA).[24] Even though the ban was removed during the spring of 1953, the studios remained sceptical. Actors and actresses needed permission to appear on television, as many of them remained under studio contracts. Some studios lent their stars for TV appearances, but only under strict contractual clauses.[25] With the gradual dismantling of the studio system and the industry's uncertain future, lending their stars to the competing medium of television was even riskier.

The Oscarcast's general director, John Green, strove to bestow uniformity and glamour on Hollywood's elite in their first televised gathering. The dress code requested all winners, past nominees, and their ladies and escorts to wear dinner jackets and formal evening dress. Presenters had to wear white tie and tails, while nominees could get away with a black-tie dress code.[26] Tuxedos were mandatory for everyone working at the event, even behind the cameras.

The first Oscarcast opened from the theatre's exterior with a crane pan shot of Hollywood Boulevard moving from Vine Street towards the entrance of the RKO Pantages. The camera zooms into the marquee and the entrance, revealing the arrival of stars waving at the fans sitting in the bleachers. The image abruptly cuts to the inside of the Pantages. 'Here in the Pantages tonight is the world's most glamorous audience', announces the narrator. Charles Brackett is the first to take the stage to introduce the ceremony's already emblematic host: Bob Hope.

NBC's sales department was proved overwhelmingly wrong in their difficulty in conceiving of an audience interested in the media event. The Nielsen ratings ranged between 42.1 and 53.9, with a share of 76.[27] As one of the most watched television shows for that year, the Oscars rapidly changed perceptions regarding its sponsorship potential, becoming an easy sale for advertising focused on rating success. *Daily Variety* estimated that 91 million people – half the country – tuned in, with 50 million watching the ceremony on television, and the rest following it on radio.[28] *Life* magazine claimed that

**Figure 4.2** NBC coverage outside the RKO Pantages Theatre, venue for the 26th Academy Awards ceremony in 1954. In the background, a billboard on Hollywood Boulevard announces the Oscarcast and its sponsor. Academy Awards Collection. Courtesy of ©A.M.P.A.S.®

Hollywood had turned to its deadly rival to publicise the award, underlining the nature of media events by observing that the stars had to arrive on time to comply with the dictates of television schedules.[29] The *Los Angeles Times* reported that the stars showed 'remarkable restraint, especially when the TV cameras panned across the theatre at the opening of the awards'.[30] During these first years, the Oscars functioned as a cross-media platform in which stars were presented as themselves, yet participated in an outstanding performance of 'stardom'.

Journalists celebrated television's final realisation of audiences' interest in movie stars. 'It took television 25 years to catch up with Hollywood's crème de la crème, but to the millions it was well worth the wait', wrote *Daily Variety*.[31] For *Chicago Daily Tribune* columnist Larry Wolters, the ceremony allowed viewers to see some stars on TV for the first time, and – for once – 'the gilded people of Hollywood seemed rather human'.[32] This parade of stardom was brought home to the viewers sitting in a virtual front row with privileged access. Some articles compared the experience to being in the bleachers. In Lynn Spigel's words, '[t]elevision was meant to democratise what had traditionally been an aristocratic, box-seat view of theatrical spectacle'.[33] Television ran with this advantage over radio by broadcasting images as well as sound, and its live broadcasting capabilities made it more authentic than film. These differences associated television with realism.[34] Pat Weaver believed in television's capacity to take people from their living room to other places.

Live transmissions allowed the viewers to 'be there' and witness events in a different location from the comfort of their home, altering the notion of space. Commercial campaigns for television sets played upon these capacities too. Audiences were located onsite or, even better, the ceremony was entering their homes, making them part of Hollywood. The home viewers were even said to have a better view than the $12 ticket holders at the RKO Pantages.[35] In his opening monologue, Hope addressed the idea of the closeness that television provided. 'Isn't it exciting to know that a lot of these glamourous stars are going to be in your homes tonight? All over America, housewives are turning to their husbands and saying: "Put on your shirt, Joan Crawford is coming"'.[36] This idea of the celebrities coming into the home, instead of the audiences going to a public space to see them, was pivotal for the televised ceremony and, consequently, to the emergence of the televised red-carpet telethons.

Television production had inevitably gravitated towards Hollywood by the mid-1950s. This relocation benefited the television industry by giving it access to a larger pool of talent and to the film industry's infrastructure. Even NBC, as the network that favoured New York the most, carried only two programmes from the East Coast.[37] The Oscars were televised solely from Hollywood starting in 1958. The show was simulcast coast-to-coast over the NBC television and radio networks under the regained sponsorship of the Motion Picture Industry. After years of discontent with sponsorship handled by NBC deals, the Academy managed to overcome the financial need by securing industry support once again. This enabled them to deliver a show without the network's requirement for commercial breaks that interrupted the ceremony's natural flow. Conversely, the PR firm Harshe-Rotman & Druck considered that this jeopardised the credibility of the Academy and the ceremony, arguing that this configuration raised suspicions about the validity of the awards among the media and the audience. The Academy had by then developed a successful television show worth keeping on air for promotional purposes. Despite the disagreements, all efforts were focused on improving the event's publicity to replicate its local success abroad. This decision marked a turning point in the process of the professionalisation of the ceremony led by globalisation.

## Accommodating the press

The attention afforded to journalists covering the show was a strategic resource behind how the event grew into the mediascape. During the banquet era, a hotel room was designated for journalists to report on the event. The Academy understood early on that efforts to improve the working conditions of the press could translate into broader coverage and better publicity. The budget constraints that led to the ceremony being held at the Academy Theatre in 1949 diluted these discussions.

In 1951, with the ceremony having settled into the RKO Pantages Theatre, *The Hollywood Reporter* celebrated the work of Howard G. Mayer, PR agent of the Academy, in aiding a (questionable) estimate of 600 national and international newscasters covering the event.[38] The demand for press tickets significantly increased after the inception of the Oscarcast. Western Union installed a press telegraph in the ceremony's premises to expedite the work of reporters, starting in 1954. As the ceremony grew and handling the press became more demanding, the Academy changed gears towards professionalisation on the PR front.

In tandem with the growing popularity of the event, the Academy restructured its PR approach by hiring Harshe-Rotman & Druck, Inc. in 1956, to manage Awards-related matters year round.[39] Foreign reporters were no longer willing to reproduce cables from news agencies, and sought to report the Oscars experience from their own culturally informed perspective. Information about the event was arguably no longer controlled or dictated by the US's cultural viewpoint via their press releases and news agencies' cables, demonstrating the cross-hybridisation of global experiences as non-unilateral.[40]

In 1958, the agency suggested changes to enhance the press room, including the construction of a press tent to improve the journalists' working conditions. The creation of this special area reduced the number of solicited theatre tickets, liberating seats for other guests. The Award Planning Committee worked together with the Academy's PR committee, the Harshe-Rotman team, and the traffic and safety committee in the creation of the first press tent, built in the car park adjoining the RKO Pantages Theatre. The new press area was divided into sections, catering to different needs. A camera area, right by the entrance, facilitated the job of photographers and newsreel crews. Another area, with telephones, was reserved for tape-recorded interviews and reporters contacting their newsrooms. A third area was equipped with teletype machines, typewriters and monitors. The set-up of the tent created an efficient working space for reporters and photographers. The streamlined stations functioned like a well-oiled machine. Presenters and winners posed for photographers with their statuettes and responded to questions from the reporters. This first station was also optimal for fashion photo-ops. Winners then moved into the lounge area for one-on-one interviews or phone interviews with selected media outlets. Finally, reporters were free to prepare their transcripts or write their articles in the typewriting room.

The downsides of this orchestration were originality, access and authenticity, values that characterised the emerging progressive media. After all, the main purpose of sending correspondents was to avoid the standardised reproduction of news agencies' cables. It did not take long until photographers demanded exclusive access to the ceremony to register more spontaneous reactions. One media outlet requested cameras backstage, in the stars' waiting area, to capture their reaction as the awards were announced. They wanted their readers to see 'how they saw what they did on their home screens'.[41] They also wanted photographers with long zoom lenses to be at the sides of the stage, to capture the immediate reactions of winners and losers at the moment the announcements were made. Some even manifested their lack of interest in the 'mass shot of the stars'. These were repetitive and depended on a pre-selection based on whom the Academy wanted to promote, which would, naturally, not include the more established names attending the ceremony in other capacities. Another demand from photographers was to capture the scene outside the Pantages Theatre and the arrival of the stars. Media outlets hoped to have a photographer out front for the pre-show, possibly in an elevated position across the street with a long lens. The visual goal was to capture the arrival of elegantly dressed stars with the Academy Awards marquee in the background. The print press argued that television failed to show the stars' gowns in full detail and hoped to capture these in their full-length photographs.

The board of governors set boundaries and decreed that no photographers would be allowed to work backstage or in the Pantages Theatre on the night of the awards.[42] The Academy's main concern was the potential conflict emerging from giving exclusive permissions to some media outlets over others. By the late 1950s, the success of the Oscarcast had put the Academy in a good negotiating position. The Academy was looking for cash flow to build its new headquarters.[43] When NBC refused to advance money against its next contract, the game opened up for ABC.

## Hollywood exodus

ABC took over the Oscarcast from NBC in 1961. The ceremony moved from Hollywood to Santa Monica. The capacity of the RKO Pantages was significantly reduced after the upper balcony and rear sides were covered with drapery for the release of *Spartacus* (Byrna Productions/Universal International, 1960). With 2,337 Academy members, escalating interest from the press and a commercial sponsor to please, the increasing demand called for a bigger venue. The Santa Monica Civic Auditorium could accommodate 2,500 attendees, about 1,000 more than the Pantages with its newly reduced capacity.[44] In addition, it had an orchestra pit, cameras, radio microphones and twenty monitors to operate a closed circuit for journalists and those involved in the production.[45]

The press did not welcome the ceremony's departure from Hollywood. Some even called it an 'exodus'.[46] *Los Angeles Herald*'s Eddy Jo Bernal ironically put Oscar in a prophetic position by saying

> just like the mountain coming to Mohammed, Hollywood came to its Oscar. For the film town pulled up stakes and staged its famous event not in Hollywood, not in Los Angeles, but in the seaside city of Santa Monica. And the geographic change cost the 12-inch prince a great deal in atmosphere and glamour.[47]

Seeking to regain media sympathy, the Academy worked on creating a comfortable and well-organised press area at the new venue.[48] Faced with the consistently good press turnout and possibly concerned by the lower ratings, the Academy acknowledged the importance of an efficiently working venue and strove to keep the journalists happy.[49] The facilities had an area designated as a press room, with thirty typewriters and three telegraphers, and separate rooms for group work that catered to the needs of reporters and photographers. The minor sponsorship of Sara Lee and the Coca-Cola Company provided free catering for participants.

A series of changes outside the Santa Monica Civic Auditorium restructured circulation on the red carpet by further delimiting space and enforcing hierarchies. The ample space between the street and the entrance to the auditorium provided more space than the thin pavements of the RKO Pantages, allowing more fans to gather. The 28 m x 91 m red carpet extended from the main road along the bleachers, through the lobby and down aisle of the venue.[50] While the wider entrance left more room for journalists and photographers to circulate, the chaotic setting made it more difficult for them to work, and for stars to enter the venue. During the first year, fans sitting in the bleachers could not recognise or attract the attention of their favourite stars among the crowd of photographers, journalists, guests and the show's staff.[51] There was room for improvement.

More than 500 reporters, columnists, photographers, and television and radio reporters were expected to cover the ceremony in 1962. The Academy spent a full year working on the PR 'battle plan' with a steady flow of press releases building up towards the event.[52] A record high attendance was registered at all press conferences before the show.[53] The plan included turning a room adjacent to the venue into a press pavilion.[54] The new facilities hosted 320 journalists, photographers, radio and television reporters. 'It would almost seem that the outside world was missing something far more exciting here in the Press Room', reflected *Hollywood Citizen-News* reporter Nadine Edwards.[55]

In 1962, new bleachers promised to accommodate more spectators, ensuring an unobstructed view of arrivals.[56] Back then, bleacher seats were available for free on a first-come-first-served basis, with 110 police officers maintaining order with regard to all aspects of the arrivals.[57] The red carpet was divided into different pathways. This sectioning allowed attendees to walk either directly into the lobby, along the press line, or closer to the fans, which later included a stop for an interview with the red-carpet greeter. From that point on, the circulation of photographers and journalists was limited to the designated press areas. As seen if facing the venue, photographers and journalists were located behind the rope to the right. The roped area to the left brought the stars closer to the fans while guiding them into the venue. Those who wanted to enter the venue directly, or to pose and interact with photographers and journalists, used the central pathway as the 'clear sailing' section. These changes to the red carpet would usher in the model we see today.

In 1964, the Academy built a platform outside the Santa Monica Civic Auditorium, visible from all seats in the bleachers, for the red-carpet greeter to interview celebrities upon arrival. The platform was located between the two bleachers on the left pathway leading into the venue. The Academy also built a ramp, extending approximately 10 metres, for the fans to see celebrities and stars up close. The first to inaugurate the podium was Army Archerd, who also became one of the most iconic red-carpet figures associated with the Oscars. Archerd's first foray into journalism was in 1945 when he started writing a column for AP after leaving the army. He moved to *Los Angeles Herald-Express* and worked with

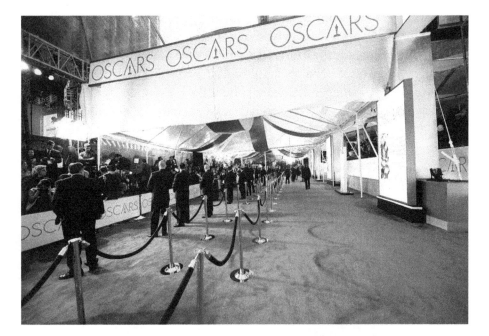

**Figure 4.3** View of the sectioned-off circulation areas of the red carpet outside the Santa Monica Civic Auditorium during the 37th Academy Awards ceremony in 1965 and the 87th Academy Awards ceremony at the Dolby Theatre in 2015. Academy Awards Collection. Courtesy of ©A.M.P.A.S.®

Harrison Carroll, a red-carpet chronicler of film stars, before moving to *Daily Variety*, where he ran a Hollywood gossip column entitled 'Just for Variety' for five decades. His first job in Hollywood as a red-carpet greeter was for the premiere of the film *The Barefoot Contessa* (Transoceanic Film/Figaro, 1954). The event was broadcast live on KTLA from Hollywood Boulevard. It was TV executive James Aubrey who allegedly saw his potential to become the reporter Hollywood needed for the small screen.[58] Like a circus ringmaster, Archerd ran his own show, addressing the roaring fans seated in the bleachers while interviewing the parade of movie stars.

The Oscars continued at the Santa Monica Civic Auditorium until it moved to the Dorothy Chandler Pavilion in downtown Los Angeles in 1969. In 1970, a second podium was added to speed up the flow of arrivals and to make the event more entertaining for those sitting in the bleachers.[59] Archerd had a group of publicists located in the limousine parking sector assisting him and delivering the names of those approaching the platform, keeping him updated on the flow. Media constructions pointed at his power to discern who was important enough to be interviewed on the red-carpet.[60] As a celebrity in his own right, Archerd appeared in the media describing his expert pre-Oscars routine and frequently played cameos in Hollywood films.[61] He held this role uninterruptedly until 2006 when *Hollywood Reporter*'s columnist Robert Osborne replaced him. The official red-carpet greeter role continued to overlap with that of media presenters, at least until Osborne's death in 2017.

The need to upgrade the PR services for the ceremony during the late 1950s and early 1960s responded to the growing interest of international media outlets that were no longer depending on local correspondents. The affluence of international journalists demanded an expansion of the press facilities and improved communication. The format and dynamics crafted during this era continue to the present day. Direct access to the venue is nowadays separate from the roped-off section, called the press line, and it is known as the red-carpet's fast track. The fast track provides a clear way for guests who do not need, or want, to interact with the press. The press line allows news photographers and media outlets to photograph and interview the nominees, presenters and performers.[62]

## The potential of international markets

Back in 1949, when the event was hosted at the Academy Theatre, the institution decided to film the ceremony and screen it for those members who could not attend.[63] This action that started as a palliative to the venue's reduced capacity became a tradition of recording the ceremony. Whether

**Figure 4.4** Army Archerd interviewing stars on the red-carpet platform. Above: Phyllis Diller at the Santa Monica Civic Auditorium for the 38th Academy Awards Ceremony in 1966. Below: Jane Fonda and her husband, Ted Turner. She is wearing a white sleeveless dress by Gianni Versace during the 65th Academy Awards ceremony at the Dorothy Chandler Pavilion in 1993. Academy Awards Collection. Courtesy of ©A.M.P.A.S.®

the event continued to be filmed for archival purposes or for export remains unanswered. The Academy circulated copies abroad. The NBC live broadcast reached Canada by 1958, and another nineteen countries received 16 mm sound film prints for local television stations.[64] The Armed Forces Television Service was broadcasting the show through kinescope to half a million US citizens abroad by 1962.[65] In 1969, ABC Films distributed the show to thirty countries within hours using colour or black-and-white 16 mm film, videotape or kinescope.[66] The show was sent in an abbreviated one-hour edit on a trial basis for prime-time delayed broadcast under the sole sponsorship of Eastman Kodak. Non-English-speaking countries were permitted to provide their own 'voice-over' translations.

After the export trials in 1969, the Academy announced its intention to expand the international market using new technologies in 1970. Balancing the economies of exports required adjustments. The payment delays from the foreign stations carrying the syndication in 1969 put the Academy in a difficult economic situation. ABC offered to reimburse the institution for all guild residual payments, assuming the costs of production and distribution for future shows directly.[67] The willingness of ABC to rapidly cover all costs in advance is evidence of its understanding of the financial potential of exporting the event. To centralise the distribution demand, the Academy and ABC agreed on the cancellation of all licences for radio transmissions of the show. ABC retained the right to broadcast inserts, live from the press area, as the programme progressed.[68] It was not a hard decision: radio had lost its weight as a dominant medium by then. Radio stations retained the rights to report the results and send live interviews with the winners via telephone from the press area as insert news reports.[69]

ABC agreed to pay a flat sum despite the cancellation of the radio broadcast, showing its commitment to the telecast's international potential. Under the terms of the new agreement, the company would work as the distributor of the show abroad, liberating the Academy from all logistics, costs and negotiations with foreign markets. The Academy's legal department posted several concerns. The first was knowing to what extent international networks could commit to broadcasting the show in its entirety and unedited. Another challenge was regulating the commercials and sponsors attached to the broadcast, considering the institution's reticence to lose control over the companies and messages attached to the Oscars brand. There were initial discussions about requiring foreign networks to submit their pool of sponsors in advance for approval. The logistics behind this made lawyers pull back. They settled on sending a copy of a document entitled 'Regulations for the Use of the Academy Awards Symbols and References to the Academy Awards' to all networks. The goal was to remind them of 'the Academy's position with regard to the copyright of the Oscar and the dignity of the Academy and its award programs'.[70]

The publicity for the international broadcast focused on 'firsts'. The 42nd Academy Awards ceremony promised to be the first live broadcast by landline to Mexico, and by satellite to Brazil and possibly other Latin American countries, with on-camera translations into Spanish and Portuguese.[71] The idea was to launch the international broadcast campaign with a major press conference from the Academy Theatre two or three weeks before the telecast. The Oscarcast allegedly became the first overseas satellite transmission of an entertainment event.[72] According to *The Hollywood Reporter*, the show added 250 million viewers in forty countries to the show's domestic attendance with the help of ABC Television.[73]

After the success attained in Latin America, the executives at ABC International were eager to continue expanding the show into other markets.[74] NBC approached the Academy offering $1,100,000 for the rights to broadcast the show for five years starting in 1971.[75] This was a generous sum considering that the actual expenses for the programme in 1970 amounted to $251,812.[76] The battle for the rights to distribute the show abroad was on. The agreement included worldwide distribution by NBC International at no cost to the Academy, with full revenues for the network. The Academy officially terminated its contract with ABC on 15 April 1970.[77] NBC International broadcast the ceremony live to Canada, Latin America and Australia in 1971.

The 1970s were foundational for building international presence. By the mid-1980s, national and international media outlets were requesting permission to cover and broadcast pre- and post-Oscars activities. The cult of celebrity, so endemic to American culture, sparked curiosity. For some, the audience's reaction to fame was a foreign concept. The Soviet Union covered the event for the first time in 1988, putting Western society under scrutiny. Correspondent Nikolai Gnisyuk explained that their main interest was not the celebrities or the event itself, but the American obsession with it: 'We journalists and photographers in the Soviet Union are amazed such a fuss is made over these awards … If I were a famous actor or singer in this country, I would go crazy'.[78] That same year, the *St. Petersburg Times* reported that elegance replaced glitz when Hollywood's royalty turned out for the Oscars.[79] These examples reveal the migratory trajectory of ideas – in this case, celebrity culture's assimilation in the US at the time – and the penetration of American popular culture in some remote locations. The ceremony was broadcast for the first time in the Soviet Union in March 1989. In November that year, the fall of the Berlin Wall marked the advent of a new era in the race for globalisation. Two years later, in 1991, the dissolution of the Soviet Union sealed it.

By 1993, the ABC Distribution Company had licensed the 65th Annual Academy Awards to ninety-five international markets, a record at that point. Of that number, forty-eight countries and territories received the telecast live via satellite.[80] The remaining markets were given a ninety-minute version of the telecast that was prepared overnight and fed via satellite for broadcast the following day.[81] A total of seventy-five correspondents from the Hollywood Foreign Press Association were accredited to cover the event. By 2016, Disney Media Networks was distributing the Oscarcast to 225 countries worldwide. The mediatisation of the Oscars ceremony became the main source of income for the Academy, sustaining the infrastructure and the many activities that the institution runs.[82]

## Notes

1. Critchlow, *When Hollywood was Right*, 53–4.
2. For a more complete list of contributors to the Republican Party, see ibid., vii–x.
3. Frank Lee Donoghue, 'Starry-Eyed Stars, Crowds Eyed Oscar', *Los Angeles Examiner*, 5 April 1950.
4. 'Darnel, Hopper Pay Bleachers a Visit', *Daily Variety*, 24 March 1950, 3.
5. 'Music Fills the Air as Academy Marks Up Brightest Awards Fete', *The Hollywood Reporter*, 21 March 1952, 5.
6. 'Recommendations', *Report of the President*, 30 April 1949, 8, Academy History Archive, MHL.
7. Ibid., 9.
8. For the full story of the Bulova watches deal and the subsequent legal issues see Elizabeth Castaldo Lundén, 'Oscar Night in Hollywood: Fashioning the Red-Carpet from the Roosevelt Hotel to International Media' (PhD dissertation, Stockholm University, 2018), 121–5.
9. Christopher Anderson, *Hollywood TV: The Studio System in the Fifties* (Austin, TX: University of Texas Press, 1994), 47–8.
10. Memo from Geo Frey, 20 January 1953, National Broadcasting Company Records, Office Files 1921–1976, Wisconsin Center for Film and Theater Research (hereafter WCFTR).
11. Lynn Spigel, *Make Room for TV: Television and the Family Ideal in Postwar America* (Chicago, IL: University of Chicago Press, 1992), 207. See also 'NBC-TV's "What's the Use?" Slant May Give Daytime Back to Affiliates', *Variety*, 3 September 1952, 20; 'Daytime TV – No. 1 Dilemma', *Variety*, 24 September 1952, 1, 56; 'NBC-TV Focus Prime Attention on Daytime Schedule', *Variety*, 24 December 1952, 22; 'NBC-TV Affiliates in Flareup', *Variety*, 6 May 1953, 23.
12. Thomas M. Pryor, 'Hollywood's Uneasy "Oscar": Motion Picture Academy is Seeking Commercial Sponsor to Underwrite Expense of Annual Ceremonies – Other Matters', *The New York Times*, 25 January 1953, X5.
13. 'TV Funds Aid "Oscar": N.B.C. and R.C.A. Set to Pay $100,000 for Rights', *The New York Times*, 5 February 1953, 20.
14. Jack Hellman, '1st Major Pix-TV Wedding Big Click', *Daily Variety*, 20 March 1953, 4.

15. James L. Baughman, *Same Time, Same Station: Creating American Television, 1948–1961* (Baltimore, MD: Johns Hopkins University Press, 2007), 31.
16. As Raymond Williams explains, it was relatively cheap to transmit something that happened on television. See Raymond Williams, *Television: Technology and Cultural Form* (New York: Routledge, 2003 [1974]), 24.
17. Walter Ames, 'Oscar Awards Rated Bargain by Sponsor; Big Story Club Organized by TV Producer', *Los Angeles Times*, 21 March 1953, A5.
18. Anderson, *Hollywood TV*, 86.
19. William Boddy, *Fifties Television: The Industry and Its Critics* (Champaign, IL: University of Illinois Press, 1993), 103.
20. Baughman, *Same Time, Same Station*, 90, 87.
21. Ibid., 90.
22. Untitled, *The Hollywood Reporter*, 20 March 1953, 7.
23. Pryor, 'Hollywood's Uneasy "Oscar"', X5.
24. Murray, *Hitch Your Antenna to the Stars*, 43.
25. See, for example, Interoffice communication Kramer, O'Shea, Dann, Hungate, Willson, MacNamara, Gillham, Scanlon, Miss Bruns, 3/21/48, Box 260, f. 4, David O. Selznick Collection, HRC.
26. Letter from John Green to Mr Sydney H. Eiges, 27 February 1953, National Broadcasting Company Records, Office Files 1921–1976, WCFTR.
27. 'Academy Awards Television Broadcast Chart', Academy Awards Ceremony Files, MHL.
28. Mike Kaplan and Bill Brogdon, 'First TV Spread in Academy Annals Heightens Drama', *Daily Variety*, 20 March 1953, 3; Hellman, '1st Major Pix-TV Wedding Big Click', 4.
29. 'Oscar on TV', *Life*, 30 March 1953, 39, 31.
30. Ames, 'Oscar Awards Rated Bargain by Sponsor', A5.
31. Hellman, '1st Major Pix-TV Wedding Big Click', 4.
32. Larry Wolters, 'Glamour Takes a Beating at Academy Show', *Chicago Daily Tribune*, 21 March 1953, A1.
33. Spigel, *Make Room for TV*, 140.
34. Lynn Spigel explains how 'television at its most ideal promised . . . a sense of "being there", a kind of *hyperrealism*'. See *Make Room for TV*, 133.
35. Kaplan and Brogdon, 'First TV Spread in Academy Annals Heightens Drama', 3.
36. Oscars, 'The First Televised Oscars Opening in 1953', *YouTube*, https://www.youtube.com/watch?v=iOtp4dli7-4/
37. Baughman, *Same Time, Same Station*, 190.
38. 'Press Relations Expertly Handled', *The Hollywood Reporter*, 30 March 1951, 5.
39. The firm had headquarters in Chicago, a branch in Los Angeles and offices in New York. The key point person was Dorothy Furman. See 'Harshe-Rotman, Inc. Named PR Counsel', *Academy Report* 1.1 (November 1956): 2, Academy History Archive, MHL.
40. Appadurai, *Modernity at Large*, 48.
41. Letter from Lumsden for Movies to Jenkisson for Zeitlin-Bevedit, 13 March 1958, David I Seitlin Papers, f. 32 Academy Awards Correspondence, MHL.
42. Letter from Zietlin Bevedit to Carmichael and Marckland and Stanton Life New York, 21 March 1958, David I Seitlin Papers, f. 32 Academy Awards Correspondence, MHL.
43. An Oral History of Howard W. Koch interviewed by Douglas Bell, 118, 1999, W1308787, Oral History Collection, MHL.

44. 'Experienced Team Set to Stage 33rd Awards', *Academy Report* 6.1 (February 1961): 2; Cecil Smith, 'Oscar's Up for Grabs', *Los Angeles Times*, 16 April 1961, 4.

45. Elizabeth Sullivan, 'Oscar Night', *Boston Globe*, 16 April 1961, A18; 'Stars Will Shine Tonight in Academy Award Show', unknown, 17 April 1961, f. 84, AMPAS 33rd (1960) Academy Awards, Hedda Hopper Papers, MHL.

46. Len Simpson, 'In the Limelight', *Limelight* 3.16 (20 April 1961): 1.

47. Eddy Jo Bernal, 'Gems and Gorgeous Gowns Gleam at Oscar Fete', *Los Angeles Herald-Express*, 18 April 1961, second front page.

48. 'Press Reaction Enthusiastic to 33rd Awards Show, Facilities', *Academy Report* 6.2 (June 1961): 2, Academy History Archive, MHL.

49. 'Year of Planning Lies Behind "Oscar" Show Promotion, Press Preparations', *Academy Report* 7.1 (April 1962): 3, Academy History Archive, MHL.

50. Sullivan, 'Oscar Night', A18; 'Officials to Complete Preparations for Academy Awards Program', *Los Angeles Times*, 8 April 1962, WS4.

51. 'Santa Monica's Biggest Night', *Daily Variety*, 18 April 1961, 11.

52. 'Top Production Staff Operating Efficiently on Awards Program', *Academy Report* 7.1 (April 1962): 4, Academy History Archive, MHL.

53. '"Oscarcast" Again Captures Lion's Share, 47.9, of Television Audience with a 37.1 Ratings', *Academy Report* 7.2 (July 1962): 4, Academy History Archive, MHL.

54. 'Year of Planning Lies Behind "Oscar" Show Promotion, Press Preparations', 3.

55. Nadine M. Edwards, 'Press Room Full of Smaze Confusion', *Hollywood Citizen-News*, 10 April 1962, 26.

56. 'Red Carpet Treatment Expanded This Year', *Academy Report* 7.1 (April 1962): 1, Academy History Archive, MHL.

57. 'Oscar Show Readied at S. M. Auditorium', *Los Angeles Times*, 1 April 1965, 167.

58. 'Army Archerd: 40 Years as Hollywood's Town Crier', *Variety*, 28 January 1993, https://variety.com/1993/more/news/army-archerd-40-years-as-hollywood-s-town-crier-103503/

59. 'Oscarcast Producer Blends Historic with the Present', *Chicago Daily Defender*, 31 March 1970, 13.

60. Traude Gomez, 'The Name of the Game is Glamour', *The News*, Frederick (from *The Kansas City Star*), 5 April 1988, D6.

61. The AP article appears in Bob Thomas, 'Army Archerd has Greeted Oscar Arrivals for 30 Years', *The Palm Beach Post*, 20 March 1987, 22; Bob Thomas, 'Archerd Has Greeted Oscar Night Arrivals for Three Decades', *The Dispatch*, 17 March 1987, 27.

62. 'Red Carpet Treatment Expanded This Year', 1.

63. *Annual Report 1948–49*, Academy History Archive, MHL.

64. 'Awards Show Attracted World-Wide Audience Estimated at More Than a Quarter Billion', *Academy Report* 3.1 (July 1958): 3, Academy History Archive, MHL. The list of countries includes Argentina, Australia, Austria, Belgium, Brazil, Colombia, Cuba, France, Great Britain, Italy, Japan, Mexico, Netherlands, Philippines, Puerto Rico, Spain, Venezuela, Uruguay and West Germany.

65. 'AFRTS Flashes Awards News to Armed Forces Across Entire World', *Academy Report* 7.1 (April 1962): 3, Academy History Archive, MHL.

66. '32 Countries Will Telecast Oscar Show', *Academy Report* 12.1 (April 1969): 1–2, Academy History Archive, MHL. ABC Films, Inc. was an internationally based subsidiary of ABC Television. The countries reached were Argentina, Australia, Austria, Belgium, Canada, Chile, Costa Rica, Dominican Republic, Ecuador, Finland, Greece, Guatemala,

Holland, Honduras, Hong Kong, Italy, Korea, Mexico, New Zealand, Nicaragua, Norway, Panama, the Philippines, Portugal, San Salvador, Singapore, Spain, Switzerland, Thailand, the UK, Uruguay, the US and Venezuela.

67. Letter from Rowe Glesen to Margaret Herrick from ABC, 1 December 1970, f. 2614 Academy of Motion Picture Arts and Sciences 42nd Annual (1969) Academy Awards, Gregory Peck Papers, MHL.

68. Letter from Margaret Herrick to Gregory Peck, 14 January 1970, f. 2614 Academy of Motion Picture Arts and Sciences 42nd Annual (1969) Academy Awards, Gregory Peck Papers, MHL; Letter to Margaret Herrick, 24 January 1970, f. 2614 Academy of Motion Picture Arts and Sciences 42nd Annual (1969) Academy Awards, Gregory Peck Papers, MHL.

69. Letter from ABC to Margaret Herrick, 5 January 1970, f. 2614 Academy of Motion Picture Arts and Sciences 42nd Annual (1969) Academy Awards, Gregory Peck Papers, MHL; Letter from ABC's Rowe Giesen to Margaret Herrick, 16 February 1970, f. 2614 Academy of Motion Picture Arts and Sciences – 42nd Annual (1969) Academy Awards Correspondence, MHL.

70. Law office letter to Margaret Herrick, 17 November 1969, f. 2614 Academy of Motion Picture Arts and Sciences 42nd Annual (1969) Academy Awards, Gregory Peck Papers, MHL.

71. ABC letter to Gregory Peck, 11 February 1970, f. 2614 Academy of Motion Picture Arts and Sciences 42nd Annual (1969) Academy Awards, Gregory Peck Papers, MHL.

72. Cecil Smith, 'International Audience Awaits Oscar Ceremony', *Los Angeles Times*, 5 April 1970, N31B.

73. John Mahoney, 'Oscars Sustain Glamor Infused Tradition', *The Hollywood Reporter*, 8 April 1970, front page.

74. Letter from Klas Lehman to Gregory Peck, 4 June 1970, f. 42nd Awards General ABC-General Correspondence, MHL.

75. Letter from Thomas W. Sarnoff to Walter Mirisch, 2 February 1970, f. 2614 Academy of Motion Picture Arts and Sciences 42nd Annual (1969) Academy Awards, Gregory Peck Papers, MHL.

76. 42nd Annual Awards-Estimated Expenses, f. 2619 Academy of Motion Picture Arts and Sciences 42nd Annual (1969) Academy Awards (Miscellaneous), Gregory Peck Papers, MHL.

77. Letter from Gregory Peck to Elton H. Rule, 15 April 1970, f. 2614 Academy of Motion Picture Arts and Sciences 42nd Annual (1969) Academy Awards Correspondence, MHL.

78. John Voland, 'Countdown to Oscar: A First: Soviets Cover the Academy Awards', *Los Angeles Times*, 11 April 1988, 1.

79. John Antczak, 'The Oscars: Elegance, Some Glitz', *St. Petersburg Times*, 12 April 1988, 4A.

80. Among these were Argentina, Australia, Austria, Bahamas, Belgium, Brazil, Canada, Chile, China, Colombia, Denmark, Dominican Republic, Dubai, Ecuador, Finland, France, Germany, Guatemala, Hong Kong, Indonesia, Ireland, Isle of Man, Israel, Italy, Jamaica, Japan, Luxembourg, Mexico, Monaco, Netherlands, New Zealand, Nicaragua, Norway, Panama, Paraguay, Portugal, Puerto Rico, Singapore, South Africa, Spain, Sweden, Thailand, Trinidad, Turkey, United Kingdom and Venezuela.

81. Press Release, 24 March 1993, f. 66th Annual (1993) Academy Awards (TV) Press Material, Arthur L. Wilde Papers, MHL.

82. An Oral History of Robert Wise interviewed by Douglas Bell, 2004, Oral History Collection, MHL.

# 5

# Creating an international fashion show for the American market

The attention awarded to fashion during the postwar era corresponded to changes in the Hollywood film industry and the power shift towards television. Interest in what stars wore to the ceremony existed before the inception of the Oscarcast in 1953, but from a fashion standpoint, the reactivation of transatlantic trade cannot be ignored. Paris's strong return to the American fashion scene, the advent of Italian fashion and the consolidation of New York as a mercantile fashion epicentre all reveal a blossoming scenario for the promotion of fashion.[1] The 1941 PR campaigns that propelled New York into becoming the new style centre of the world diluted the efforts of the 1930s to establish Hollywood as the new Paris. By the time the international fashion scene got back on track, Hollywood had consolidated its power as a promotional platform for designers, in part due to the widespread interest in what stars were wearing, and the consequent notoriety of Hollywood designers under the studio system.

Between 1948 and the first telecast in 1953, designer names increasingly appeared in extensive media coverage of Oscars fashion. Don Loper, Hattie Carnegie, Howard Shoup, Orry-Kelly, Kay Nelson, Rosemary Odell, Christian Dior, Adrian and Mitchell Leisen were at the forefront. For the Oscars and the studios, fashion remained a useful cross-promotional tool for the telecast and, consequently, the nominated films. The full-blown branding of the Oscars as a fashion show was not provided by the power of the new medium *per se*, but by discourses articulated to promote the Oscarcast embedded in ongoing changes within the fashion industry. The Oscarcast became the perfect window display for fashion, in which the stars functioned as mannequins. As the studios were slowly dismantling their structures, the star system entered a transition that constrained the influx of studio resources, which led to less control over the star commodity. With the emergence of television, the idea of the distant stars was rapidly shifting. Instead, a new form of fame was proposed that paved the way for the notion of 'celebrities'.

European designers were increasingly interested in entering the wealthy American market. Parallel to this, the transatlantic flow of cinematic productions and talent facilitated the exchange between European designers and Hollywood stars. American actresses had access to European creations, and European actresses were the perfect vessel for introducing new names into the US media. The focus on fashion as an epiphenomenon to the event, in combination with the reactivation of transatlantic commerce and the exchange between actresses and designers facilitated by the propagation of air travel and runaway productions, made for an increasing presence of European designer names on the red-carpet.

Even though the international coverage of the Oscars focused primarily on nominees and winners for much longer, fashion became central for promoting the ceremony in the US. The sudden growth of fashion journalism allowed newspapers to focus exclusively on the gowns worn to the ceremony, and the cross-media input of these columns helped associate designer names with the gowns worn. The role of television was pivotal. As a visual medium, television was a powerful vehicle to display fashion. Audiences were no longer limited to the fashion expert's descriptions on the radio or in the printed press.

This chapter explains the consolidation of the ceremony as an international fashion show free-for-all in the US. In doing so, it anchors the contemporary global red-carpet mania to a phenomenon that emerged in the American context during the first two decades of the Oscarcast, the second period of fashion at the Academy Awards. It describes the events that brought fashion to the forefront as a promotional force for the televised ceremony, exploring the media coverage and the production of the first fashion pre-show.

## Fashion's showtime

Network executives believed that fashion could be a powerful promotional tool to engage the female audience. The strategy was implemented from both production and promotional angles through creating the position of fashion consultant and launching press campaigns that promoted the event as a unique opportunity to see what stars were wearing. Television gave audiences the illusion of seeing the stars as 'their real selves' – out of character, living their seemingly luxurious lifestyles, casting a halo of authenticity to their equally constructed public personas.

The first Oscarcast came with a legion of publicists and PR strategies. It gathered together the PR departments of NBC, RCA, the Academy and a group of external representatives from the Carl Byoir and Associates PR agency.[2] More than thirty-one publicity strategies were outlined, most of which targeted female audiences. Fashion and beauty discourses became central to this promotion amid the 1950s boom of fashion journalism and its predominantly female readership. Integrated plugs and pre-recorded introductions calling attention to the Oscarcast were presented in shows through sketches, interviews and musical numbers.[3] Special stories were plugged to fashion and beauty editors. Photos of prominent female guests in special gowns were a priority for editors of women's magazines, encouraging their readers to organise home viewing parties and dress up for the occasion. Movie stars' press agents and studios' publicity departments provided material suitable for stories in women's pages relating to fashion, hairstyles and similar topics.[4] Publicist Maury Foladare joined the team for developing exclusive strategies for Louella Parsons, Hedda Hopper and other syndicated gossip columnists.[5] These opinion-makers were to participate in a saturation campaign through their columns, to get all available movie fans to tune in that night.[6] Besides customised stories for gossip, beauty and fashion editors, a separate deal was made with *Photoplay*.[7]

## First show coverage

All promotional efforts to establish the Oscarcast as a fashionable event paid off. The press headlines presented it as a fashion show. Besides referring to the event as 'Hollywood's annual fashion parade', the media ruled that the first Oscarcast 'may well go down in history as television's greatest fashion show'.[8] Mink coats and capes were said to be the stars of the night. *Daily Variety*'s fashion column celebrated how the Oscarcast allowed audiences to get 'more than a word picture of the fashions' designed by local and international couturiers.[9] According to Hedda Hopper, appearing on live television put pressure on what to wear. Previously, stars were 'dressed to the teeth, but some of the most gorgeous gowns didn't show up well on television. Now the girls [paid] a great deal of attention to their garbs before stepping in front of a television camera'.[10]

Edith Head designed Loretta Young's gown, Terry Moore's dress and her own ivory faille dress embroidered in black. For Moore, she used pale pearl-pink French satin with a full wraparound skirt covered in pink satin poppies.[11] Joan Crawford was nominated for Best Actress in a Leading Role for *Sudden Fear* (Joseph Kaufmann Productions, 1952). Sheila O'Brien – the film's costume designer who was also nominated for Best Costume Design in Black and White that night – designed Crawford's gown for the ceremony.[12] Howard Greer designed a décolleté ballgown in black over pink net with mauve and pink lilacs draped over the bodice for leading vocalist Peggy Lee. Adrian designed a strapless gown in pink silk organza, embroidered with gold and amber oak leaves for his wife, Janet Gaynor. Don Loper captured media

**Figure 5.1** Janet Gaynor and her husband, Hollywood designer Adrian, arriving at the 25th Academy Awards ceremony in 1953. She is wearing an Adrian original. Academy Awards Collection. Courtesy of ©A.M.P.A.S.®

attention for at least three of his creations: Maureen O'Hara's short strapless gown in a fine gold fabric, accessorised with diamond and emerald earrings and a white ermine wrap; Teresa Wright's gown with a halter neck, lace bodice and skirt in the polonaise style; and Kathryn Grayson's gown in white nylon net and lace, with a bodice embroidered with pearls and rhinestones. Italian actress Pier Angeli promoted the new Italian trends by wearing a dress with a green and white strapless bodice, trimmed with green and white tulle, designed by Carosa di Roma.[13]

Fashion designers were increasingly showcased, but costume designers also continued to dress actresses despite the studio system's demise. Besides Head, other costume designers appearing during this period included Sheila O'Brien, Don Loper, John Moore, Charles La Maire, Travilla, Howard Shoup, Bill Thomas, Mitchell Leisen, Cecil Beaton, Ray Aghayan, Jean Louis, Theadora Van Runkle and Helen Rose.[14] Former Hollywood designers also continued dressing actresses for the event, now on behalf of their own fashion houses. The most popular were Adrian, Howard Greer, Orry-Kelly and Irene. New York-based designers were also frequent choices for the Oscars. Among these were Galanos, Arnold Scaasi, Oscar de la Renta, Marusia, Giorgio di Sant' Angelo, Donald Brooks, Jeffrey Bean, George Halley and Marilyn Lewis's brand Cardinalli.[15] International designers receiving media attention included Christian Dior, Hubert de Givenchy, Pierre Balmain, Pierre Cardin, Pauline Trigère, Yves Saint Laurent, Jean Desses, Jacques Fath, Bob Bugnand, Antonio Castillo, Carosa di Roma, Sorelle Fontana, Emilio Schuberth, John Cavanagh, Hardy Amies and Jean Pacot.

## The emergence of the fashion consultant

Edith Head was appointed as the first fashion consultant for the show in 1953, a crucial appointment for promoting fashion at the ceremony.[16] She fostered a strong media presence as an American fashion expert, audiences were familiar with her since she had been put in charge of Paramount's costume department in 1938 and her predisposition for media appearances made her an ideal spokesperson for the promotional campaigns leading up to the event. In return, her public exposure helped her transition into new business ventures in a seemingly declining film industry. Aside from the personal benefits she derived from the exposure, there were other, more political reasons behind the costume designer's lobbying for visibility.

The demise of the studio system triggered certain anxieties regarding the consequences of the studios' loss of profitability. As Peter Lev asserts, '[t]he changes of the late 1940s and early 1950s in Hollywood brought a share of

**Figure 5.2** Shirley Jones, dressed by Don Loper, arriving at the 33rd Academy Awards ceremony in 1961 with husband Jack Cassidy. Photographer: Howard Ballew, *Los Angeles Herald Examiner* Photo Collection. Courtesy of Los Angeles Public Library.

instability, unemployment, even panic; but they also pushed the industry toward a different, more entrepreneurial, model of filmmaking'.[17] Costume designers were not immune to increasing redundancies. A series of actions were launched in 1948. The costume designers, then aligned under the Art Directors Guild, demanded screen credits, a minimum wage scale, reciprocal agreements regarding the use of external designers and eligibility for an Academy Award for Costume Design. Edith Head became a board member of the Academy and joined the Art Directors Branch for the preparations of the 22nd Academy Awards Presentation Committee in 1948.[18] As a result of all the lobbying, the Academy introduced two statuettes for Best Achievement in Costume Design – 'Black and White' and 'Colour' – in 1949.

Head also participated in a series of actions launched by the Academy to promote the film industry at large. As a PR strategy to alleviate audience decline, a series of twelve industrial films under the title *The Industry Film Project* were produced between 1949 and 1950, as a joint venture with all Hollywood guilds, unions and the Producers Association.[19] Aside from their distribution in the cinema circuit, 16 mm copies were sent to schools, libraries and universities through Teaching Film Custodians, Inc., a company that had been distributing educational films to promote the value of motion pictures in schools, colleges and universities since the 1920s.[20] Prints were dubbed into foreign languages and made available for television purposes on a non-sponsored basis.[21] Each short documentary introduced a different aspect of movie-making. Head appears in the leading role for *The Costume Designer* (RKO Radio Pictures, 1950). This production, lasting 8 minutes and 55 seconds, combines costume tests and scenes from different films with other scenes especially shot for the storyline, in which the audience can see Head 'at work'. She also participated in a forum for 300 entrepreneurs from the National Retail Dry Goods Association at the Biltmore Hotel in Los Angeles.[22] The panel, under the title 'Motion Picture Techniques Applicable to Modern Visual Merchandising', gathered six Academy members: art director Paul Groesse; set decorator Henry Grace; cinematographer Victor Milner; the Academy's PR counsellor Howard G. Mayer; and Edith Head.[23] Head mentored industrialists in the art of using motion pictures for selling fashion to American women. All these actions raised visibility for the costume designers' profession, leading to the formation of the Costume Designers Guild in 1953.

As the Oscars fashion consultant, Head became an inventive promotional machine bringing attention to the media event. As a result, the media increasingly focused on fashion. Audiences identified Head as the woman who helped craft the image of Hollywood stars, but she also developed a voice within the retail industry due to her connection with female audiences, her endorsements as an expert, and her mail-order patterns and other tie-ins that had been available in department stores since the 1930s. Besides being an endorser of fashion products, Head also became an endorser of Hollywood itself and saw actresses as performing the same role. In a conversation with her publicist, she explained:

> When an actress goes on the stage, I like the audiences to say 'hooray' not because they know her but because she is exciting and typifies a star. We're not selling women and we're not selling dresses. We're selling Hollywood and that's our star system, and when these gals appear with their beautiful jewels, their beautiful make-up and their beautiful hair and beautiful dresses, they should represent what makes motion pictures.[24]

For her, the ceremony's allure was not determined by the role, the actress-model or the fashions, but by the glory of Hollywood's star system as a nostalgic force that she was highly invested in.

The fashion consultant's job description remains vague and not adequately documented. Head's job title indicates that it was her advice and not her work as a designer that was offered to the stars. It is plausible that her services as a fashion consultant were primarily rendered to award presenters and nominees. Following the promotional restructuring of the ceremony in 1958, an invitation letter was sent on her behalf, establishing clear guidelines of attire. All-black or pure-white dresses, busy patterns and sparkling jewellery were discouraged. Attendees were reminded of the importance of formal wear with floor-length gowns to give the occasion the importance it deserved. The letter highlighted her services for consultation, but it also suggested that attendees could consult other studio costume designers, and recommended Helen Rose, Bill Thomas, Jean Louis, Howard Shoup, Charles LeMaire, Renie Conley, Edward Stevenson and Gwen Wakeling.[25]

The closest to an official description of her role can be found in a promotional film for the 42nd Academy Awards ceremony in which she narrates, in the first person:

> I come to each of the stars, describe the colour of the set and discuss with them the colour they are going to wear, the silhouette, so we try to get a differentiation of costumes on all of the actresses. You must remember that this is the one time that an actress presents herself as their own image, not a character in film. Now, the Academy does not tell a star what she can or cannot wear, but 'since this is the most important time of the year in Hollywood, since the Academy Awards go all over the entire world, it represents not only our industry but the entire country, we feel sure that the stars aren't gonna wear any of the freaky far-out unusual fashion, and we feel that this year it is going to be the most beautiful fashion show it has ever been … Well, I don't have crises because, you see, I have a crush crew backstage. There are women prepared with needles, liquid cement,

scotch tape, all sort of things. You know, one time, we had a star who was just ready to go onstage, stepped over her dress, all of the skirt almost came off and she said: 'I can't go on'. So, we pinned it together and on she went. We had so many strange fashions the last two years; we had the micro, the mini, the midi, we had see-through clothes, we even had unisex. Nobody, not even the designers, knows exactly what is gonna happen. But I know one thing, that on 7 April, you are going to see at the Academy Awards I think the world's greatest fashion show because you are gonna have fashions from every great designer all over the world, modelled by the most beautiful women in the world: the Hollywood stars.[26]

This promotional film was produced in 1970, in the context of the first international Oscarcast broadcast via satellite.

Head's activities can be grouped into two categories. The first set of activities would take place before the ceremony, and would include meetings with set designers and producers to get information about the venue, ambience and décor. She would then contact the attendees to ask what they planned to wear, providing fashion advice, suggesting which colours would better suit that year's decorations and even designing gowns if requested. She also ensured that no two movie stars showed up wearing the same dress.[27] The second set of activities would take place during the show, supervising an 'emergency crew'. Head's availability backstage should be questioned, however, considering that she was the radio broadcast's fashion commentator at least during the 1960s, which required her presence in the radio booth. Head frequently described this onsite role as that of a censor. The backstage crew supervised and enforced morality guidelines that would ensure appropriate femininity and decency, without disturbing the viewers at home.

It was an alleged incident with the cameras during the first Oscarcast that paved the way for Head's role as a censor. During that first televised event, 'the cameras in the balcony of the Pantages Theatre peered deep down inside the décolletage of the already low-cut glamour gowns as many an actress on the floor below walked toward the platform'.[28] Making sure the garments were television-appropriate became one of the primary challenges. The backstage staff were 'equipped with fashion emergency kits – a large supply of tulle to tuck into bosoms, scotch tape, pins, needles, waxing spray to dim jewellery, shoes, stockings and gloves in every shape, size and description to meet all possible emergencies'.[29] In 1959, Shirley MacLaine's zipper broke, and the crew had to put her dress together with safety pins before she went on stage. 'That's why she looked like she was backing off the stage and down the stairs. She was trying to keep her safety pins off-camera', Head explained to the media.[30] Aside from the dictates that prevented overexposure, Head's conservative ideals opposed any figure-hugging clothes on and off screen, unless a portrayed character required them.[31]

Head's so-called role of censor must be embedded in the historical landscape that marked the emergence of the Oscarcast. In 1952, the National Association of Radio and Television Broadcasters (NARTB) passed an industry-wide censorship code for television.[32] Worried about the new medium's influence on children and juvenile delinquency, the code regulated the portrayal of crime, law enforcement, sex and other matters. Several clauses in the section for 'Decency and Decorum' addressed appropriate bodily exposure:

1. The costuming of all performers shall be within the bounds of propriety, and shall avoid such exposure or such emphasis on anatomical detail as would embarrass or offend home viewers.
2. The movements of dancers, actors, or other performers shall be kept within the bounds of decency, and lewdness and impropriety shall not be suggested in the positions assumed by performers.
3. Camera angles shall avoid such views of performers as to emphasise anatomical details indecently.[33]

American postwar discourses centred on the importance of family values and the delineation of gender roles, with the mother as the central figure keeping the home running. Television was questioned constantly as a bad influence, potentially undermining patriarchal authority and disrupting family dynamics. Religious organisations actively monitored 'unsavoury content'.[34] These family-centred discourses, a conservative configuration of femininity and the heavy regulations applied to television in order to protect younger audiences made executives extremely careful of what they broadcast. The two leading networks were cautious not to offend audiences. The US code of practices for television broadcasters was upheld between 1952 and 1970, which comprises the entire second period of fashion at the Academy Awards run by Edith Head.

Not all of Head's observations were driven by contemporary concerns. Some of her advice worked in the actresses' best interests with regard to functionality. 'A too-tight dress only makes them appear ridiculous if they have to go up and down the ramp from the auditorium'.[35] A garment had to enable the actress's mobility at the ceremony, and allow for the star to sit comfortably, walk the red carpet, climb stairs and go up and down ramps, as well as preventing heels from getting stuck somewhere along the way.[36]

A third set of (tacit) activities for Head were her media appearances promoting the ceremony. Aside from anticipating Oscars fashions, she focused on describing her role by relating anecdotes that constructed the illusion that audiences were being given behind-the-scenes access to the organisation of the ceremony. Through her carefully practised and reproduced anecdotes, Head's main role may actually have been as a spokesperson to discuss fashion, in order to generate, and capitalise on, the promotion. An essential aspect of her speech emphasised the idea of putting attention on the star instead of the dress. 'The dress should be understandable. Not so extreme that it might provoke laughter. The ensemble should depict the actress's personality and not look as though it was designed for someone else'.[37] In other words, it was the dress that enhanced the star commodity. Gowns had to be 'photogenic' and still look 'equally good to the live audience at the awards and to the television audience at home'.[38] According to Head, a design for television should concentrate on the waist up, taking advantage of the camera framing that rarely took in the whole silhouette.[39] This commentary portrayed her as a knowledgeable designer. The observation is true for television, but it reveals the lack of understanding for the intermedial reach of fashion coverage that already circulated thousands of photographs in the printed press.

By the 1960s, the understanding of the event as a fashion parade had already permeated fans' perceptions. The red-carpet offered the possibility of witnessing the fashion parade upfront. The audience's reaction to being able to see the stars' allure up close added to media constructions of the red-carpet as a fashion show free-for-all. An audience member sitting in the bleachers during the ceremony in 1961 described the experience as 'worth it just to see the pretty dresses', even though she did not 'go to the movies enough to recognize all the stars'.[40] Fashion was rapidly becoming a standalone vehicle for attracting audiences to the bleachers, which implied that audiences at home were expecting to see more fashion.

## The emergence of the Academy Awards fashion pre-show

On 4 April 1960, NBC broadcast what may be considered a predecessor of today's Oscars red-carpet pre-show. It was a thirty-minute segment called *Oscar Night in Hollywood* (*ONH*), featuring Edith Head as the fashion authority. Live television broadcasts of the ceremony's arrivals, as well as other Oscars pre-shows, existed before *ONH*, but none was orchestrated entirely around fashion. Head claimed that the only thing done before was 'to have a camera in the lobby with someone saying "here comes so-and-so, as they scurry to their seats"'.[41] The creation of *ONH* captures the materialisation of discourse into a concrete social practice after years of promoting the ceremony as a fashion event.

The show was not an initiative from the Academy, PR teams or Head herself. *ONH* was the brainchild of Al Hollander, of Grey Advertising Agency Inc., for its client, Procter & Gamble (P&G). Having advertising agencies and sponsors work as artistic and executive producers in the development of TV shows was common practice, particularly during the 1950s and 1960s.[42] Sponsors decided on programming within their purchase slots, and some programmes were created by advertising agencies and designed entirely around the sponsors' goals.[43] In this dynamic, agencies would develop not only the idea but also full scripts. Audience recall of TV advertising was twice as high as that of radio, magazine or newspaper advertisements, but, as Gallup Robinson analysis also showed, long commercials making exaggerated claims were disliked.[44] Factual demonstration commercials were more effective, especially when integrated with the programme and if a star delivered the message. This was the case of *ONH*. The show was a half-hour product placement for P&G's Lilt Home Permanent, a do-it-yourself hair perming kit, hidden beneath a veneer of fashion commentary in keeping with the 'expert advice' delivered by Head.

## The sponsor

Star-studded sponsored TV shows were in vogue at the time with programmes such as The Drugstores of America's *Cavalcade of Stars* (DuMont, 1949–52/ CBS, 1952–7), Ford's *Startime* (NBC, 1959–60) and *Here's Hollywood* (NBC, 1960–2), sponsored by Colgate, Jergens and Heinz, among others.[45] The decision to put together the Oscars pre-show suggests that the main audience for the Oscarcast was the target market for P&G's product and, consequently, an audience familiar with Head's media appearances. Head's perception of what was fashionably appropriate was aligned with P&G's ideal consumers: middle-class American housewives. P&G's corporate image has consistently represented American postwar values, and this translated into applying strict rules that aligned with contemporary moral standards.[46] The company's familiarity with the medium made it follow closely the television censorship code as a given, and Head's persona aligned with the company's interests. The show also contributed to Head's branding as a fashion expert, setting her up as the Oscars' fashion authority.

By the end of the 1950s, P&G had significantly increased its investment in television, becoming the corporation with the largest investment in TV commercials.[47] P&G had already invested 80.6 per cent of its advertising budget in TV by 1957 and 84.4 per cent by 1960.[48] According to *Fortune* 500 rankings for 1959, P&G was the twenty-first most profitable American company.[49] In 1961, trade magazine *Television Age* labelled P&G 'a marketing machine'.[50] In 1960, when *ONH* was broadcast, P&G was indisputably the biggest TV advertiser.[51]

Ratings were a key element providing advertisers with an assessment of the reach and pull of their investments. Television could be extremely cost-effective, with easily calculated results in terms of cost-per-thousand.[52] In this regard, the sponsor was essential to monetise the medium. Ratings are meaningless *per se*; they gain meaning only insofar as they enable the selling of airtime at a higher rate within a specific target market. Audiences were the commodities indirectly sold to the advertisers. Sponsors relied on Nielsen ratings to ascertain reach.[53] A relatively low cost-per-minute was doubtless an essential parameter, but marketing strategies were increasingly oriented towards target markets and television was the way to demonstrate a product in action and so reach a niche audience.[54]

A comparative study conducted by JWT in 1958 concluded that audience memory was stronger when commercials were contextualised in a continuous programme rather than in isolated TV spots.[55] Television provided the perfect educational platform to showcase step-by-step instructions, suiting the 1950s shift towards do-it-yourself hair styling products for women.[56] In *ONH*, a selected model underwent an 'Oscars makeover', demonstrating how Lilt worked. This audiovisual experience facilitated the use of the product, making it more accessible to audiences.

## Lilt's 1960 aesthetics and the imagined Oscar audience

The prime selling point of Lilt Home Permanent was its practicality. Television commercials in the 1960s showed the perils of housewives attempting to perm their own hair. In one of the commercials, 'Marge' asks her friends if they can help her, but finds that all of them are busy. She looks at the camera and expresses her frustration: 'I need a home permanent, but nobody will help me'. The male voiceover replies, 'Nobody needs to, Marge. Now Lilt gives you all the help you need'. Scenes of Marge applying the home perming kit appear while the product's features are described. 'You're done. Beautifully. Alone'. The scene cuts to Marge on the phone, telling her friend, 'Yes Gloria, alone! Helped myself with Lilt'.[57] Another spot shows a group of people lugging heavy hair salon equipment and furniture down the street. A car stops. The woman driving the car exclaims, 'They are bringing the beauty shop home!' A traffic policeman replies in awe, 'Beauty shop home?!' The woman in the car wonders out loud, 'Why?' The woman leading the parade replies, 'Finally, I can get a professional looking permanent at home'. The voiceover intervenes, suggesting, 'There is an easier way. Now Lilt home permanents are almost like bringing the beauty shop home'.[58] The third commercial shows a similar configuration.[59] All three commercials close with the slogan 'Get the professional look'.

Several aspects stand out concerning the advertising campaign for Lilt, providing a glimpse into P&G's perception of their target market. First is the relegation of women to their homes, subservient to the romanticised contemporary construction of the suburban lifestyle. In one of the commercials, the first friend 'Marge' visits while asking for help is standing at the door, whisking up something in a bowl while talking to her. This is what keeps her busy, making her unable to help her friend. All subsequent interactions happen over the phone. In the other two spots, the emphasis is put on 'bringing the beauty shop home', as if women would not want to leave the house even to indulge in a beauty treatment. Cost-benefit analysis is not addressed. The choice of a home perm is not tied to economic advantage; instead, it emphasises the comfort of the home. The brand also highlighted that the product could be self-applied. With Lilt, women did not need to leave the home, but neither did they need to invite someone over. The third observation ties Lilt's 1960 TV commercials directly to *ONH*. The whole campaign plays with the notion of 'professional'. It is not just any home perm. It is not just any results. Despite doing it themselves, women get, as the slogan promises, a professional look. Coincidentally or not, the selection of Head as the most prominent fashion expert in her field underpins a notion of authority, playing along the lines of the brand's key messages for 1960.

## Promotional synergies

*ONH* played with three different promotional figures for the show: Head, as the expert; Janet Leigh, as the star to emulate; and Sharon as the aspiring actress who gets closer to stardom through the transformative qualities of the product. Leigh does not appear in the show, but she was the central feature of the promotional campaign, setting the ideal for emulation. This was by no means problematic. Endorsements were entering a novel period that focused attention away from personalities and onto the self. P&G was leading this trend. According to Vance Packard, 'studies of narcissism indicated that nothing appeals more to people than themselves'.[60] This propelled the use of anonymous endorsers with whom audiences could identify, turning consumers into 'self-image buyers'. The FTC had released a revised primer for testimonial advertising in 1955 warning about the limitations of associating a product with the wrong endorser. This could result in more publicity for the personality than reputation for the product; loss of point, and loss of weight; loss of face by the maker; and even resentment on the buyer's side.[61] The key to successful testimonial advertising in the mid-1950s relied on it being truthful, the personality and product being logically connected, and the testimony being simple, sincere and honest.

In the case of *ONH*, the direct endorsement came by way of a relatable and unknown model aspiring to emulate stars like Leigh. In order to achieve this, she follows the recommendations of an expert, someone who understands better than anybody the creation of stardom: Edith Head. Head had designed Leigh's dress for the ceremony that year and was there to design a gown for the model. She stressed the importance of hair and make-up to 'make or break a look'. Lilt was looking after the styling, giving professional results, and Head trusted her gown to shine under the brand's accomplishments.

Publicist Cecile Gray Bazelon, from PR agency Rogers & Cowan, was in charge of the promotional campaign for the show in conjunction with the release of *The Dress Doctor*, Head's book. Head capitalised on the additional publicity by making herself available to promote the show.[62] Rogers & Cowan organised interviews with major media and press agencies at the Hotel Plaza in New York, a lunch with AP, a large number of phone interviews, tape-recorded sessions and meetings. The show included multiple selling points around which the promotion was articulated, which included discussing:

1. the idea of being close up to Hollywood royalty
2. Head's role as a fashion expert
3. the Oscars' status as an international fashion show
4. the show's democratising aspect
5. the show's educational aspect.

Referring to stars as 'Hollywood royalty' was a central feature throughout the campaign, prompted by the agency in letters sent to journalists.

The show was sold as inspirational to women. The educational aspect manifested through the product's step-by-step demonstration and the opportunity to copy ideas from Hollywood styles.

> By watching the parade of Hollywood actresses, many women of any age and type may claim worthwhile ideas and suggestions for her own wardrobe. It wouldn't be possible for any woman to buy a ticket for this kind of fashion show, yet just a flick of the TV dial will give her the greatest show on earth.[63]

This statement also underscores the democratising wherewithal of television, capable of bringing the most expensive fashion show, in terms of star/price and designers, directly to the comfort of the home.

Head exploited her branding as a fashion expert in 1960 to support the release of her first book. In a letter to United Press International, Bazelon announced Head as 'Hollywood's top fashion designer'. Her intention to emphasise this role rather than her costume designer position should not be seen as a transition or rebranding. Instead, it was a continuous contradiction throughout her career that responded to the different strands of fashion politics she encountered along the way. Head juggled both labels interchangeably to suit her needs. Notwithstanding this, she distanced herself from fashion designers' artistic whims by pushing the idea of creating clothes to fit each woman's personality: 'This is not a fashion show reflecting the originality and talent of the designer. It's a personal presentation'.[64] In this sense, she would continue to differentiate her work from that of fashion designers at large by flattering the female body instead of focusing on her creations as artistic expressions. This type of argument was not uncommon among American designers, who often used this marketing strategy to differentiate themselves from the 'genius' halo constructed around Parisian fashion while underlining the functionality of ready-to-wear.

In order to make the interviews more attractive to media outlets, and to avoid journalists' annoyance in the event of overlapping stories, multiple stories were plugged. The idea of seeing stars out of character was one angle. In a letter to *New York Journal-American*, Bazelon described how '[t]here is a fascinating story in the gowns that are worn for the Academy Award presentations, for this is the night the actress is selling herself as herself and not as a character in a movie'.[65] Head played upon the idea of closeness to satisfy audience demand. She made a comparison to previous shows in which 'the cameras were too far away and they couldn't really get a good look at the stars. This year, there are going to be cameras literally in their teeth'.[66] 'For the first time', she claimed, 'we are going to have a pre-Academy Award presentation in Hollywood so that people can actually see what the stars are wearing, and how they look in real life'.[67] Stripped away from their characters, actresses would appear as what they really were, or what Hollywood consistently created through years of publicity, an annotation of American royalty. The public image of Hollywood figures was, of course, equally constructed. Nevertheless, the stars were at least performing stardom even in these seemingly ordinary settings.

Aspects of Head's career were also pitched to the journalists as a string of convoluted Hollywood anecdotes that included her eight years' experience as the official fashion consultant of the show.[68] The bait worked. Newspaper articles anticipated the fashion spectacle at the ceremony:

> 'Glamour cannot be oversold' is the estimation of this woman who holds stellar rights to fame as fashion creator to many of the movie capital's most-alluring stars. So strong is her conviction, that 'even the broadcaster of the commercials will be glamorized' by the clever hand of Head. This year's event will amount to an International Fashion show, with every model a star.[69]

The promotion built up expectations for what stars would wear, and NBC did not hesitate to sell the pre-show and the Oscarcast as the biggest fashion show free-for-all.

Newspaper articles promised the telecast would offer a chance to see a show where 'almost every designer in the world would be represented'.[70] This created a perception of an international community eager to partake. When contacting the press, Bazelon emphasised this international relevance:

> The Academy telecast has world-wide repercussions. Designers in Rome and Paris, as well as America, pull all possible strings to get their clothes on display. The designer, however, has to have a perfect sense of drama and exploitation, for in the final analysis, the gown must not overpower the actress because the actress must sell herself. It's a great international race.[71]

Loyal to her Hollywood-centred discourse, Head ensured that 'the parade of fashions [would] surpass any Paris opening', because it combined designers from Hollywood, New York and Europe with the glamorous high-priced models: the Hollywood stars.[72] 'It's the highest priced fashion show in the world – one that money couldn't buy', she said, implying the democratising qualities of television.[73]

The show was a great chance to communicate Head's expertise, putting her at the same level as other national and international fashion designers, something the national press had been doing for decades. As Head designed many of the stars' gowns, she would have a chance to discuss her creations for the night during the pre-show. Journalist Eleanor Roberts joked about the selection of gowns being the 'most closely-guarded secrets in America right now', listing these, in reference to the Cold War, above issues of atomic power or national defence.[74] Adding to the mystique, Roberts gave assurances that only Head knew these secrets. Designs were anticipated in the media, but one of them took centre stage in the show's promotion.

### Dress for success

Actress Janet Leigh was the centre of the promotional campaign, announced as the big star of the night. Information about her gown, designed by Head and commissioned by Leigh's husband, Tony Curtis, flooded the pages of newspapers. The dress was said to weigh 9.5 kg and was made of nude-coloured chiffon, with 186,000 imported Czechoslovakian silver-lined bugle beads, producing a solid diamond effect.[75] The actress accessorised the creation with flesh-coloured gloves, diamond earrings and a white mink stole.[76] The dress took six months to finish, and no one was willing to disclose its price.

According to Head, the price of an Oscars gown ranged from $4,000 to 'as little as the price of the fabric'.[77] Leigh said the dress 'might easily be traded for a Cadillac', while *Los Angeles Times* estimated its cost at $3,000.[78]

The gown itself became a pseudo-event, generating much media coverage for Leigh, Curtis, Head, *ONH* and the Oscarcast. Rogers & Cowan distributed press images of Leigh wearing Head's creation next to Head and her Oscar statuettes. Sketches of the dress also illustrated many articles. The reason behind selecting Leigh for the promotion of *ONH* is not documented. A pattern can also be derived from close observation of Oscars promotion over the years. Leigh was presenting the award for Best Original Screenplay together with Tony Curtis.

Presenters, the only stars confirmed for the show in advance, were recruited to promote the media event. Nominees, in contrast, had to maintain a low media profile and show no association with promotional activities in order to avoid heated accusations of campaigning. Leigh was the new 'blonde beauty' in Hitchcock's upcoming movie, *Psycho* (Shamley Productions, 1960), and both she and Head used William Morris as their talent agency. Rogers & Cowan, in charge of the promotion for the pre-show, also represented Leigh, making it plausible that the actress joined the campaign in order to create synergy.[79] The actress captured all the attention of photographers on the red carpet, despite not participating in the pre-show.[80]

Leigh and Curtis were enjoying wide audience recognition at the time, with promotional efforts to present them as a Hollywood royal couple. In November 1960, JWT evaluated the popularity and familiarity of 275 personalities among 2,045 respondents of mail surveys, using a method called the Q-score system.[81] The performers were divided into categories (singer, comedian, emcee and so on), and tested in familiarity (categorised as 'unknown', 'moderately known' and 'established') and popularity ('well-liked', 'average' and 'less-liked'). Familiarity measured the number of people who knew of the performer, while popularity measured to what extent the audience liked them. Janet Leigh scored 72 for familiarity, with a total TV-Q of 17, meaning that she was as well-known and popular as Audrey Hepburn.[82] These actresses were more recognisable than Lauren Bacall, Shirley MacLaine, Ann Baxter and Brigitte Bardot, but less so than Marilyn Monroe, Zsa Zsa Gabor, Debbie Reynolds, Joan Crawford and Ingrid Bergman. Regarding popularity, Leigh ranked much higher than Gabor, Bacall and Ava Gardner, but was less influential than Bergman, Jane Wyman, Elizabeth Taylor or Debbie Reynolds. Tony Curtis's total familiarity score was 82, ranking him 'average' in popularity, with a total TV-Q of 22. Other actors ranking 'average' in popularity and considered 'established' were Burt Lancaster, Fred Astaire and Rock Hudson. Cary Grant is an example of an established actor ranked above 'well-liked'. Despite her husband's popularity,

**Figure 5.3** Janet Leigh and Edith Head. Promotional picture distributed by Rogers & Cowan as publicity material for the TV show *Oscar Night in Hollywood* (NBC, 1960). Courtesy of the Wisconsin Center for Film and Theater Research.

Janet Leigh became the photo-op for the night owing to the wide promotional campaign lead for *ONH*.

## *Oscar Night in Hollywood* is brought to you by P&G

Edith Head was key for the show's exposure, but she was not an experienced TV host. Hosts were predominantly vaudevillians who could memorise long texts, improvise when unexpected situations emerged and entertain the audiences by ad lib and script. Tony Randall and Betsy Palmer were recruited for the job. Market research showed that Palmer was regarded as 'warm and personable and very lovely' among television stars.[83] She was ranked second to Lucille Ball in popularity, and thereby considered an 'established' female television personality.[84] Tony Randall was not as established among male comedians. His familiarity had the lowest score among the 'moderately known' category. According to the show's rundown, Randall and Palmer had to open the telecast, interview Head and stop at the tables to interview the stars. The show was framed by four short P&G Lilt commercials. The pre-recorded in-show product demonstration was divided into three sections integrated into the overall programme and consisting of interviews with the stars at the dinner party. The estimated cost of this informal buffet dinner was between $27,500 and $30,000.[85] The gathering was supposedly rehearsed for hours the day before. Everyone had to stick to the black-tie dress code, including the NBC crew behind their cameras.[86]

The pre-show was broadcast from the Hollywood Brown Derby, conveniently located a stone's throw away from the RKO Pantages Theatre. By the early 1960s, broadcasters did not see live programming as a priority. NBC tried a new technology that delayed transmission. The show would be recorded between 6.15 and 6.45 p.m., and broadcast between 7.00 and 7.30 p.m., giving the stars enough time to arrive at the RKO Pantages for the ceremony. Presumably, this also allowed for greater control of the flow of the show, for example, when combining product demonstration and results, or when segueing into the live Oscarcast. By pre-recording, artists could avoid 'flubbed lines or costuming accidents'.[87] This technological experimentation carried consequences, as the pre-recorded transmission was played later unedited, with all errors. Randall made four failed attempts at introducing and opening the show. He excused himself later, alleging that he was following instruction from the on-set producer and that he did not know they were on air. 'Whenever you do an adlib show, you're at the mercy of people giving signals. I figured they were starting and stopping the videotape. It was only afterward I found out we were on the air – live', he explained.[88] To make things worse, the sound did not work at first. When it finally came back, the first words to be heard came from an irritated Randall saying, 'Are we ready now?'[89]

The first segment of the show was the interview with Head. She was introduced as the fashion consultant for the Academy Awards ceremony and the woman who had won most Oscars. That night, Head had two nominations, one for *Career* (Hal Wallis Productions, 1959) and one for *The Five Pennies* (Dena Productions, 1959), but won neither. In the main interview with Palmer, she presented sketches of what stars would be wearing and discussed the upcoming trends in Paris and Rome. She was also expected to interview those present at the dinner party.

After the main interview, Palmer and Head introduced the first part of the product demonstration, a series of steps before revealing Head's creation for the model to complete the '1960 Academy Awards look'.

> PALMER: Tonight, to sum up everything Miss Head has talked about, we've asked her to show you a special gown she designed for this evening.
>
> HEAD: Let's step into the Record Room, Betsy. I have the sketch on an easel there. I call it the 1960 Academy Award Look. [The sketch is set up spotted by lights. Head describes the dress briefly as camera shows it in detail.]
>
> PALMER: Now, we're going to bring Edith Head's Academy Award Look to life on beautiful young star, Sharon Thomas.
>
> HEAD: You know Betsy, the most critical part of any look is this ... the close-up ... from neckline up. Too many women fail to realize what they do with their hair can 'make or break' a design.[90]

By deflecting attention away from her creation into styling as a critical factor of building the desired look, Head was functional to the product.

For the second pre-recorded segment, Palmer and the model, Sharon, discuss the difficulties of curling hair at home before the launch of P&G's Lilt perming lotion, while Sharon applies the product. The scene rundown describes Palmer standing in front of Sharon. The camera focus is on Palmer while she explains to the audience, 'We're on tape now so that later in the show, we can pick up Sharon and see how her hair turns out ... and how it goes with Head's beautiful Academy Awards look.'[91] The final section opens with Palmer holding up Head's sketch, revealing Sharon's complete look:

> Earlier tonight you saw Sharon Thomas wearing Head's ball gown symbolizing the Academy Awards look. She was right in the middle of a permanent to complete the look. Now here she is to show us how her hair turned out.[92]

As Sharon walks into frame, Palmer and Head discuss the results and recommend that viewers buy Lilt.

The Oscar pre-show was a complete disaster, and its critical reception devastating. Eugenia Sheppard was unimpressed by Head's fashion agenda for the 1960s ceremony. She described the dress Head had made for the P&G commercial as 'a homely ball gown and oversized stole', adding that the model looked slightly dazed by the fumes of the hair product.[93] Not only did she say that Elizabeth Taylor had been either over- or underdressed for the event, she also took aim directly at Head by calling the pre-show 'a real dog'. She further pontificated: 'Hollywood longs for fashion leadership but leadership is a lot more than this parade of girls who never looked lovelier', in a clear reference to a description given by Head during the promotional campaign.[94] Another piece of unnecessary drama was created around Head having forgotten to compliment and ask Palmer about her gown. The gossip columns used the incident to spread rumours of a confrontation between Head and the gown's designer, Ceil Chapman, thus creating a media rivalry.[95]

The critique was not limited to hostile fashion columnists. Bill Fiset described the show as

> so poorly prepared it was like a comedy of errors ... Edith Head is a dress designer and for weeks the industry has been sending out thousands of words from her lips about last night's clothes. But last night she heard her name and became rigid in fright and speechless for several full minutes ... a waiter blocked [Betsy Palmer] completely from the camera for two minutes at $1,000 a minute.[96]

The 'waiter' was Buster Keaton, trying to provide comic relief for the telecast in a comedy move that did not translate well on camera.[97] Keaton was also a special guest at the Oscars ceremony that night to receive an honorary award.[98]

Betsy Palmer was also targeted. Hal Humphrey described how she managed to tangle Head in the microphone cables, in what he described as 'a near lynching experience'.[99] Once Head untangled herself, none of the three knew what was coming next. In an acerbic tone, Humphrey commented with irony:

> Nearly everyone in town maintains he could put on a better TV show than that aromatic fish-fry which preceded the Oscar Awards Monday night ... I have no idea what NBC intends doing with the tape of this show, but if it were mine, I would light right out for New York and Madison Avenue. It's the funniest pilot for a situation comedy series that I've seen in a long time.[100]

For Arch McKay Jr, the show was uninspiring; 'a long commercial for Edith Head, some hair goop inspired in her, and a design class'.[101] Others tried to redeem the hosts by arguing that these two accomplished stars should not have been ridiculed for having been recruited to make small talk with the stars, concluding that 'The talk was so small it's not worth repeating'.[102]

Despite a media flogging, the Oscarcast ran steadily as number one with a total audience share of 53.6 per cent that night.[103] The mismatch between ratings and critiques may be indicative of a clash between the evaluations of emergent and dominant audiences. Many had already embarked on a cultural shift towards the emerging trends signalled by The New Hollywood. At the same time, a large section of the mid-American audience still praised the value of old Hollywood entertainment. With the changing winds of the swinging sixties, designer Orry-Kelly took a personal stand against Head's role, ridiculing the idea of dictating long formal dresses for the Oscars in favour of shorter dresses that showed women's legs.[104] Together with Hedda Hopper, he challenged the idea of having someone telling movie stars what they could or not wear after decades of being fashion trendsetters.

Head claimed that hundreds of women across the country wrote to her once the telecast was over, asking where they could get a gown worn by a certain actress, or asking if she could send them any 'left-over gowns'.[105] She did receive numerous letters from colleagues and sponsors congratulating her on having conducted herself gracefully. In an apologetic note, the sponsor showed its gratitude: 'Dear Miss Head: I know we have brought you a lot of problems, but Procter and Gamble loves you, from our standpoint you couldn't have been more wonderful'.[106] Regardless of its success or failure, ONH marked a turning point in the history of the Academy Awards. It reflected a strongly emerging cultural shift leading to the replacement of Head as the awards' consultant and marked the peak of her popularity and the beginning of the demise of her discourses and ideals. It was also the first and last transmission for this fashion pre-show that can be considered the precursor of today's red-carpet media parades.

## An international fashion show free-for-all

Turning fashion into a central promotional vehicle for the Oscars was not only the result of Head's promotional skills or her appointment as fashion consultant. The turmoil in which Hollywood was immersed, the emergence of television, the postwar reactivation of consumption and the PR actions that actively worked to disseminate the Oscarcast all helped to showcase fashion. By the 1950s, interest in fashion had escalated as a result of the professionalisation of fashion journalism, the formalisation of fashion education in the US, the reactivation of transcontinental commerce, the emergence of new European fashion capitals and the increasing promotion of American designers. These painted a promising picture for the circulation of fashion discourses in association with the Oscars. Fashion represented an attractive tool for developing epiphenomena that would benefit the Oscarcast. The repetitive presentation of the event as an international fashion show free-for-all lingered on in the mind of the social spectator already familiar with the idea of Hollywood stars and designers as fashion figures. These already established satellite discourses, in tandem with the widespread promotion of the media event as a fashion parade, consecrated the Oscars as the foremost display window of fashion in popular culture.

## Notes

1. For more about Italy's postwar fashion scene see Eugenia Paulicelli, 'Fashion: The Cultural Economy of *Made in Italy*', *Fashion Practice* 6, no. 2 (2015): 155–74; Chiara Faggella, 'Not So Simple: Reassessing 1951, G.B. Giorgini and the Launch of Italian Fashion' (PhD dissertation, Stockholm University, 2019).
2. Interdepartmental correspondence from Robert W. McFayden to Mr John K. Herbert, 9 February 1953, National Broadcasting Company Records, Office Files 1921–1976, WCFTR; NBC interdepartmental correspondence from Syd Eiges to all concerned, Oscar Awards Program, National Broadcasting Company Records, Office Files 1921–1976, WCFTR.
3. Memo from Frank Young to Mr Carl Stanton, Oscar Awards, 20 February 1953, National Broadcasting Company Records, Office Files 1921–1976, WCFTR.
4. NBC Interoffice Correspondence, from Norm Pader to Mr Syd Eiges, Oscar Awards Campaign, 27 February 1953, National Broadcasting Company Records, Office Files 1921–1976, WCFTR.
5. Ibid.
6. Report from R. H. Coffin to Mr C. M. Odorissi, Report on Advertising, Promotion, Publicity and Exploitation of the 25th Annual Awards of the Academy of Motion Picture Arts and Sciences, 19 March, Simulcast over NBC TV and AM Networks, 3 March 1953, National Broadcasting Company Records, Office Files 1921–1976, WCFTR.
7. Ibid.
8. 'Glittering Gowns Grab Gasps, Gushes as Gals Greet Oscar', *Daily Variety*, 20 March 1953, 12.
9. Ibid., 12.
10. Hedda Hopper, 'Looking at Hollywood: Ronda Fleming Steps Out of One Film into Another', *Chicago Daily Tribune*, 11 April 1953, 14.
11. 'Glittering Gowns Grab Gasps', 12.
12. 'Movie Queens Don Best Togs for Television', *The Hutchinson News Herald*, 18 March 1953, 13.
13. 'Glittering Gowns Grab Gasps', 12.
14. Helen Rose left MGM and opened her own fashion house towards the end of this period.

15. Marusia Radunska was based in California. Besides being a fashion designer, she is credited as working as a costume designer in television, and for starting a brief partnership with Travis Banton a few years before his death in 1958. See 'Designer Du Jour: Marusia', Past Perfect Vintage, 15 December 2013, http://pastperfectvintage.blogspot.se/2013/12/designer-du-jour-marusia.html/

16. Jay Jorgensen, *Edith Head: The Fifty-Year Career of Hollywood's Greatest Costume Designer* (Philadelphia, PA: Running Press, 2010), 184.

17. Lev, *The Fifties*, 32.

18. Academy Committees 1949–50, *Report of the President to the Members of the Academy of Motion Picture Arts and Sciences, 1949–50*, April 1950, 10.

19. 'The Academy and Santa Claus', *For Your Information* 4.1 (September 1950): 7, Academy History Archive, MHL.

20. Academy Committees 1949–50, *Annual Report 1949–50*, 6, Academy History Archive, MHL.

21. 'Industry Shorts to Be Given Wide School Distribution', *For Your Information* 3.7 (Winter 1949): 2, Academy History Archive, MHL.

22. 'Academy Forum for National Retail Dry Goods Association', *For Your Information* 4.1 (September 1950): 3, Academy History Archive, MHL.

23. Ibid.

24. 'Letter from Cecile Gray Balezon to Romola Metzner', 17 March 1960, Edith Head Papers, 1934–1965, WCFTR.

25. Letter from Jerry Ward to Gene Allen, 13 March 1958, f. 268 Academy of Motion Picture Arts and Sciences – Academy Awards (30th), Gene Allen Papers, MHL.

26. Edith Head discusses fashion and nominees for the 42nd Academy Awards, 1970, Pickford Center, AMPAS.

27. James Bacon, 'No Dior Look – Oscar Night Gowns Neat and Dignified', *Press Telegram*, 29 March 1955, 5.

28. '"Oscar"' Fashions Are a Secret, Too', *The Atlanta Constitution*, 4 April 1960, 30.

29. Letter from Cecile Gray Bazelon to Elenor Klein, 16 March 1960, Box 22, f. 6, Edith Head Papers, WCFTR.

30. Nancy Gallagher, 'Dressing for Oscars Takes a Good Head', *Ohio Press and News*, 2 April 1960, Box 22, f. 7, Edith Head Papers, WCFTR.

31. 'Hollywood Disregards Paris Trend', *Victoria Texas Advocate*, 18 April 1961, Box 23, f. 4, Edith Head Papers, WCFTR.

32. Spigel, *Make Room for TV*, 54.

33. 'US Code of Practices for Television Broadcasters', http://www.tvhistory.tv/SEAL-Good-Practice.htm/

34. Spigel, *Make Room for TV*, 54.

35. 'From the Mouth of the "Clotheshorse"', *Tucson Daily Citizen*, 19 March 1960, 15.

36. 'Fashions Compete with Talent at Academy Awards Tonight', *Asbury Park Press*, 17 April 1961, 28.

37. Bob Brock, 'Hollywood's "Second Secret" is Oscar Night Apparel', *Texas Times-Herald*, 3 April 1960, Box 22, f. 7, Edith Head Papers, WCFTR.

38. Dora May Priester, 'Edith Head Dresses Stars and Audience', *Santa Monica Outlook*, 13 April 1961, Box 23, f. 4, Edith Head Papers, WCFTR.

39. Gallagher, 'Dressing for Oscars Takes a Good Head'.

40. 'Bleacher News: Bigger Cheers', *Citizen-News*, 18 April 1961, 24.

41. Dave McIntyre, 'Front Row', *Evening Tribune Entertainment Editor*, 22 March 1960, Box 22, f. 7, Edith Head Papers, WCFTR.

42. The J. Walter Thompson agency claimed to pioneer these practices, sponsoring the first full-hour sponsored show, *Hour Glass* (WNBT, 1946). See JWT's Role in Television, Newsletter, 18 November 1946, JWT: TV. Radio Department 1930–1964, n.d., Box 14, The Colin Dawkins Papers, JWT, Duke Archives.

43. Erik Barnouw, *The Sponsor: Notes on a Modern Potentate* (Oxford: Oxford University Press, 1979), 33. See also Lawrence R. Samuel, *Brought to You By: Postwar Television Advertising and the American Dream* (Austin, TX: University of Texas Press, 2003).

44. Percentages of people recalling advertisements in each medium by 1953: television 43 per cent; radio 16 per cent; magazines 18 per cent; and newspapers 14 per cent. Source: Gallup-Robinson, from 'The Audience and the Commercial', *Television Magazine*, 21 November 1953, Box 14, The Colin Dawkins Papers, JWT, Duke Archives.

45. For more on *Cavalcade of Stars* during the DuMont period, see David Weinstein, *The Forgotten Network: DuMont and the Birth of American Television* (Philadelphia, PA: Temple University Press, 2006), 111–36. JWT, for example, developed *Startime*.

46. Baughman, *Same Time, Same Station*, 26.

47. Ibid., 202; 'The New Look at Lever', *Madison Avenue*, May 1958, 15.

48. 'The House that Lever Built', *Television Age*, 30 October 1961, 33, 44. P&G was expected to raise its TV budget for 1961 to 90 per cent, with an investment of $110 million.

49. 'Fortune 500 Data for Procter & Gamble', *Fortune* 1959, http://archive.fortune.com/magazines/fortune/fortune500_archive/snapshots/1959/1389.html/; 'Fortune 500 Data for Lever Brothers', *Fortune* 1959, http://archive.fortune.com/magazines/fortune/fortune500_archive/snapshots/1959/3254.html/

50. 'The House that Lever Built', 31. Sales and earnings for P&G 'rose to still new highs in fiscal 1960 and fiscal 1961'.

51. Untitled, *Television Age*, 31 October 1960.

52. Cost-per-thousand is a measure used in marketing and refers to the price of an advertisement per 1,000 impressions (i.e. per 1,000 people who will view it).

53. Calculations were based on audiometers installed in a sample of homes. See Barnouw, *The Sponsor*, 70.

54. 'J. W. T. Stages the World's First Television Advertising Program', *J. W. T. News*, September 1930. JWT: TV. Radio Department 1930–1964, Box 14, The Colin Dawkins Papers, JWT, Duke Archives.

55. An Analysis of Syndicated Film Vs. Spot Television Announcements, July 1958, 53, Nos 58–9, Box 23, Information Center Records, 1890, 1987, JWT, Duke Archives.

56. See Jane Farrell-Beck and Jean Parsons, *20th Century Dress in the United States* (New York, NY: Fairchild Publication, Inc., 2007), 157. Sumiko Higashi also refers to do-it-yourself discourses to achieve star looks in *Photoplay* during the 1950s, in Sumiko Higashi, *Stars, Fans, and Consumption in the 1950s: Reading Photoplay* (New York, NY: Palgrave Macmillan, 2014), 169–87.

57. Vintage Fanatic, 1960s Lilt Home Perm Commercial 1, *YouTube*, https://www.youtube.com/watch?v=c5-8Kpiq11k/

58. Vintage Fanatic, 1960s Lilt Home Perm Commercial 2, *YouTube*, https://www.youtube.com/watch?v=sMEEitvFIdw

59. Vintage Fanatic, 1960s Lilt Home Perm Commercial 3, *YouTube*, https://www.youtube.com/watch?v=2Qtn_u3s2WA

60. Vance Packard, *The Hidden Persuaders* (New York, NY: Ig Publishing, 2007 [1957]), 66–7.

61. The revised primer of testimonial advertising, Box 99, Advertising Vertical File, 1950–1994, JWT, Duke Archives.
62. To contextualise her popularity at the time it is worth noting that in the previous year, 1959, she was recognised by the *Los Angeles Times* as one of the top ten women of the year for outstanding achievement. See '10 Names 1959 Times Women of the Year for Outstanding Achievement and Service', *Los Angeles Times*, 20 December 1959, cA.
63. Letter from Cecile Gray to Miss Pat Mc Cornick, 16 March 1960, Box 22, f. 6, Edith Head Papers, WCFTR.
64. Kay Gardella, 'Edith Head's Spinning Over the Oscar Awards', *N.Y. Daily News*, 30 March 1960, 74.
65. Letter from Cecile Gray Balezon to Romola Metzner, 17 March 1960, Box 22, f. 6, Edith Head Papers, WCFTR.
66. Bob Williams, 'On the Air', *New York Post*, 29 March 1960, Box 22, f. 7, Edith Head Papers, WCFTR.
67. Romola Metzner, 'Heart of Edith Head Belongs to Hollywood', *N.Y. Journal-American*, undated, 1960, Box 22, f. 7, Edith Head Papers, WCFTR.
68. Letter from Cecile Gray Bazelon to Elenor Klein, 16 March 1960, Box 22, f. 6, Edith Head Papers, WCFTR.
69. Metzner, 'Heart of Edith Head Belongs to Hollywood'.
70. Brock, 'Hollywood's "Second Secret" is Oscar Night Apparel'.
71. Letter from Cecile Gray Bazelon to Bob Williams, 17 March 1960, Box 22, f. 6, Edith Head Papers, WCFTR.
72. '"Oscar" Festivities to Present Exciting Parade of Fashions', *Alhambra Post-Advocate*, 15 April 1961, Box 22, f. 7, Edith Head Papers, WCFTR.
73. 'Academy Awards Gowns: Fashion Free-For-All Will Highlight Show', *Los Angeles Times*, 17 April 1961, B1.
74. Roberts, 'Big Question for Oscar Party Tonight: Who Will Wear What?'.
75. Text from news release accompanying sketch for dress, Rogers & Cowan, Inc., Box 22, f. 6, Edith Head Papers, WCFTR. Leigh also wore the dress for a cameo role in Cantinflas's film *Pepe* (Columbia Pictures, 1960) and to the film's premiere.
76. Arlene Dahl, 'Academy Awards Show Gowns: Stars' Dresses Will Have Roman Look', *Chicago Daily Tribune*, 4 April 1960, B1.
77. Letter from Cecile Gray Balezon to Romola Metzner, 17 March 1960, Box 22, f. 6, Edith Head Papers, WCFTR.
78. Dahl, 'Academy Awards Show Gowns: Stars' Dresses Will Have Roman Look', B1; Eddy Jo Bernal, 'Million Dollars in Gowns Thrill Oscar Viewers', *Los Angeles Evening Herald Express*, 5 April 1960, Box 22, f. 7, Edith Head Papers, WCFTR. Adjusted for inflation, $3,000 is $26,719 in 2020.
79. See Diary entry 5. f. 99 Leigh Janet 1961, David I. Zeitlin papers, MHL.
80. 'Janet Leigh Arriving at the 32nd Academy Awards', newsreel footage, *Producers Library*, http://www.producerslibrary.com/displayProduct1.do?product_id=6301&product_name=CRV-0003_012/
81. The Q-score was developed for measuring 'how much a star is liked or disliked by the public and how familiar the public is with the star'. The star was graded by the public on a scale of six indicators: 1 = One of my favourites, 2 = Very good, 3 = Good, 4 = Fair, 5 = Poor, 6 = Someone you have never seen or heard of. The method was frequently used for selecting endorsers. See Irving Rein et al., *High Visibility: Transforming Your Personal and Professional Brand* (New York, NY: McGraw-Hill, 2006), 105.

82. Audrey Hepburn ranked 74 in familiarity and had a total TV-Q of 17. See 'Performer Popularity Analysis, May 1961', Box 10, Centre for Sales, Advertising, and Marketing History, The Papers of Dan Seymour, JWT, Duke Archives.

83. The Road to Beauty from a woman's point of view for Lever Brothers Company Lux soap, August 1958, Account Files, JWT, Duke Archives.

84. Lucille Ball scored 97 points in familiarity and had a total TV-Q score of 38, while Palmer scored 76 points in familiarity with a total TV-Q score of 33. Shari Lewis, whose total TV-Q score was 34, did not benefit from the established familiarity Palmer enjoyed. She accumulated only 50 points, placing her in the 'moderately known' category. See Performer Popularity Analysis, Box 9, Dan Seymour Papers, JWT, Duke Archives.

85. 'Oscar Night Show on TV from Derby', *Hollywood Daily Reporter*, 22 March 1960, Box 22, f. 7, Edith Head Papers, WCFTR.

86. Larry Tubelle, 'Stars Work Gratis on P&G-Sponsored Pre-Derby Derby', *Daily Variety*, 5 April 1960, 3.

87. Baughman, *Same Time, Same Station*, 300.

88. Sturgis Hedrik, 'That Awards Show', *Daily News*, 9 April 1960, Box 22, f. 7, Edith Head Papers, WCFTR.

89. Hal Humphrey, 'They Did it Again!', *L.A. Mirror News*, 6 April 1960, Box 22, f. 7, Edith Head Papers, WCFTR.

90. Grey Advertising Agency, INC. Script for Procter & Gamble Lilt, 3/21/60, Box 14, f. 12, Barbara A. Fishel Papers, 1951–1965, WCFTR.

91. Ibid.

92. Ibid.

93. Eugenia Sheppard, 'They Never Looked Lovelier', *Journal-Herald Dayton*, 14 April 1960, 33.

94. Ibid.

95. 'So now don't invite Edith and Ceil to the same fashion show'. Atra Baer, 'Stars Balking Over "Pitching" Commercials', unnamed publication, 14 April 1960, Box 22, f. 7, Edith Head Papers, WCFTR.

96. Bill Fiset, 'These TV People', *The Oakland Tribune*, 5 April 1960, E21.

97. Tubelle, 'Stars Work Gratis on P&G-Sponsored Pre-Derby Derby', 3.

98. Ceremonies database, Oscars.org, https://www.oscars.org/oscars/ceremonies/2020

99. Hedrik, 'That Awards Show'.

100. Humphrey, 'They Did it Again!'.

101. Arch McKay Jr, 'Oscar Night Improved . . . Still Needs Improvising', *Alabama Journal*, 5 April 1960, 4-B.

102. Marie Torre, '"Oscar" Telecast Review', *N.Y. Herald Tribune*, 6 April 1960, Box 22, f. 7, Edith Head Papers, WCFTR.

103. 'Nielsen, Top Ten Programs', *Broadcasting Magazine*, 16 May 1960, 49; Top Ten Television Shows 1950–1964, A.C. Nielsen Company Ratings, Television Department, Box 8, Sidney Ralph Bernstein-Company History Files, JWT, Duke Archives.

104. Hedda Hopper, 'Orry-Kelly Mixes Fashions, Humour', *Los Angeles Times*, 29 March 1960, 8.

105. Hal Humphrey, 'Oscar Stars Will Be Pretty for "Oscar" Presentations', *The Daily Sentinel*, 4 April 1960, 12.

106. Letter from P&G president to Edith Head, Box 22, f. 6, Edith Head Papers, WCFTR.

# 6

# Style arbiters and the genesis of best- and worst-dressed lists

Minutes after celebrities hit the red carpet, online editors and fans flood cyberspace with their selections for the best- and worst-dressed lists. In the main, these lists historically served as promotional vessels and pseudo-events, bringing designers, institutions, the personalities listed and even their creators under the spotlight. They continue to function as such in the context of the red-carpet. Achieving fashion success or failure has equally captured media attention and immortalised celebrities in the context of the Academy Awards. Landing on the worst-dressed list can mean publicity for lesser-known celebrities. Being featured on the best-dressed list can turn an actress into a style icon, portrayed on the cover of fashion magazines as a newly found fashion muse, increasing her cachet and her chances to seal an endorsement contract. For a designer, this translates into positive media exposure and brand equity. To understand the phenomenon of best- and worst-dressed lists, it is necessary to trace the origins of *Vanity Fair*'s emblematic best-dressed list and the success of harsh criticism.

Eleanor Lambert was a pivotal figure in the development of the US fashion industry and the structuring of the entrance of European fashion houses into the American market. Her role is both crucial and controversial. Lambert gained prestige through her international clients despite her agenda for developing an American fashion scene. She built a stage for international designers to land in the local market. Producing international fashion shows for the American press, she managed to present her local clients alongside the most prestigious European names. A counter figure to Lambert's power was a man known simply as Mr Blackwell, supposedly the creator of the worst-dressed lists. Blackwell was a provocative performer who openly criticised the French fashion scene in ways Lambert never could, despite her efforts to promote the American fashion enterprise. Lambert figuratively bridged the European and American fashion markets. Mr Blackwell, on the other hand, unapologetically broke the rigid conventions imposed by the French fashion community through his celebrity persona, leading fashion into entertainment.

Figures like Lambert and Blackwell contributed to the emergence of red-carpet reporters such as Joan Rivers. These players set a precedent for the propagation of best- and worst-dressed lists that populate the internet, but also helped fuel discussions about fashion and take them outside elite circles and into popular culture as marketing tools. The juxtaposition of these figures reflects an underlying tension in discourses of prestige that associated couture with Paris, as a rival scene to the American ready-to-wear market. The outcome of the cultural and economic negotiation of such rivalry is essential for an understanding of the contemporary luxury market managed by multinational conglomerates on the red-carpet today. This chapter discusses the role of style arbiters as gatekeepers and cultural intermediaries. It provides a brief account of the genesis of these lists in the US context, unravelling a reconfiguration of the international fashion system that led to the combination of fashion and spectacle.

## The meaning and power of expertise

Before delving into an analysis of style arbiters, we must first address the notion of fashion experts. In 1999, Peter Walsh coined the notion of the 'expert paradigm', inspired by discussions regarding the democratisation of opinion and the function of the 'expert' following the propagation of the internet. Walsh describes this paradigm as a dialectical interaction, 'a social construct, a dialogue between the experts and the rest of society' that rejects self-proclamation as the sole criterion.[1]

Expertise crystallises once a society acknowledges the expert's position and responds in accordance. Followers, in the form of readers or viewers, are essential for the validation of expert knowledge. These audiences internalise, credit and reproduce the message as followers in a religious manner, contributing through referencing to the growth of the expert's status.

Fashion columns have been informative and educational, with fashion experts playing a crucial role in the cultural construction of femininity. Grant McCracken labels intermediaries, in the form of publicists, journalists and advertisers, as 'agents of meaning transfer'.[2] Popular magazines have contributed to the emergence of experts and the reliance of working- and middle-class women on them. For those living outside capital cities, glamour could only be experienced at the theatre or through media.[3] Through experts, the media played its part in the construction, representation, circulation and consumption of Hollywood glamour.

In the context of the US, fashion expertise developed alongside the involvement of Hollywood in fashion journalism. Pioneering figures such as Peggy Hamilton became fashion columnists and used this platform to promote Hollywood activities while propelling the notion of a thriving local fashion industry.[4] Fashion experts' connection with Hollywood set the basis for intertwining fashion and popular culture, articulating fashion discourses that catered to mass audiences. The act of bringing experts to confirm media statements has been a fundamental part of what Noam Chomsky and Edward Herman call the 'propaganda model'.[5] While the countless selections made by anonymous fans today may be acts of preference, established fashion columns, as well as official lists, have mostly functioned as promotional vehicles to mobilise the fashion industry in various ways, introducing new designers or launching personalities into celebrity.

## Style arbiters

The expression 'style arbiter' is even more fitting for these lists. The denomination of style arbiters encompasses a specific type of cultural intermediary that exerts the right to say who is 'in' or 'out'. The word arbiter also denotes that the decision is arbitrary but binding, 'based on a random choice of personal whim rather than any reason or system'.[6] Their judgement is not measured through knowledge and established rules, but through the acceptance they enjoy within a community that follows their rulings and pontifications.

Arbiters managed to break into these roles by positioning themselves as gatekeepers. Some even capitalised on reverting the interplay of inclusion/exclusion by siding with the masses and rejecting the elites. By being outsiders to the elite groups, they found an alternative way into power, establishing their authority while eliciting resistance from more established circles of fashion expertise. The function of style arbiters relates to the gatekeeping activities of social arbiters, such as Ward McAllister, who determined who was worthy of being invited to society's exclusive parties. A figure linking these two roles was party-giver Elsa Maxwell, who suggested that meeting her was the parameter to establish whether someone had made it into society.[7] Maxwell wrote a gossip column for Press Alliance, Inc. from 1942 in which she presented her best-dressed list.[8]

The 1950s were vital for the international fashion scene. Kate Nelson Best regards this decade as the golden age in which 'fashion journalism became perceived as a serious profession'.[9] She attributes this partially to the work of the Fashion Group, the emergence of new organisations with similar goals and the incorporation of fashion into higher education with the creation of the

Fashion Institute of Technology in 1944 and the BSc in Fashion at Parson's School of Design in 1952. The proliferation of fashion experts' columns in newspapers increased fashion coverage. *Los Angeles Times'* Faye Hammond, *New York Herald Tribune's* Eugenia Sheppard, *The New York Times'* Nan Robertson and Marylin Bender, *Chicago Tribune's* Arlene Dahl and *Boston Globe's* Elizabeth Sullivan became celebrity columnists, providing outlets for detailed descriptions of fashions at the Oscars featuring designer names. The emergence of celebrity culture and the powerful reach of media culture helped the fashion industry break into the mass market. American gatekeepers, in the form of style arbiters, played a significant role in this, partially due to the American fashion industry's development and promotion.

## Simply the best

The history of best-dressed lists can be traced back to seventeenth-century French court circles.[10] In the US, the importance for society women to be regarded among the best-dressed can be found in *Godey's Ladies Book* in 1840, where being fashionable appeared along with considerations about beauty and femininity as desired features for women.[11] Best-dressed lists functioned as templates for women to replicate these attributes, which were reinforced in early society columns, and later continued in gossip and beauty columns. Best-dressed lists also functioned as promotional platforms. New York department store Hamilton Garment Co. featured best-dressed women from the worlds of society and entertainment in their mail-order catalogue advertisements during the 1920s to attract consumers. These women were presented as being part of the selection process of merchandise for sale, appealing to the emulation of good taste. In Paris, the French fashion community organised the Concours d'Élegance, a parade in which the French couture houses' female clientele supposedly competed to be named the best-dressed.[12] The event was sponsored by the Chambre Syndicale de la Couture.[13]

Random 'best-dressed' lists appeared sporadically, while other lists appeared more regularly and thus gained authority and recognition. American publisher John Fairchild claimed that one of his publications, *W*, invented the 'in-out lists'.[14] These lists included brands, locations, designers, celebrities and all sorts of commodities that could be dictated as fashionable or not at any given point. They generated enormous controversy and the magazine even lost several advertisers who had found their products listed in the 'out' category. Besides Fairchild's narcissistic rant, a wide range of organisations have released a number of lists for various purposes. The Black-Tie Bureau, an organisation of formalwear manufacturers and marketers based in Chicago, released its own lists. Even the Costume

Designers Guild had a list, giving awards to the best-dressed American and foreign entertainers. However, it was Eleanor Lambert's best-dressed list that set the pace in legitimacy.

## The Fashion Academy

The New York Fashion Academy, presided over by Emil A. Hartman, had awarded medals to female fashion leaders every spring since the 1930s, in the hope of making 'American women more clothes conscious'.[15] Since the 1910s, Hartman had advertised lectures for those willing to enter the growing profession of costume design through his art school, the Fashion Academy. In a conference held at the Rockefeller Center in 1936, he pleaded for '[t]he cultivation of an educational point of view, rather than a commercial attitude towards fashions'.[16] Aside from its best-dressed list, the institution released lists of outstanding designers in the fashion world, which seem to work mostly as publicity for American designers.[17] Both lists naturally brought attention and prestige to Hartman's main profitable enterprise: the design school.

The Fashion Academy's list was supposedly compiled from the results of a poll among America's leading fashion designers, under the criteria of 'personality, charm, and ability to wear clothes'.[18] Hartman's list captured the eclecticism of café society, gathering women into categories ranging from the arts and journalism to society and nightlife, with one even labelled 'adventure'.[19] Hartman notified the winners by correspondence.[20] News agency AP was in charge of the list's distribution, a role it would also take with other listings that emerged later. As in most other American fashion-related enterprises, Eleanor Roosevelt featured frequently.

The list had several detractors. New York columnist Alice Hughes questioned the inexplicable cultural impact of such arbitrary information: 'These things mean absolutely nothing and yet they do have a certain interest'.[21] Photographer Arthur O'Neill challenged who should, or should not, be a part of it, arguing that professional models were the best candidates; after all, they were paid to look good. 'Society women cannot hold a candle to professional models when it comes to dress', expressed his partner, John Robert Powers, to the press.[22] Powers was the head of a clearing house for model services, which reveals a personal interest in promoting the profession. Criticism against the predominance of Western women appeared in 1936. American artist Thomas Handforth singled out Chinese women's superiority, pinpointing how unrepresented the Far East was on the list.[23] What made Chinese women special in his eyes was not that they followed the extreme styles or latest modes, but instead their elevating traditional dress into an art form. This stands as an early critique of the already noticeable imposition of Western beauty ideals circulating through mass media. It also discloses the intricate nature of these lists and their connection to business instead of aesthetics. Despite all criticism, the list persisted and overlapped with other similar lists that gained prominence. While this was by no means the only list, it was the one with the most widespread media circulation in the US until the arrival of Eleanor Lambert's.

## The caretaker of the French list turns New York's fashion empress

*Vanity Fair*'s best-dressed list holds a seemingly official status within the vortextuality of Oscars fashion. The origins of this list are linked to the annual International Best-Dressed List orchestrated by Eleanor Lambert. The original list started in Paris in 1922 – or 1924 according to Lambert – when journalists asked French designers for a list of their most elegant clients. It was controlled by Main Rousseau Bocher to – supposedly – strategically favour his clients.[24] The list combined American and French personalities, and was distributed by wire services around the globe under the anonymous tag of 'the French Couture Community'. Lambert claimed the list was created as 'a record of taste and taste-making of the time, whether those tastemakers were rich or poor', and went on to explain how personalities become a symbol of their times.[25]

The trade restrictions between Europe and the US, and the German occupation of Paris, impacted on the French fashion industry, forcing many designers into exile as some ateliers closed indefinitely.[26] Among the migratory patterns that took place as a consequence of World War II, publicist Eleanor Lambert became the guardian of the International Best-Dressed List. Looking back at the events, Lambert described how 'the 1940 best-dressed list recorded the sudden shift of mood from the hectic, hedonist 1930s to the grim reality of war against a power-mad dictator'.[27]

Lambert is a central figure in the history of fashion, both in the US and Europe, particularly during the second half of the twentieth century. She started as a novice in the PR business, with a few artists' accounts, while working as a press director at the Whitney Museum of American Arts in the 1930s. Her marriage to Seymour Berkson, chief of the International News Service and publisher of the *New York Journal American*, in 1936 may have contributed to the escalation of her power. In May that year, she joined the Fashion Group, as a representative for Helen Wills's company.[28] She joined the New York Dress Institute (NYDI) in 1940, the year it was created, amid the campaigns to turn New York into the style centre of the world. The NYDI gathered labour unions and clothes manufacturers seeking propaganda for an industry in crisis. They counted on the support of advertising agency JWT to target female consumers but soon decided that subtle PR actions would benefit them more than advertising.[29] As a novice PR professional in the field of fashion, representing an institution like the NYDI, despite it being newly formed, captured the journalists' attention. Lambert delivered her first version of the list as a press release for the NYDI on 27 December 1940.[30] Publishing the list during World War II became a PR stunt for keeping the fashion scene alive during wartime, with its shortage of supplies. The list continued to appear on behalf of the NYDI, with mentions of Lambert as press agent or commentary on her behalf, for at least two decades.

Lambert was not an established name by the time she picked up the list's publication, but eventually established herself in a privileged position through an ethically questionable triple gatekeeping function as an event organiser, publicist and journalist with a syndicated column. Her clients thus garnered guaranteed coverage through her 'vertically integrated' empire. Lambert's mythologised persona has fuelled her influence within the industry, and is often credited for initiating what was already ongoing at the time. By the time the European fashion industry had reactivated trade with the US, during the postwar era, Lambert had built a network and a name as a PR agent that positioned her as a gatekeeper to the American media and market.

The process for compiling the list would involve three stages. The first was a ballot conducted among fashion designers, fashion editors, executives and restaurant owners. According to one version, Lambert would organise a cocktail party for around fifty guests and suggest 100 names from which to choose. Another version, however, refers to a closed committee of twenty experts that later discussed the results during an annual luncheon at Lambert's apartment. 'The meeting is wildly vocal and sometimes chaotic, but in the end it makes sense', explained Lambert in one of her columns.[31] During the 1960s, fashion journalists Eugenia Sheppard, Diana Vreeland, Margaret Case, Nancy White and Sally Kirkland were committee members.[32]

Fashion PR man Percy Savage was also part of the committee. In his recollection, the list was a vessel for promoting designer names by showcasing prominent clients.[33] He was asked to contribute the names of people whom he wanted to promote.[34] Looking for natural elegance, preferably from among French couture clientele, he frequently suggested women who were unknown to the general public such as Italian Princess Paola, later to become queen of Belgium, or Gloria Guinness. Savage himself made it on the list, as did several fashion journalists and editors.[35]

Stories surrounding the mythologised figure of Eleanor Lambert can be compared to the contemporary representation of Anna Wintour's power and influence in the fashion industry. According to *The Washington Post*

> [w]hen one of her clients asked Eleanor Lambert what she really had to offer his company, she didn't hesitate, saying 'I own every fashion editor in America'. She then went on to except *WWD* from her blanket statement, but added that as far as the rest of this country's fashion editors were concerned, 'I can deliver them'.[36]

These power plays unravel the elitism required by the fashion industry to maintain its mystique. Lambert's fight against fashion editors who favoured Parisian above American designers replicated the same snobbery others questioned in her list.

Lambert had her fair share of detractors despite her status within the fashion industry. *Women's Wear Daily*'s editor-in-chief John Fairchild represented a strong contender. Fairchild would not only ban designers she represented from appearing in his publication, but he would also refuse to participate in the list's committee or allow his journalists to serve on it.[37] 'We thought her Best-Dressed list was a joke, and we had an animus for PR people generally', explained James Brady, the magazine's publisher between 1965 and 1971.[38] The resistance to Lambert's list extended to *Harper's Bazaar*'s Carmel Snow, whose preference for French fashion dovetailed with Fairchild's.

Lambert was also criticised for praising wealth as the conduit for elegance and good taste. Gossip columnist Hedda Hopper was a fierce detractor of Lambert's position. She slammed the list for containing 'the names of wives of rich men mostly'.[39] Arguably, the list was indeed elitist and ignored Hollywood. By listing society women, royalty and nobility, Lambert reinforced the idea of entitlement, wealth and style. In this, she stratified society by excluding the majority of women. These women did not represent a potential target market of the high-priced goods portrayed in the list at the time. Building the mythology behind the list's weight, an article in *Vanity Fair* suggested that Eleanor Roosevelt had complained about not being included, and that 'MGM tried to influence Lambert by offering motion-picture work for her clients in exchange for a citation of one of its stars'.[40]

According to Lambert, being visible was as crucial as wearing the right clothes for being influential and making it onto the list. Interestingly, many of the best-dressed women had also voiced misgivings for a variety of reasons. It was reported that husbands disliked their wives' exposure for portraying an ostentatious expenditure on clothes that could set their businesses under Washington's radar.[41] The Duchess of Windsor, who frequently found her way onto the list, was quoted as saying, 'How could such a list be anything but phony when most of the judges seldom see me or the other people they are voting for?'[42]

Because of her profession, Eleanor Lambert did not need to rely on news agencies to distribute the list, even though AP took over the task after some years. Her own company's listing comprised international, national and local fashion journalists from radio, television and the printed press to whom she periodically sent material such as press releases, event invitations etc. relating to her clients.[43] Lambert also wrote a weekly syndicated column entitled 'She', and organised a biannual fashion press week in New York.[44] The column, handled by Field Enterprises Inc., targeted audiences in small towns, combining advice and how-to information.

In the late 1970s, Lambert became a square peg among the reigning counter-cultural movements. *Boston Globe*'s fashion editor, Marian Christy, was one of the experts asked to participate in the ballots who refused to vote. 'The turnoff is relatively simple. I don't have the foggiest notion about most of the names on the ballot', she explained.[45] On more than one occasion, she utilised her column to criticise both Lambert and her list, favouring instead new lists such as the one produced by California fashion designer Mr Blackwell. In contrast to Lambert's list, Mr Blackwell's was considered controversial and amusing, while not relying on any ballots or committees.

The general criticism made by the press that the list was irrelevant, elitist and favoured certain individuals left Lambert in limbo between the fashion system and the mass audience. Accusations of elitism persisted well into the 1980s. Lambert tried to dispel prejudice against society in her column instead of explaining the reasons why these women had been selected.[46] Rather than providing reasonable arguments for her decisions, she ended up defending a social elite her mother had taught her to admire and emulate. Lambert tried several ways to become more popular and to stay relevant. She launched an 'American Cities' Best-Dressed List' sponsored by Cadillac. In the 1970s and 1980s, she began including TV celebrities and rock stars on her list.[47]

In 1993, the committee decided to publish five separate lists to express the opposing points of view in the fashion industry given by that year's 'clash between classic fashion evolution and jump-start experiments like "grunge"'.[48] A similar action had been taken in 1967 when the clash between hippy culture and traditional fashion led the committee to produce two different lists. Percy Savage marked the selection of Tina Turner in 1996 as a breaking point of direction in order to remain current. Lambert's conservative visions of femininity were also under fire among her readers, demonstrating her residual thinking and her lack of ability to adapt to the current era. She was still published through Editor's Press Services in a few newspapers in the US and abroad in 1992. After receiving letters from a few newspapers cancelling their subscription to her column in 1998, Lambert personally contacted editors of the remaining ones to announce her retirement as a columnist.

Lambert was an energetic entrepreneur whose goals were a good match for the contemporary economic, political and cultural state of affairs. Over the years, the list produced its fair share of epiphenomena, including two coffee table books and the exhibition entitled 'The Best of the Best-Dressed List 1934–1984' at the Museum of the City of New York in 1987.[49] The exhibition was financed with a grant from Gucci America, Inc. Rather than a guardian, as she liked to describe herself with regard to her involvement in producing the list, Lambert was actually an appropriator. Once World War II ended, she never handed back the reins to the Parisian fashion community. Nor did she do so when she decided to retire. She claimed that the French never took the list back after the war, even though she was expecting them to do so.[50] Before she died, Lambert decided to leave the legacy of compiling the International Best-Dressed List to *Vanity Fair*, which has continued its publication since 2004.

## Who cares about the best dressed?

Along with the proliferation of best-dressed lists, many produced worst-dressed ones. In a humorous turn, character actor Allen Jenkins wrote a worst-dressed list to include himself in it, as early as 1942.[51] A Hollywood designer called Clinton Stoner suggested 'a new way to analyze your friends by looking at their clothes', picking Hollywood's best- and worst-dressed in 1952. Orson Welles topped Stoner's worst-dressed list. Cary Grant, who was conveniently one of his clients, made it to the top of the best-dressed selection.[52] President Harry S. Truman's tailor, Irving Heller, submitted lists of best- and worst-dressed male celebrities.[53]

Those who created best-dressed lists strove for authority and prestige. Unlike them, their worst-dressed counterparts unapologetically blended provocation and entertainment, building their branding power around this. The popularity of worst-dressed lists seems to be a phenomenon linked with celebrity culture and gossip. Mr Blackwell released the most popular worst-dressed list, often erroneously referred to as the first one. While countless listings of negative fashion choices may have appeared in the media, the creator of one in particular may have inspired Mr Blackwell's outrageous public persona.

## The bad boy of fashion arbitrage

Raymond Driscoll started his career designing for the House of Worth in London during the mid-1930s. He returned to the US in the mid-1940s and opened a jewellery store in New York. The business did not prosper, so instead he became a waiter at the Waldorf Astoria. Driscoll eventually moved to Los Angeles and lectured on fashion and jewellery at the Chouinard Art Institute while creating extravagant garments for a private clientele. Once settled in California, he became the fashion editor of *The Beverly Hills Bulletin*. Driscoll bragged about designing for the Duchess of Kent and Magda Lupescu during the interwar years in Europe, and for actresses such as Carmen Miranda after disembarking in Hollywood.[54] His transition into entertainment came when he became a costume designer, working primarily for the Mexican film industry but also freelancing for Hollywood. As a fashion designer, Driscoll continued working for private clients and even designed small, popular-priced collections in association with other brands, such as Norma Lane Sportswear and Lichtenstein robes. These co-brandings suggest that his name carried some degree of popularity.

Self-labelled as 'the bad boy designer of the international jet set', Driscoll released his annual worst-dressed list in December for eleven years, roughly between the 1940s and the 1950s. Among the most controversial listings were Judy Garland and French couturier Christian Dior. Garland, who topped the 1946 list, sued Driscoll for 'defamation of character' when he described her style as that of 'a tired club woman'.[55] Dior was featured in the 1954 worst-dressed list. Driscoll proclaimed that a designer 'should know how to dress well himself', alleging that Dior's clothes gave him a 'look of dated decadence in mothballs'.[56] In an interview with *Enquirer*, he claimed that compiling his list was a labour of love.[57] The list was not published by one specific media outlet or carried by a wire agency but still he successfully managed to reach newspaper columnists who replicated it.[58] Due to his continuous performance as his own press agent, Louella Parsons labelled him 'the designer who always has something to report'.[59]

Driscoll also compiled a best-dressed list with the names of 'those chosen few who have pierced the iron curtain of mediocrity by dressing with glamour, drama, excitement and originality'.[60] His whimsical choices included picking himself for the best-dressed list in 1954, allegedly tired of waiting for Christian Dior to do so. Driscoll flirted with politicians and fashion elites by including them in his best-dressed list and tried to get close to the rich and famous through correspondence, in explicit acts of demagogy.[61] This shows his understanding of the pastiche nature of the contemporary jet set. While no audiovisual records of Driscoll have been found so far, remaining photographs reveal a vaudevillian comedic personality. References in the printed press support this contention.

Even though his career in Mexico seemed to be paying off, Driscoll wished to return to Hollywood. He vanished soon after the mid-1950s and died in 2004. The success of worst-dressed lists remained alive in those who followed him.

## Mr Blackwell's infamous list and the art of self-branding

Californian fashion designer Mr Blackwell became a celebrity after releasing the most popular worst-dressed list to date. Like his predecessor Ray Driscoll, he also released a best-dressed list, but the latter vanished in the shadow of the more controversial one. Blackwell reflected on how he had tried to be nice during the first two years of his career, but that it was not until he became more mean-spirited that real attention arrived.[62] From his perspective, the success of the worst-dressed list came about because nobody wanted to hear anything but the negative. His lists premiered in *The American Weekly* on 30 October 1960, and were soon taken over by AP and distributed around the world. From this point, the list took on a life of its own and the creator's renown was sealed. Once they achieved popularity, the lists were announced yearly with a champagne brunch and a fashion show framing a press conference at Mr Blackwell's mansion.

**Figure 6.1** Mr Blackwell holding a picture of Bette Midler's arrival at the 54th Academy Awards ceremony while announcing his annual worst-dressed list for 1982. Her Oscar look got her fourth place in the ranking. AP Photo/Lennox McLendon.

Blackwell's real achievement was mastering the art of celebrity through self-branding. He sought to enter the entertainment world at several stages in his life, undergoing a series of reinventions along with his career, shifting identities from Richard Sylvian Seltzer, Dick Seltzer, Dick Ellis and Richard Blackwell to Mr Blackwell. Several plastic surgeries accompanied these transformations. His life oscillated between the East Coast and West Coast during the many times he tried to become famous. Blackwell's career path comprised, first, a brief performance as a child actor off-Broadway and on film; radio theatre; Broadway back-up dancer; male escort; Las Vegas showgirls' manager; hat seller; and, finally, fashion designer.[63] Three years into his career in the fashion industry, selling both exclusive pieces to private clients and mass-produced garments at department stores, Mr Blackwell became president of the Guild of American Creative Fashion Designers.

Whether or not he was aware of Driscoll's approach to his worst-dressed list, Mr Blackwell's fashion criticism followed similar strategies. He consciously targeted celebrities, expecting replies that would generate more media coverage. Those who were granted spots on other best-dressed lists were also targeted. He followed a pattern of targeting divas, implying that if a name was on either list, that meant the celebrity was 'hot'.[64] Not afraid of being the centre of criticism, Blackwell explained his strategy by saying that celebrities could appear on television saying 'This guy's nuts', which would generate more publicity for him.[65] What made the list attractive was not only the lampooning of successful women's putative fashion failures but also the edgy comments that accompanied their names, comments that often lacked any direct reference to fashion. Celebrities took offence, but their press agents knew that getting clients on the list would get them international publicity overnight.[66] The worst-dressed list was, in Blackwell's perception, 'the most brilliant idea any press agent could have dreamed of'.[67]

Despite attempts to get worst-dressed lists under the spotlight, none achieved recognition on a par with Mr Blackwell's. A feature that set him apart from other arbiters was his commitment to his constructed persona, embracing this role instead of pushing to enter exclusive circles. Mr Blackwell made it his business to be blunt and unpleasant in a business that seemed to be all about keeping up the illusion of politeness. Caustic gossip columnists such as Hedda Hopper and Louella Parsons referred to celebrities as their friends, creating the myth of a Hollywood community in which they were not outsiders. Even when they were being critical, the veneer of politeness was still intact. Mr Blackwell embraced spite and ire, convinced it would develop his brand, which in turn translated into money.

Mr Blackwell stands as a symbol of an emerging celebrity culture, fuelled by the contemporary success of a more scandalous approach to gossip journalism that revamped the idea of 'there's no such thing as bad publicity'.[68] He described his list as 'purely camp, not cruel. It's just a reaction to Eleanor Lambert's Best-Dressed list that's filled with names nobody knows'.[69] His enemies and critics were unable to understand his acerbic comments as mere entertainment. Media reports described an encounter between Mr Blackwell and Lambert at an event in 1995. Mr Blackwell was said to have asked her if she would work as his PR agent. Her dry answer was, allegedly, 'I don't see any need to have me. If there's anything good to say about you, you've said it yourself'.[70]

Lambert and Blackwell unexpectedly shared points of convergence in their intention to defend the American fashion enterprise. While she followed rules of etiquette, he played with controversy beyond merely listing his worst-dressed choices. Distancing himself from French fashion while zooming in on his domestic target market was a key element of his press campaigns.[71] Part of this involved setting American fashion against French artistry. With provocative headlines against Parisian creations such as 'Who Needs Paris?', 'Dress Designer Declares War on French Couturiers' or 'Don Quixote of Fashion World Fighting Paris', Mr Blackwell charged against the fashion elites through press cables reproduced in newspapers around the world. About Parisian designers, he said, 'Those clowns would move women's bosoms to their backs if they thought it would make the papers'.[72] The anti-Paris diatribes should not be credited to branding genius only. It was part of the same political trend that had begun much earlier, promoting local industries as an act of patriotism. Blackwell capitalised on the residuals of such campaigns to approach a different market.

His attacks on Paris created circles of enemies. Robert L. Green, fashion director of *Playboy*, described him as 'a salesman, a self-proclaimed underprivileged who, unfortunately, ha[d] become overpublicized'.[73] *Vogue*, *Harper's Bazaar*, *Glamour*, *Seventeen* and *Women's Wear Daily* even refused to attend the mansion gatherings. The celebrity designer did not muffle his opinion of them as 'snob fashion editors who dictate one disaster after another'.[74] Local fashion hot spots also got their fair share of comments, such as 'New Yorkers are sheep. What one says or does, the other mimics. No one wants to be out of step'.[75] He targeted Mid-Americans who would buy his clothes at local department stores, listen to his KABC radio show, read his columns or buy a ticket to meet him. Paris, Italy, New York, *Vogue* all represented nothing but a privileged minority.

In his game of self-promotion, he became the self-acclaimed pioneer in multiple registers: the first designer to premiere a fashion line with a TV show; the first designer to host a television fashion show; the first designer to release a record; the first to launch a special plus-size designer collection in association with Lane Bryant; the first to start a worst-list of something; the first American designer to have his own signature fragrance; and the only fashion designer internationally known outside the industry as a personality by 1977.[76] Among the many side enterprises he ran were live presentations in theatres that combined stand-up comedy, musicals, fashion shows and a series of sarcastic on-site critiques of the worst-dressed people in the audience. He softened his comments when addressing his fans, claiming that he asked first if anybody wanted to be critiqued and always took into account the fact that these were people who had done the best they could.[77] His media popularity won him appearances as a guest actor in TV series, his own radio show and other activities that eventually interfered with his work as a designer, leading to the closure of his atelier in the mid-1980s. Mr Blackwell became a cult figure in popular culture, often portrayed in newspaper cartoons as the ultimate judge of what to wear or not, and immortalised in TV shows such as *The Simpsons* (Fox, 1989– ) and *Two and a Half Men* (CBS, 2003–15).[78] All these accomplishments seem to be the result of shrewd showmanship.

Mr Blackwell took it upon himself to criticise Oscars fashions early on with an annual Academy Awards Fashion Review.[79] Through his achieved standing as the ultimate arbiter of style, he participated in the televised fashion coverage during the 1980s and 1990s.[80] He also took his Oscar fashion commentary to the printed press.[81] Interviewed for the 66th Academy Awards fashion pre-show in 1994, he reflected:

> I think the minute you hear Oscars we want GOWNS. We want women to say: I am a woman, and I am proud of it. Too many of the things that we saw were chosen by the star. And to condemn the designer for a bad choice of the star, would not be fair.[82]

By then, Mr Blackwell was no longer presented humorously, but as an authority with a reputation as the world harshest fashion critic. In the 2000s, he became part of the internet coverage of the red-carpet when he broadcast live commentary on www.eStar.com.[83] The *Pittsburgh Post-Gazette* announced:

> On television, E! will have the most fun of all, presenting Joan and Melissa Rivers' catty fashion commentary as the wannabes and never-weres arrive at the Shrine Auditorium. The only version of the show has highlights from the previous year's coverage … www.estar.com – Mr Blackwell comments live on the fashions on this celebrity site. www.people.com – The magazine's site offers some interesting Oscar insights, and it posts some of the earliest fashion photos up from tonight's show.[84]

The coverage appeared in a broader context of emergent internet outlets offering alternatives to the ceremony's official telecast. Authors of worst-dressed lists became precursors of the over-opinionated scrutiny of celebrity fashion. They claimed to democratise opinion in the name of audiences by rejecting the establishment in saying, 'what we [the audiences] all want to say'.[85] The advent of Web 2.0 would seal this.

## The legacy is everyone's

Best- and worst-dressed lists are efficient vehicles for circulating fashion discourses branding the Oscars' red carpet as a fashion event today. Their replication, multiplication and persistence over time have consistently fed the idea that what famous elites are wearing is newsworthy. By shifting attention from society women to celebrities, these lists levelled their standing as fashion icons. In this sense, Eleanor Lambert's best-dressed list unintentionally documented the fashion industry's transition from a royalty-nobility society into an emergent celebrity culture and, with it, the unsuccessful striving of the residual to remain dominant. Blackwell's accomplishment was taking the best- and worst-dressed lists from insular promotion to worldwide entertainment.

Figures like Driscoll and Mr Blackwell challenged the status quo as they dared to criticise influential personalities, anticipating the democratisation of criticism enabled by the mediascape in the digital era. The emergence of the internet entitled everyone to a potentially valued opinion, leading countless magazines, websites, blogs, YouTube channels and Instagram accounts to produce their versions of both best- and worst-dressed lists for any red-carpet event available.

## Notes

1. Peter Walsh, 'The Withered Paradigm: The Web, the Expert and the Information Hegemony', in Henry Jenkins and David Thornurn, eds, *Democracy and New Media* (Cambridge, MA: MIT Press, 2003), 365–72.
2. Grant McCracken, 'Culture and Consumption: A Theoretical Account of the Structure and Movement of the Cultural Meaning of Consumer Goods', *Journal of Consumer Research* 13 (June 1986): 71–89.
3. Gundle, *Glamour*, 389.
4. Tolini Finamore, *Hollywood Before Glamour*, 141–67.
5. Edward S. Herman and Noam Chomsky, *Manufacturing Consent: The Political Economy of the Mass Media* (New York, NY: Pantheon Books, 2002 [1988]), 3, 23–4.
6. According to the *Oxford English Dictionary*, the origin of the word 'arbitrary' derives from the Latin word *arbitrarius*, from *arbiter* 'judge, supreme ruler', and perhaps influenced by French *arbitraire*.
7. 'The Mike Wallace Interview. Guest: Elsa Maxwell', 16 November 1957, HRC.

8. Sam G. Riley, *Biographical Dictionary of American Newspaper Columnists* (Santa Barbara, CA.: Greenwood Publishing Group, 1995), 201.

9. Kate Nelson Best, *The History of Fashion Journalism* (New York, NY: Bloomsbury, 2017), 134.

10. Joan DeJean, *The Essence of Style* (New York: Free Press, 2005), 62, 71–2.

11. See Mrs Emma C. Embury, 'The Village Bride', in *Godey's Lady's Book-Magazine* 20–1 (1840): 125–30.

12. Percy Savage, interview by Linda Sandino, June–July 2004, C1046/09, transcript, An Oral History of British Fashion Collection, British Library Sound Archive (hereafter Oral History).

13. Percy Savage, Oral History, 238.

14. Kathleen L. Endres and Therese L. Lueck, eds. *Women's Periodicals in the United States: Consumer Magazines* (Santa Barbara, CA: Greenwood Publishing Group, 1995), 425.

15. 'Style Leaders for 1937 Chosen from 8 Fields by Designers', *The Washington Post*, 23 March 1937, 3.

16. 'Study of Fashion Urged', *The New York Times*, 17 June 1936, 27.

17. See, for example, Jean Spadea, 'The Glass of Fashion: Academy Awards', *The Sun*, 24 January 1950, 10.

18. 'Best Dressed Women Selected in Washington and New York', *The Washington Post*, 29 March 1936, M1.

19. See Alice Hughes, 'A Woman's New York', *The Washington Post*, 31 March 1937, 17; 'Fashion Designers Pick 11 "Best Dressed" Women', *The Sun*, 19 March 1939, 13.

20. Letter from Emil Alvin Harman to Miss Hagen, 17 May 1854, Box 46, Uta Hagen/ Herbert Berghof Papers, Billy Rose Theatre Division, The New York Public Library for the Performing Arts, Dorothy and Lewis B. Cullman Center (hereafter NYPLPA).

21. Hughes, 'A Woman's New York', 17.

22. 'Professional Models Said Best Dressed Women in America', *Harrisburg Telegraph*, 4 December 1935, 1. This article was also distributed by AP.

23. Carol Bird, 'Chinese Women World's Best Stylists', *The Charleston Daily Mail*, 26 January 1936, 29.

24. 'The Lady, the List, the Legacy', *Vanity Fair*, April 2004, 267. Main Rousseau Bocher was an American couturier established in Paris, and founder of the couture house Mainbocher. He was also an illustrator for *Harper's Bazaar* and editor-in-chief of French *Vogue*. Bocher moved back to New York during the occupation of Paris.

25. Eleanor Lambert, Oral History, FIT.

26. For more about French fashion during World War II, see Dominique Veillon, *Fashion Under the Occupation* (New York: Berg Publishers, 2002); Steele, *Paris Fashion*, 268–72.

27. Manuscript for column, Box 47, f. February 1991, Eleanor Lambert Collection, 1943–2003, FIT.

28. *Fashion Group Bulletin*, May 1936, 4, f. 8 1936, Fashion Group International records, Manuscripts and Archives Division, NYPL.

29. 'The Lady, the List, the Legacy', 262.

30. Eleanor Lambert and Bettina Zilkha, *Ultimate Style: The Best of the Best Dressed List* (New York, NY: Assouline, 2004), 7.

31. Manuscript for column dated February 1992, Box 17, Eleanor Lambert Collection, 1943–1993 columns, series 1966–1998, FIT.

32. 'The Lady, the List, the Legacy', 329.

33. Percy Savage, Oral History, 238–9.

34. Ibid., 238.

35. Ibid., 240.
36. 'The Woman Who Owns Fashion Editors', *The Washington Post and Times Herald*, 17 December 1968, B6.
37. 'The Lady, the List, the Legacy', 329.
38. Patricia Linden, 'Fashion's Grande Dame', *Harper's Bazaar*, February 1993, 201.
39. Hedda Hopper, 'Drama: Columnist Questions Box-Office Pollsters', *Los Angeles Times*, 9 January 1951, A6.
40. 'The Lady, the List, the Legacy', 272.
41. Ninay Hyde, 'Pick of the List', *The Washington Post*, 14 April 1985, C2; Gabrielle Williams, 'Mistress of the Lists', *The Irish Times*, 12 July 1982, 9; Gloria Emerson, 'Grumbles as Well as Acclaim Greet Women Named the Best-Dressed', *The New York Times*, 5 January 1959, 35.
42. Emerson, 'Grumbles as Well as Acclaim Greet Women Named the Best-Dressed', 35.
43. Random examples of these lists can be found attached to her clients' promotional pictures; see for example Box 1, Box 2 and Box 3, New York Dress Institute Press Clippings, Special Collections and Archives, FIT.
44. List of Editors – Fashion Week Press Show Box 47, Eleanor Lambert Collection, 1943–2003, FIT; Letter from Eleanor Lambert to Mr Le Salem, 8 November 1982, 1943–1993 columns, series 1966–1998, Box 17, Eleanor Lambert Collection, FIT.
45. Marian Christy, 'The Absurd World of the "Best-Dressed"', *Boston Globe*, 7 August 1978, 13. See also Marian Christy, 'The Best Dressed List – It Ain't Necessarily So', *Boston Globe*, 7 January 1972, 23.
46. Manuscript dated 1–2 February 1986, f. January, February, March 1986, Eleanor Lambert Collection, 1943–2003, FIT.
47. Particularly during the reign of the 'Beautiful People' in the 1970s, Lambert flirted with exponents of this emerging eclectic celebrity milieu.
48. Manuscript for column, Box 47, f. March 1993, Eleanor Lambert Collection, 1943–2003, FIT.
49. Lambert and Zilkha, *Ultimate Style*; Amy Fine Collins, *The International Best-Dressed List: The Official Story* (New York: Rizzoli, 2019); THE BEST OF THE BEST DRESSED LIST, exhibition brochure, Museum of the City of New York.
50. Morris, 'Perspectives: Eleanor Lambert', 26, 30. Accessible at Eleanor Lambert clippings, Thomas J. Watson Library, The Metropolitan Museum of Art.
51. 'These Are Screen's 10 Worst', *The Salt Lake Tribune*, 7 June 1942, 38.
52. Bob Thomas, 'Screen Designer Tells Men by What They Wear', *The Times (San Mateo California)*, 4 November 1952, 11. Distributed by AP.
53. 'Presley Lister as One of Ten Worst Dressed', *The Brownsville Herald*, 20 February 1957, 14.
54. Erskine Johnson, 'Fashion Expert Picks Worst-Dressed Stars', *The Winnipeg Tribune*, 10 February 1947, 2. This article was syndicated and appeared in many other local media.
55. 'People', *Time*, 25 February 1946; see also Clippings, Raymond Driscoll Collection, Anna-Maria and Stephen Kellen Design Archives, the Parsons New School for Design (hereafter PNSD).
56. 'Dior Put on List of "Worst-Dressed"', *Los Angeles Times*, 11 December 1954, 12.
57. Gene Coughlin, 'Choosing Worst Dressed Gals is Labor of Love', unidentified clipping, available in Series II. Scrapbook circa 1942–circa 1961, Raymond Driscoll Collection, PNSD.
58. Correspondence between Driscoll and Mike Connolly also indicates that he personally submitted his lists to journalists.

59. Louella O. Parsons, 'Rita and Dick Plan Honeymoon in Philly', *Los Angeles Examiner*, 16 September 1953.

60. Louella Parsons, 'Hollywood and Mexico Dress Designer Announces His Best-Dressed List', *The News*, 31 December 1954.

61. Letter from Edna Chase to Raymond Driscoll, Series II. Scrapbook circa 1942–circa 1961, Raymond Driscoll Collection, PNSD.

62. 'His Annual Dressings-Down Have Made Nasty Mr Blackwell L.A's Dreaded Designer', *People*, 4 February 1985, 53.

63. Richard Blackwell, *From Rags to Bitches* (Los Angeles, CA: General Publishing Group, Inc., 1995), 51, 53, 82, 100. Blackwell believed that Hedda Hopper ruined his last chance for success in Hollywood when she ran a story in her column revealing that he was former child actor Dick Ellis, one of the Dead End kids in Sidney Kingsley's Broadway production, when Howard Hughes casted him for the film *Vendetta* (Hughes Productions, 1950).

64. 'The Best and Worst of Blackwell', *Pittsburg Post Gazette*, 16 April 2000, G-12.

65. Clifford Terry, 'Behind Every 10 Worst-Dressed Women There's This Man', *Chicago Tribune*, 4 December 1977, G79.

66. Ibid., G79.

67. Linda Deutch, 'Mr Blackwell: Drapery the World in Cloak of Whimsy', *Los Angeles Times*, 5 June 1983, 3.

68. The expression is attributed to American politician, showman and circus owner Phineas T. Barnum during the early to mid-twentieth century, and said to be a paraphrase of Oscar Wilde.

69. Paddy Calistro, 'Dresses to Tresses', *Los Angeles Times*, 29 February 1980, J8.

70. Victoria McKee, 'Best Dressed? Worst Dressed!', *The Guardian*, 18 January 1995, A12.

71. Joseph Finnigan, 'Dress Designer Declares War Against French Couturiers', *Enterprise-Record*, 7 June 1963; Joseph Finnigan, 'Hollywood Designer Says: Buy American', *Outlook*, 6 June 1963.

72. Calistro, 'Dresses to Tresses', J8.

73. Marylou Luther, 'Worst-dressed Makes Best Out of It', *Los Angeles Times*, 9 January 1973, F1.

74. Ibid., F1.

75. Marian Christy, 'Mr Blackwell Says: "It's All for Fur"', *Boston Globe*, 8 February 1979, 57.

76. Gina Horan, 'Mr Blackwell: The Man Behind the List', *Chicago Tribune*, 27 June 1998, 26; Lane Bryant: Retailing BIG Business, unidentified medium, 7 July 1972, clippings, Mr Blackwell Special Collection, Avenir Museum, Colorado State University (hereafter CSU); 'Curvy California Fashions Make Los Angeles Debut', *The Indianapolis Times*, 17 November 1963; 'Designer Blackwell Continues to Flatter the Fuller Figure', unidentified newspaper source, clippings, Mr Blackwell Special Collection, CSU; Terry, 'Behind Every 10 Worst-Dressed Women', G79.

77. Aurora Mackey Amstrong, 'Blackwell Has Words for a Few Fashion Statements: The Designer Puts on a Show to Benefit the Symphony, Dresses Down some Dressed-up Attendees and Also Bares a Personal Redesign', *Los Angeles Times*, 18 November 1990, 1.

78. Blackwell's character appears in *The Simpsons* as Mr Boswell, a judge of a beauty contest in Episode 61, 'A Streetcar Named Marge', original broadcast 1 October 1992. He is mentioned in an episode called 'Winky-Ding Time' of the TV series *Two and a Half Men*, original broadcast 14 April 2008.

79. 'Fashion Showtime with Mr. Blackwell', *Valley Times*, 7 May 1964, 1, 9.

80. Mary Rourke, 'Mr Blackwell (Richard Sylvan Selzer) 1933–2008: Wrote Acerbic Lists of "Worst Dressed" Celebs', *Los Angeles Times*, 20 October 2008, B7.

81. Mr Blackwell, 'Dressing Down for the Oscars Fashion Flops', unidentified clipping c. 1992, Mr Blackwell Papers, CSU.

82. W065234 66th Academy Awards AMPAS FASHION SHOW – TV coverage E! M11985, Pickford Center, AMPAS.

83. Gary Dretzka, 'Sorting Out Media Credentials is One of Academy's Toughest Jobs', *Chicago Tribune*, 24 March 2000, 5.1.

84. Ken Zapinski and the San Jose Mercury News, 'Sites to See/Oscar Edition', *Pittsburgh Post-Gazette*, 26 March 2000, C-3.

85. Lean Rozen, '... as Rivers Takes Aim at the Stars' Wardrobes', *The New York Times*, 7 March 2010, ST1.

# 7

# The emergence of fashion conglomerates turns couture into prêt-à-porter

Eleanor Lambert and Gérald Van der Kemp, curator for the Palace of Versailles, organised an event known as 'The Battle of Versailles' in 1973.[1] This fashion showdown pitted five French designers (Yves Saint Laurent, Christian Dior, Emanuel Ungaro, Hubert de Givenchy and Pierre Cardin) against five American designers (Halston, Bill Blass, Oscar de la Renta, Anne Klein and Stephen Burrows) in an ultimate battle for fashion leadership at the Palace of Versailles. This PR stunt illustrates a turning point regarding fashion, commerce and spectacle, as it put American designers at the forefront of their French counterparts in European territory. Allegedly, the success of the Americans rested on their understanding of spectacle. Their flamboyance, including a musical performance by Liza Minnelli, outshone the dullness of the French, whose creations were perceived as 'old' in this 'new' age. The Battle of Versailles symbolises the triumph of American ready-to-wear over the French tradition. This unravelling of events marked a point of disjuncture in which the ideoscape surrendered to the financescape.[2] In other words, it was a turning point in which the national identity of French fashion as synonymous with couture was confronted with a financial need to join the fast growth and economic success of the American business model. As Lambert put it in 1983, couture was an 'old-fashion' term that used to mean 'only made-to-order, but now it's used for high-priced clothes that are not much more exclusive than the general run.'[3] This validation of American designers and the expansion of European fashion houses into the American ready-to-wear market worked as stepping-stones for this moment in fashion history.

During this period, the attention awarded to fashion at the Oscars fluctuated, reflecting the multiplicity of perspectives that the new era brought about. The friction between new and old Hollywood brought glamour in and out of the Oscars, following the preferences of assigned producers. The lower ratings during the glamour-less years may be a testimony to the 'cult' status achieved by the ceremony, with audiences expecting to see Hollywood glamour. It may also speak for residual audiences only interested in what was familiar to them. During this period, Edith Head was replaced by a group of costume designers who focused primarily on staging the show's performances.

This transitional period could only be described as uncertain. This uncertainty significantly impacted the media attention afforded to the event in the US. Fashion's prevalence in the promotional build-ups decreased. Conversely, the show was rapidly growing abroad as a result of the agreements for satellite transmissions that started in the 1970s. This chapter departs from a cultural shift emerging in the 1960s that manifested as dominant throughout the 1970s and prompted a search to fit the new times. This period can be seen as chaotic for fashion at the Oscars, partly because the fashion, film and media industries underwent a significant re-structuring of their business models. The consolidation of The New Hollywood and the fashion industry's reconfiguration into fashion conglomerates marked these changes, paving the way for an ideological turning point towards 'big business' during the 1980s. This era also witnessed a proliferation of Oscars pre-shows that demonstrated the potential of these television slots leading to the main event, slots that would become fashion's new central stage in the following period.

## Cultural turmoil

By the mid-1960s, the cultural landscape of the US was rapidly changing. Head's ideas regarding fashion and femininity were becoming outdated. Overall, the conventional gender roles that characterised the previous generation were questioned, parallel to advocacy for the liberation of women from the home. The second wave of feminism and the sexual revolution reclaimed the female body, promoted the use of the pill, advocated the legalisation of abortion and paved the way for the gay liberation movement. The increasing, albeit slow, inclusion of women in corporate positions led many to 'adopt an anti-fashion look intended as a feminisation of the men's suit'.[4] These changes inspired designers to produce garments that prioritised movement and comfort.[5]

The Oscars red-carpet became a platform for political protests that garnered massive attention. The postwar attitude towards consumer culture encountered resistance among young Americans. Government mistrust and peace movements advocating the end of the Vietnam War replaced sentiments of nationalism that supported the war and challenged consumer society values that characterised the postwar period. These social and cultural changes brought a new perception, or even disregard, of fashion among younger generations in the US. William Stadiem describes a 'generational ignore for materialism', in which 'the 1967 San Francisco Summer of Love-inspired New Bohemia didn't exactly result in making poverty chic, but rather, elegance passé, the stuff of out-of-it parents.[6] The fashion industry was not immune to this cultural turmoil.

During the late 1960s, clothes functioned as a counter-cultural device that proposed an alternative view of society.[7] The influence of European trends coming from the UK and France became popular among younger and more avant-garde sectors of society. In 1964, André Courrèges launched the Space Age collection, introducing the catsuit and go-go boots, and encouraging women to wear trousers. Yves Saint Laurent, Pierre Cardin and Paco Rabanne were also part of this fashion revolution. British fashion, or more particularly British culture at large, enjoyed a global cultural cachet during this period. Mary Quant's popularisation of the miniskirt caused controversy and resistance in the US market.[8] These trends, reflected in art, music and fashion, called for the use of unconventional materials such as vinyl, synthetics, rhodoid plastic, paper, metal and PVC. The new styles either avoided contouring the female body through geometric shapes or overexposed it by using see-through materials or less fabric. These postmodern designs aimed to be provocative and reflected the pluralism of this experimental era expanding towards popular culture.[9]

## The beginning of the end

Edith Head was concerned about the influence of new trends among young actresses. In 1967, Inger Stevens stepped on the red carpet wearing a miniskirt. The following year, Head circulated a letter to all attendants, explicitly requesting actresses to wear 'formal evening gowns either maxi or floor length', emphasising that 'long dresses (no mini or day-length) look more graceful on stage and on camera' and that the 'dignity' of such a traditional affair as the Oscars deserved formal dressing.[10] This statement was a response to the increasing new trends seen on the red-carpet. Miniskirts, trousers and geometric-shaped dresses threatened to disrupt Head's under-standing of femininity and classical Hollywood glamour. She called these new trends the 'anti-woman look' imposed by European designers trying to be different.[11] In her stand against fashion, she alleged that trends were only for teenagers, defending 'the normal figure dress' that 'puts bust, waist and hip where they are intended', unlike the new styles from Paris and London.[12] She alleged that the so-called 'sister look' was so widespread that very important people appeared in all sorts of places wearing pyjamas, miniskirts and far-out costumes, and claimed that the Academy had 'an inventive foolproof secret' that would 'guarantee that nobody, of any age, size or shape can get on the Academy stage in a miniskirt'.[13]

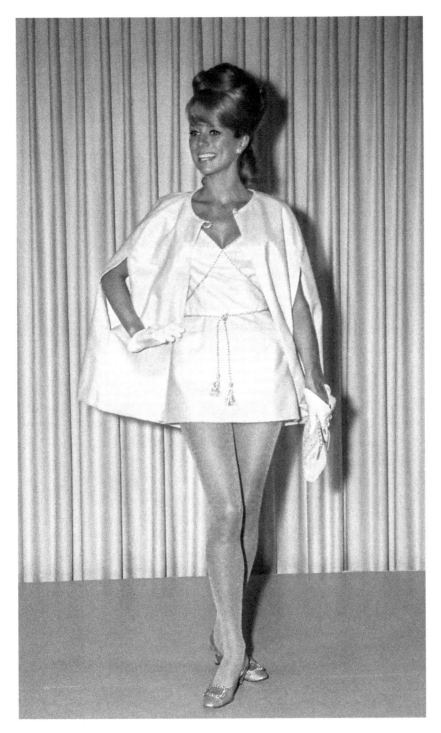

**Figure 7.1** Inger Stevens scandalising the Oscars dress code as she poses at the Santa Monica Civic Auditorium's press pavilion on 10 April 1967 for the 39th Academy Awards ceremony. Academy Awards Collection. Courtesy of ©A.M.P.A.S.®

The mid-1960s were challenging times for the Academy and for Head, as both struggled to fit in the new era. In 1965, they decided to appeal to nostalgia in order to boost ratings, by honouring silent stars during the ceremony, but the days of tuxedos and furs were over.[14] Head also faced her own struggles to stay *au courant* in and outside Hollywood. In 1964, Mr Blackwell criticised her role at the Oscars and her attempts to design off-screen garments. Blackwell was the archetype of a new form of style arbiter aligned with the emerging celebrity culture. Hal Humphrey reported that:

> Blackwell wouldn't even watch the array of femininity on the big Oscar show without aspirin and an ice-pack. 'Edith Head always supervises the clothes for the bash, and she is the worst commercial designer. She is a great costumer for the movies, but her personal stuff is years behind'... 'One can't tell where the bumps are on women in the Oscar presentations, and some of the backs would look great in front. Ugh.'[15]

This comment came at a point in Head's career in which the discourses she aligned herself with were passé and her fashion authority at the Oscars flimsy.

Head needed to boost her reputation as a costume designer. She survived the massive redundancies brought about by the demise of the studio system, mostly through politics and self-branding. By the mid-1960s, the rumour in Hollywood was that majors were entering a new business era. She renewed her contract with Paramount in 1965, but these agreements had been on a year-to-year basis since 1923. In 1966, the studio was sold to Gulf + Western Industries Inc., a company that had its origins in the car parts industry. The takeover of Paramount, as Paul Monaco explains, 'was the first example of a buyout of a Hollywood major from outside the entertainment industry'.[16] The acquisition was received with scepticism and suspicion regarding their capacity to run the business and their overall intentions. Head could no longer charm her way in among these young business school executives with for-profit corporate mindsets who focused on turnouts instead of Hollywood nostalgia. While Head signed the consent to transfer her contract to New Paramount on 28 October 1966, the new owners refused to renew it the following year.[17] In 1967, Head left Paramount after forty-four years to join Universal, and was given an office inside the Universal Studios lot. Like in a Hollywood zoo, she was now an attraction, coming out of her office, driving around in her golf cart and waving at the tourists. Lew Wasserman was keeping Hollywood history alive.

## Off with her head

Edith Head also faced challenges at the Academy Awards. Throughout the 1960s, they hired younger designers to complement her role. Donfeld was appointed from 1959 to 1962, initially as special coordinator and later as costume coordinator. Her position was rebranded as costume supervisor in 1965, when Michael Travis was assigned to work with her as the show's costume designer. While no records justify this decision, she may have wanted to assert some hierarchy over these younger designers. The title of costume supervisor resolved this. Someone else was the costume designer, but she 'supervised'.

One of the many new challenges that Head faced was the long-awaited arrival of colour for the Oscarcast in 1966. This technology would show gowns in full splendour, but it also presented new challenges. '"Our staff can control the lights," [show director Richard Dunlap declared] "but it is up to Edith Head, the Academy's Costume Consultant, to convince the presenters that they make no last-minute changes in their gowns colorwise".[18] Head asked actresses to 'play it cool this first time', and most of them wore solid pastel colours.[19] What the advent of colour was calling for was the expertise of costume designers familiar with this new technology on the small screen, expertise she lacked.

Head was replaced in 1969, following a series of changes introduced by the Academy – or more precisely by producer-director Gower Champion – to rebrand the ceremony. It was the first time in sixteen years that she was not assigned a role at the ceremony. Instead, Champion recruited Ray Aghayan as the costume consultant for the show.[20] Aghayan worked *ad honorem*, as a favour for Champion.[21] Despite having points of connection with Head's legacy of femininity, Aghayan's approach differed. He had no intention of laying down rules on the length of gowns, even though he preferred long gowns for the occasion, declaring himself

> on a crusade for a prettier, more-feminine look in American women ... If you think that statement is too bland or over-simplifies a fashion concept, please hear me out ... I'm thoroughly convinced that the vogue of the brittle, constructed look in women's wear is, at long last, giving way to a softer, clinging type of apparel for street or evening wear.[22]

An article circulated by AP enhanced the novelty of a new era, announcing, 'Oscar Show is Revamped'.[23] Champion's background as a dancer and choreographer hinted at a musical aesthetic for the upcoming ceremony. Aghayan promised to work on glamour, but the meaning of glamour was slowly turning into a Las Vegas showgirl style.

Fans blamed Champion for 'the smallest fan turnout in years'.[24] For some Academy members, Champion was fit to be the show's choreographer but not its producer; this grandiloquent staging needed 'a general showman' like Howard W. Koch.[25]

Head returned as a costume consultant in 1970, with Moss Marby as costume coordinator. Marby worked as a costume designer for Warner Bros. in the 1950s, and later freelanced for MGM, Fox and Columbia. The Oscars' media campaign launched Head's return as a comeback of Hollywood stardom. She designed Elizabeth Taylor's gown for that night and described it as a 'return to the 50s'. *The Hollywood Reporter* described it as an amalgamation of old and new, honouring the ageless so that the younger may be heard.[26] Arguably, this full touting of old Hollywood was a promotional strategy to propel the international satellite broadcast, showing what the world expected from Hollywood despite ongoing cultural and economic changes in the US.

Bob Mackie replaced Moss Marby as the costume designer in 1971. The show's press release acclaimed Head as the costume designer with most Oscar statuettes, but that only certified her 'excellence' as a film costume designer. Mackie was promoted separately, with emphasis on his work in television. He was introduced as 'the only designer to have won three Emmy Awards', a statement that reflects the importance of medium specificity at the time.[27] Determined to be back for good, Head thrived on keeping an open mind and adapting to the new times. She decided not to restrict the actresses' agency in their attire:

> These are our times and we must reflect them in every way possible. That is why Robert Wise, the producer of this year's Academy Awards Show, feels that we should impose no absolute restrictions upon the dress of presenters or recipients of awards. He will depend on the intelligence and good taste of these actresses in their fashion selection as to type, silhouette, colour, fabric, etc. Since there is so much beautiful fashion from which to choose, this year's Academy Awards should reflect the best of fashion today. As Mr. Wise says, 'The Academy is completely in tune with today and wishes the people who are working with the Academy this year to realize how very important their visual contribution to the Awards Show will be.'[28]

That was not precisely what Wise expected. He felt uneasy with this approach, suggesting that Head's new discourse was too much of an open invitation 'for the ladies to go completely wild'.[29] His vision was finding a balance between classic and new. The 1971 show was declared a total success in the eye of Daniel Taradash, president of the Academy.[30] Despite the accolades, this was Edith Head's second and final goodbye from the Oscars. After her departure, a succession of costume designers, who worked both in film and in television, filled the role for years to come.

## The anarchy of style

The demise of the studio system had left only memories of the old days of Hollywood. The movie industry turned corporate writ large, absorbed by large conglomerates and managed by business school graduates with no particular experience in it.[31] Culturally, the new era was all about youth – being youthful, looking young and challenging the establishment. The emergence of youth culture impacted the world just as the emergence of the jet set had done, although in radically different ways. William Stadiem describes the new Hollywood generation as 'anti-stars' who wanted to be 'cool'.[32] During this turmoil, the ways to approach what to wear at the Oscars differed significantly.

The eclectic looks are generally ascribed to the lack of guidance resulting from the studio system's demise. From a fashion perspective, this was merely the result of the contemporary fashion landscape. Valerie Steele explains that 'fashion was not in fashion' in the 1970s thanks to the 'freedom to wear what you want' that proclaimed it as 'the me decade', combining a continuation of the trends seen from the late 1960s to the mid-1970s, and a 'simultaneously harsher and more conservative' look in the second half of the decade, preparing the stage for the 'dress for success' attitude of the aggressive 1980s.[33]

On this anarchic fashion ground, the Academy went hands-off, keeping only costume designers to dress the entertainers on stage. In 1969, Aghayan explained:

> I don't want to ask that any of the feminine stars wear any specific gowns … They wouldn't be stars if they didn't have taste and style. All I'm going to ask is respect for Gower Champion's [producer and director of the show for 1969] concept in their choices of gowns and restrain in their coiffures. I'm an active enemy of the horrendous hairdos that make heads look like a massive construction job.[34]

The consolidation of the show as a TV spectacular finally crystallised. The show was treated as a television product in which the stage was the designers' priority. In a press release, Aghayan continued:

> I'm with him [Gower Champion]. His ideas are good. Sound. Tasteful. We can work together on the project of convincing the five hostesses that they can dress according to their own individuality, and still have an eye appealing unity when they appear on stage together.[35]

Aghayan was called back in 1972 after Head left her position for good. Bob Mackie, the last costume designer to work with Head, became Aghayan's assistant.

Aghayan's job was to design costumes for the musical parts. He compared his work for the ceremony with his experience in television variety shows: 'It's money, it's got prestige . . . it makes demands on you, and there is a reason you do it.'[36] The costume designers' job began after the score and choreography were completed, leaving twelve weeks to deliver the costumes. Elizabeth Courtney, a costume design and rental company in Studio City, manufactured most costumes.[37] The backstage emergency team was still functioning during this period, ready to solve any potential wardrobe crisis or malfunction.

Aghayan's appointment in 1972 attracted moderate media attention. It would be Mackie, his subordinate, who would make most of the headlines through his fashion design side gig. As in the case of Aghayan, Mackie designed costumes for the musical numbers, but he would also dress some of the attendees by personal request.[38] Mackie worked extensively with Cher on her TV shows; he was also responsible for most of her memorable Oscar-fashion moments, for good or bad. During this period, many took advantage of their relationship with costume and fashion designers, some paid little attention to what they were wearing and others embarked on shopping sprees in department stores. Sally Kellerman wore a white jersey chemise by Donfeld. Ann Margret wore George Hallis and Raquel Welch went for a powder blue slip dress designed by Ron Talsky. Jennifer O'Neill wore a black dress and cape by Halston that she bought at a local boutique called Giorgio Beverly Hills.[39] The store became one of the main hubs for Oscars fashions throughout the 1970s.[40]

As Mackie's popularity grew, and his expected upgrade from his role as Aghayan's sidekick never arrived, their partnership came to an end.[41] Mackie alleged that the show overlapped with New York Fashion Week, which made it impossible for him to continue.[42] Both designers would work for the Academy again, most often separately but once together in 1988. Other successful television costume designers alternated during this period. Michael Travis and Waldo Angelo worked on the ceremony in 1974, Walt Hoffman in 1975 and Ret Turner in 1976.[43]

## Celanese deals

Despite the event's focus on finding a TV aesthetic, the tension between the old and new Hollywood manifested in discussions about the best way to put together the show. The Academy juggled the fluctuating domestic interest and the increasing international demand for Hollywood glamour. In 1975, Howard

W. Koch insisted on the importance of using more arrival shots during the programme's opening. He believed that women wanted to see more full-figure shots of the stars because the event was 'a spectacular fashion show' and he wanted audiences to see the gowns.[44] After all, only a few of them would make it on stage where their full attire could be seen.

The following year, he reflected on the importance of fashion at the event in the *Los Angeles Times*:

> We realize that the girls on the show got a lot of publicity for the way they looked – bad or good ... People from all over the world were writing in telling us to show more of the fashion. The marketing's surveys showed us that people actually care more about the clothes than who wins. So we are paying strict attention this year to giving the public what it wants. A night of high glamour and the greatest fashion spectacle going in the world today.[45]

In order to enhance the fashionable side of the show, Koch joined forces with Celanese, one of the world's largest fibre firms.[46] Companies like Celanese and DuPont, a leading chemical company, became marketing machines in the postwar context, helping shape the fashion industry.[47] Celanese and Hollywood had a long history of collaborations harking back to the Great Depression, when the company joint ventured with Hollywood Fashions.[48] Ads encouraged women to be 'twins' of their favourite star by using the same fabrics as Hollywood.[49] During the 1940s, Celanese taffeta provided a technical solution for reducing the noise produced by silk gowns.[50] Part of Celanese's commercial technique to lead the market consisted of offering marketing services to manufacturers and designers willing to use its fabrics for their collections. It offered retail assistance through regional representatives, free reports on every aspect of the fashion industry, sales training aids and press kits through its merchandising, fashion and advertising programmes. The sale of Celanese reproductions mimicking the stars' looks continued throughout the 1950s.[51] Also in the 1950s, the corporation developed designer collections for department stores under the label 'Celanese International Collection of Couturier Fashions'.[52] Celanese continued promoting its products through magazine ads that featured garments produced by American designers using Celanese fibres throughout the 1970s.

In 1975, the company provided fabrics for manufacturing costumes for the Oscars' staged performances and for American fashion designers to create looks for nominees and presenters.[53] Under this deal, for example, Arnold Scaasi designed Diahann Carroll's gown.[54] Celanese planned to sell reproductions of some of these dresses.[55] The strategy of matching celebrities and designers to create their gowns for Celanese continued in 1976. The list of designers included Giorgio di Sant' Angelo, Holly Harp and Jean Louis. Simplicity Patterns Co. president Lilyan Affinito regarded the Oscars as a trendsetting arena and wished to issue an 'Academy Award Collection' featuring the gowns worn by the presenters recreated in Celanese fibres.[56]

In 1976 and 1978, the International Ladies Garment Workers Union sponsored the ceremony. These were the two years in which Koch was supposed to bring back Hollywood glamour with a strongly fashion-oriented campaign that included the collaboration with Celanese, associating actresses with American fashion designers. During this period, the union was fighting offshore manufacturing practices that sought to reduce costs in an increasingly globalised world. The president of the union, Louis Stulberg, argued that, while they had historically supported free trade, they would not tolerate competition from countries that exploited labour, paying 10–25 cents an hour.[57] In 1976, dress contractors in metropolitan areas had been protesting against the high wages imposed by the union.[58] The union's seal frequently appeared in advertisements for American brands as a guarantee of a full national product. That same year, they launched the 'Look for the Union Label' campaign with a series of TV commercials.[59] The 1978 commercial explicitly explained what looking for the union label implied:

> there used to be more of us in the International Ladies Garment Workers Union, but a lot of our jobs have disappeared. A lot of the clothes Americans are buying for women and kids are imports. They are being made in foreign places. When the work's done here, we can support our families and pay our taxes, and buy the things other Americans make. That's what the label means when it says union.[60]

In other words, the union strove to educate consumers by invoking a nationalist sentiment, in the hope of changing the market trend through consumer demand.

The arrangement with Celanese fits into this larger matrix of expansion of the American fashion business using local products and labour. In 1976, most of the designers were, not surprisingly, New York-based. Among these were Donald Brooks, Halston and Clovis Ruffin.[61] Aghayan and Mackie were designated costume designers of the event together with Ret Turner, who also dressed some of the stars. Mackie dressed Ann Margret for the event and costume designer Theoni V. Aldredge dressed Best Actress nominee Carol Kane. The 1976 ceremony broke an audience record, with 70 million people watching on ABC alone.[62]

## The New Hollywood's view of old Hollywood glamour

The emergence of portable video technology provided new opportunities for independent filmmakers, documentary makers and video artists. In 1972, a group of young documentary makers from San Francisco influenced by the so-called 'new journalism' of the day started a media collective called TVTV (Top Value Television). They provided an intimate and satirical look at American popular culture. The producers defined their work as 'nonfiction entertainment'. These 'mockumentaries' were broadcast on public television.

In 1976, they embarked on a special about the 46th Academy Awards ceremony entitled *TVTV Looks at the Oscars*, starring Lily Tomlin playing both herself and the part of Judy Beasley, a housewife from Illinois who was a big Oscars fan.[63] The producers described the insertion of a fictional character as 'an appropriate, deflatingly [sic] wry contrast to the pomp and circumstance of the movie industry's gala self-tribute'.[64] The show goes back and forth from the fictional character watching the Oscarcast to different celebrities getting ready to attend the ceremony.

The on-screen graphic reveals the crew is in Calumet City, Illinois. As the camera travels towards the entrance to a house, the sound of screaming fans coming from the TV set reaches a crescendo. The door opens. Lily Tomlin, in character as Judy Beasley, invites the camera into her home. 'Come in, hurry, the show has started and I don't want to miss it', she says while rushing back towards a big sofa beside a fireplace. Her character seems straight out of the 1950s. She is wearing a knee-length shirt dress with a flared skirt, in a fuchsia-and white check pattern, a pin with a picture of Lassie in her lapel and a black cardigan on top. Her hair is styled in a bob, pinned with two clips to keep it off her face. Judy looks at her cocker spaniel and asks, 'Did you eat this?' as she picks up the bowl of snacks she left on the sofa when she was opening the door. Later, she confesses to the camera that the dog is named after TV star Lucille Ball, who she always liked because she made 'good clean movies', and that every year it is her and 'Lucille' watching the Oscarcast together.

Judy announces to the cameraman that Elizabeth Taylor is on the TV. The camera pans left to show a big, bulky, wooden TV set from the 1950s; Taylor is being interviewed on the red carpet. As the camera returns to a close-up on Judy, she announces that Taylor said, 'I AM the awards', and continues sharing her observations about the Hollywood icon: 'She's beautiful, you can't take that away from her. I guess she and Richard aren't together anymore . . . Richard Burton. Well, I guess they will get back together though . . . sooner or later'.

After some passages about celebrities getting ready for the Oscars, they return to Judy. She has fallen asleep on the sofa by the time they are about to announce the award for Best Picture. This scene criticises the length of the ceremony and the difficulty it has keeping the audience's attention. By showing Judy asleep, the producers are suggesting that not even the most loyal fans can endure the entire show. Discussions about the length of the Oscarcast and how to make it more dynamic have taken place even since the first full radio broadcast. The search for new ways to update the show and to keep audiences engaged throughout the event persist to this day.

The phone rings and Judy wakes up. It is her friend, Glenda, making sure she is not missing Taylor onstage. Judy asks her to keep quiet. She continues holding the phone to her ear, sharing the moment with her friend in the presence of a Hollywood legend. A few days before the ceremony, Koch declared to the *Los Angeles Times* that Taylor's attendance would be the big event of the night. He referred to her as a fashion act of 'unparalleled glamor'. In his eyes, she was 'all those young girls out there wanted to see. She's Hollywood'.[65] The context given to Taylor in the mockumentary, in contrast with Koch's media discourses, evidences a generational clash. While, in Koch's perception, Taylor was what all 'young' girls wanted to see, Tomlin's character represents a middle-aged, conservative woman following postwar traditions.

Taylor is a paradigmatic figure in Hollywood history, and possibly the most emblematic in the transition from stardom to celebrity culture. She managed to master both worlds, living through the transition that went hand in hand with the changes in media culture.[66] Consequently, Taylor can be read as an old movie star but also, retrospectively, as a bridge between the old and the new Hollywood. She appeared on the red carpet wearing a striking strapless red dress designed by Halston, who was on his way to represent the American fashion industry at the Battle of Versailles later that year.

Special attention is given to fashion and celebrity in the documentary parts, but emphasising the banal instead of the opulent. A limousine arrives in Malibu, California, to pick up actress Lee Grant. She is getting ready for the ceremony and telling a young girl to tighten the belt of her dress. The actress, nominated for her performance in *Shampoo* (Persky-Bright/Vista, 1975), is wearing a second-hand wedding dress. She tells the camera that she wanted to wear something with a history, something that 'had a value', 'something that had roots'. Once in the limo, her anxiety is a far remove from the composure expected from a Hollywood personality used to glamorous gatherings. 'I feel like I am going to my high school prom', she says. Intentionally or not, the mockumentary unravels the contrast between the backstage scenes of celebrities' ordinary lives and the idealised constructed images that audiences get at home, capturing what Dyer defined as the paradox of the stars – both ordinary and extraordinary, and both present and absent.[67] The footage shows all these dimensions and contrasts the seen with the unseen. It also provides the perspective of presence and absence in the perception of the fans, watching the arrivals, and the audience, represented by a fictional character at home.

This critical take on glamour is brought to an extreme in Lily Tomlin's satirical approach when she attended the ceremony as a nominee for Best Actress in a Supporting Role for her work on *Nashville* (Paramount Pictures, 1975). Tomlin did not shop for a gown at a department store or a second-hand store, nor did she pick one from her supply of party dresses. Instead, she heads to Elizabeth Courtney Costumes, where she tries on an outfit and discusses details with one of the sales assistants. She is wearing a silver sheath sequin dress, a fashionable style in 1960 and 1961, and a white fur stole worn the wrong way round, leaving her back uncovered. The assistant suggests decorating the fur with scraps of silver sparkly fabric to turn the piece into 'a real ensemble'. Ornamentation functions as a mockery of the old Hollywood excess. 'Ok, what else do we need? Don't I need a bracelet to go with my gloves?' asks Tomlin as the camera zooms in to diamond-coloured accessories piled on a table. She takes three large bracelets to slip on top of her elbow-length gloves, a pair of dangling earrings and a tiara. She wonders if she should take the satire even further by wearing full clown make-up. In the event that she wins, she plans to say, 'I know many of you have thought about me as only a comedienne, and it is such a wonderful opportunity to be acknowledged as a dramatic actress'.

**Figure 7.2** Actress Lily Tomlin satirises the old Hollywood look at the 48th Academy Awards ceremony in 1976. Academy Awards Collection. Courtesy of ©A.M.P.A.S.®

On her way to the ceremony, Tomlin enters the rented limousine with the help of the chauffeur, asking him what the proper way to get into the car is. Interviewed by the crew, Tomlin is asked how it feels to be a star.

> There's no words to express this kind of thing because it is not quite eh ... well, look out here, look at what surrounds us: I've got a blue house and all kinds of trees and things, and there is my '68 Pontiac that I brought back from New York when I was first starting out. I'll never give it up. You can say that, well, all in all, it's been a fulfilling life.

Tomlin's performance encapsulates the contemporary clash between old and new Hollywood. The circulation of the mockumentary serves as a cross-media reference to her appearance at the Oscars. Isolated from all contextual meanings that this text provides, her look could have been evaluated by so-called style arbiters and deemed a success or a failure. Through the intertextual meanings enabled by the documentary, her performance stands as a mockery of Hollywood's tinselled glamour that challenged the glorified status of fame. Her Oscars look was a wink to a new generation of celebrities that marked the arrival of a new era in Hollywood.

In 1972, Jane Fonda took to the stage to collect her Oscar for Best Actress in a Leading Role for *Klute* (Warner Bros., 1971) wearing a ready-to-wear Yves Saint Laurent black wool trouser suit she had bought in Paris four years earlier. It was the time of the Vietnam War, and a politically involved Fonda did not want to indulge in glamour. Saint Laurent was the first French couturier to open a ready-to-wear store under his name in Paris and New York, in 1966 and 1968 respectively. Fonda refused to speak her mind when on stage, but paraphrased her father's advice instead: 'There's a great deal to say, but I am not going to say it tonight'.[68] Her unglamorous statement was not unfashionable but avant-garde. Fashion had not gone; it was only mutating.

## The New Hollywood takes over the Oscars

Ray Aghayan resigned from his positions at the ceremony alleging 'artistic differences' with the show's producer, William Friedkin, in 1977. After only one meeting, Aghayan told Friedkin: 'You know what, you don't want me. It's not something I want to do anyway. You need somebody else'.[69]

Friedkin was a representative of the new Hollywood, a minimalist who wanted to eliminate the glamour of the arrivals. He did not believe in the Oscars being about limousines and luxurious clothes because, he argued, these values did not reflect the lifestyles of the filmmakers of his time.[70] Theoni V. Aldredge replaced Aghayan and Mackie as the show's costume designer in 1977.[71] Friedkin was explicitly against the beads and glitter, and wanted to 'show culture over kitsch'.[72] Ellen Burstyn, the show's co-host, planned to wear a Donald Brooks golden beaded gown, but Friedkin asked her to 'eliminate the flash in her wardrobe' and sent her to Jean Louis for 'a more down to earth look'.[73] Instead, she wore a black tuxedo with a lavender ruffled shirt and a large, sheer, black bow tie, the same look as Best Cinematography winner Haskell Wexler.

Regarding the reception of Friedkin's vision, the waters were divided. Academy president Walter Mirisch told the press the show had its 'high points and some flaws'.[74] Friedkin received plenty of letters congratulating him on having produced the best version of the Oscars ever seen. The letters commented on the show's relaxed tone and how entertaining it was in comparison to previous ceremonies. Most of them came from management agencies and other representatives of The New Hollywood. Mackie emphatically disagreed with Friedkin's vision in the press. A large sector of the media agreed with Mackie. The consensus was that the show was 'dull'. Bill Carter, from *The Sun*, called the show 'boring', pointing out that the dress code imposed 'led to the dullest fashion parade in Oscar history, one facet of the show that some viewers have always enjoyed'.[75] The 1977 Oscarcast lost 4.4 points in ratings from Koch's 1976 Hollywood extravaganza.[76] Head was not invited to the ceremony that year. In a statement to the press, she said, 'It's a very funny town [Hollywood]. You know, this year I'm not even going to the Oscars. I'm just going to sit home and watch them on TV and hoot and holler like everyone else'.[77]

## Say yes to the (ready-to-wear) dress

The Academy summoned Koch as producer and Bob Hope as emcee for another trip down memory lane in 1978. Koch staged a fashion show in the middle of the Oscarcast, with models showing the nominated costumes and a fashion collection inspired by them designed by Aldredge who was working as a costume designer with Mabry for that year's ceremony. The segment opened with Lauren Bacall describing how Hollywood had historically inspired fashion trends and ready-to-wear collections. On the fashion front, some of the designers mentioned in media reports included Chloé, Ralph Lauren, James Reva, Norma Kamali and Stephen Borrows. Borrows dressed Farrah Fawcett that night. The intermediary was not Celanese this time, but a Beverly Hills retailer called Fred Hayman from Giorgio Beverly Hills. Hayman would become a crucial player in the restructuring of Oscars fashion in the following period.

When Ron Talsky became the costume designer for the ceremony in 1979, he called for a tribute to Hollywood high style, warning presenters that he wanted glamour. 'Not comfort, not what's in fashion, but Glamor with a capital G', he declared in the *Los Angeles Times*.[78] Talsky started his career as a costume designer at the Western Costume Company, one of the largest in the business since the silent days.

Some actresses had direct access to exclusive creations from designers such as George Stavropoulos or Givenchy, others consulted boutique owners. Department store Bonwit-Teller became a big contender for actresses searching for the right Oscar look. By the 1980s, the fashion scene had shifted towards a consolidation into conglomerates, which became visibly dominant in the 1990s.[79] Under the global uncertainty of the financial markets, designers sought refuge for their businesses in other firms.[80] Already by 1971, three of the leading conglomerates – Richton Group, Kenton Corporation and Benjamin Shaw – owned at least twenty-five department stores and seventeen fashion brands, including Valentino, Oscar de la Renta, Giorgio Sant' Angelo and a percentage of Cartier. According to *The New York Times*, '[t]hese marriages of convenience [were] becoming an increasingly important survival route for well-known fashion names'.[81] This model provided funding for the designers to stay in business while giving companies profits for a brand that already enjoyed a certain degree of market recognition. The visibility of Oscar de la Renta in society columns, for example, was seen as an asset by the head of the Richton Group, who understood such exposure as a requirement for absorbing a brand. The strategies that launched Hollywood designers into international recognition during the studio era seemed vital to the fashion industry at large.

A sharper corporate look would also become a frequent feature for women at the ceremony during this era. When Ron Talsky returned as costume designer for the ceremony in 1984, he worked with Los Angeles fashion designer Carole Little to create gowns for the presenters and performers.[82] Little designed for the ready-to-wear label St. Tropez West that retailed in major department stores such as Saks Fifth Avenue and Bullock's. Her designs were described as ideal for 'women intent on scaling the corporate ladder'.[83]

Talsky defined the theme as 'elegance, *not* tackiness; opulence, *not* decadence'.[84] He also expressed his preference for satins, velvets and jerseys, and hoped the women they were dressing would not go home to 'burn the gowns' and 'show up in leather skirts with holes in them'. 'I'll be backstage, so they'll have to face me'.[85] The *Philadelphia Inquirer* pointed out the importance of fashion at the ceremony and its potential for the show:

> If you are still awake tonight after the Academy awards grind to an end, note the credits after the show. They will say, 'All costumes designed by

Ron Talsky'. But the 'costumes' that matter will have come from Seventh Avenue's finest. I mean things like Mary Tyler Moore's purple puffy sleeves, a train, a bustle – all from the hot New York creator Tracy Miller. The clothes are part of the show, and if Oscar ever gets this fashion statement, it will be an improvement.[86]

By then, the *Los Angeles Times* had announced that Shirley MacLaine and Debra Winger, both nominees for Best Actress, would wear glamorous ready-to-wear gowns by New York designer Fabrice. Audrey Hepburn remained faithful to Givenchy, Lauren Bacall appeared in Fortuny, Amy Irving in Ralph Lauren and Cher, once again, teamed up with Bob Mackie. Julie Walters had a dress by London's David and Elizabeth Emanuel, the couple who designed Lady Diana's wedding dress. Loyal to her status as a fashion icon, Joan Collins prepared two outfits; a black and gold gown in lurex, imported from France, for a recorded sequence, and a red and black bugle beaded dress, for presenting the Science and Technical Achievement Award. Alfre Woodard wore Claude Riha. Glenn Close wore costume designer Ann Roth's creation. Department stores became the principal repositories for Oscar looks, but the ceremony was getting ready for a long-lasting fashion comeback.

## The official pre-shows

The Academy produced its first official Oscars pre-show in 1975, as a response to an escalating number of pre-shows capitalising on the event, but it did not focus on fashion. *The Academy Presents Oscar's Greatest Music* (ABC, 1975) was a one-hour special comprising clips of Academy Awards musical numbers.[87] It was a five-year agreement between the Academy and ABC, but whether it continued after the first year is uncertain. *Sunday at the Oscars* (ABC, 1999) was a thirty-minute show that promised red-carpet arrivals and behind-the-scenes segments preceding the ceremony. It featured Geena Davis as host and Jim Moret as the red-carpet correspondent.[88] By the time the Academy aired its first pre-show in 1999, the red-carpet live broadcast made by cable TV channel E! was already in the lead around the globe through cable television. In terms of fashion coverage, E!'s transmission became unrivalled.

## Notes

1. See Robin Givhan, *The Battle of Versailles: The Night American Fashion Stumbled into the Spotlight and Made History* (New York, NY: Flatiron Books, 2016).

2. This relates to the consumer revolution mentioned in Appadurai, *Modernity at Large*, 72–3.

3. Barbara Bradley, 'Glamor: Say Goodbye to Mystique of Couture', *Chicago Tribune*, 28 November 1984, e6.

4. English, *A Cultural History of Fashion*, 198.

5. Daniel Delis Hill, *Fashion: From Victoria to the New Millennium* (London: Pearson, 2012), 307.

6. Stadiem, *Jet Set*, 327.

7. English, *A Cultural History of Fashion*, 77–8.

8. See Delis Hill, *Fashion*, 309.

9. English, *A Cultural History of Fashion*, 77.

10. Letter from Edith Head, 25 March 1968, f. 204, Academy Awards Press Releases, Academy Awards Ceremony files, MHL.

11. Judy Jacob, 'Edith: Designing Woman with a Head for Fashion', *Detroit News*, 7 February 1966.

12. 'Hollywood Disregards Paris Trend'.

13. W118217 39th Annual Academy Awards – electronic press kit select bites, Head Edith and Freed, Arthur, 1967, Pickford Center, AMPAS.

14. 'Letter to Arthur Freed', 18 January 1965, and 'Letter from Gregory Peck to Joe Pasternak', 4 March 1965, f. 2585, Academy of Motion Picture Arts and Sciences – 37th Annual (1964) Academy Awards, Gregory Peck Papers, MHL.

15. Hal Humphrey, 'Ten Worst Dressed Women', *The Sun*, 3 May 1964, TV7.

16. Paul Monaco, *The Sixties, 1960–1969* (New York: Charles Scribner's Sons, 2001), 31.

17. Employment and consulting agreement, 28 October 1966, f. 156 contracts – Paramount, Edith Head Papers, MHL.

18. Elizabeth Sullivan, '1st Colorcast for Oscar Presentations', *Boston Globe*, 17 April 1966, A10.

19. Television Reviews, 'Tint and Hope's Nifties Liven Up Old Script of Annual Oscarcast', *Variety*, 20 April 1966, 43.

20. 'Champion Completes Production Staff; Show Plans on Schedule', *Academy Report* 12.1 (April 1969), 2, MHL.

21. Ray Aghayan, interviewed by Karen Herman, 26 August 1998, Video, Oral History, People, Archives of American Television.

22. '"Prettier Women This Year" Says Oscar Costume Consultant', Press Release, undated 1969, Academy Awards Ceremony Files, MHL.

23. Gene Handsaker, 'Oscar Show is Revamped', *The Atlanta Constitution*, 14 April 1969, 8.

24. John Mahoney, 'Oscars Sustain Glamor, Infused with Tradition', *The Hollywood Reporter*, 8 April 1970, 4.

25. An Oral History of Elias Hal interviewed by Douglas Bell, OH122, Oral History Collection, MHL.

26. Mahoney, 'Oscars Sustain Glamor, Infused with Tradition', Front page.

27. 'Bob Mackie Named Costume Designer for Oscar Awards', Press Release, 29 March 1971, Academy Awards Ceremony Files, MHL.

28. Paraphrasing Head's comments to a third party in Letter from Robert Wise to Edith Head, March 22, 1971, f. 141, Edith Head Papers, MHL.

29. Letter from Robert Wise to Edith Head, 22 March 1971, f. 141, Edith Head Papers, MHL.

30. Letter from Daniel Taradash to Edith Head, 23 April 1971, Edith Head Papers, MHL.

31. Monaco, *The Sixties*, 265.

32. Stadiem, *Jet Set*, 326.
33. Valerie Steele, 'Anti-Fashion: The 1970s', *Fashion Theory* 1, no. 3 (1997): 280–1.
34. 'Oscar Costume Consultant Outlines His Plans', Press Release, 1969, Academy Awards Ceremony Files, MHL.
35. Ibid.
36. Ray Aghayan, Oral history.
37. Ibid.
38. Bob Mackie, interviewed by Jennifer Howard, 29 June 2000, Video, Oral History, People, Archives of American Television.
39. Eye, *Woman's Wear Daily*, 17 April 1972, 6.
40. Ibid., 10 April 1972, 12 and 2 April 1974, 12.
41. Mackie, Oral History. They worked together at the Oscars in 1972, 1973, 1976, 1977 and 1988.
42. Ibid.
43. See Shari Okamoto, 'His Work's Cut Out', *Los Angeles Times*, 3 March 1986, 9. Hoffman specialised in costume design for television, and was working with Cher in *Cher* (CBS, 1975–6) and *The Sonny and Cher Show* (CBS, 1976–7). Nolan Miller, costume designer on the international TV hit *Dynasty* (ABC, 1981–9), was hired in 1986.
44. 'Producer Koch Hopes to Top Previous Academy Awards with 47th Ceremony', *The Bulletin* 8 (Winter 1975): 4, MHL.
45. Alan Cartnal, 'What They'll Wear Tonight: Best Dressed for the Oscars', *Los Angeles Times*, 29 March 1976, E1.
46. Eye, *Women's Wear Daily*, 28 March 1975, 63.
47. Regina Lee Blaszczyk, 'The Hidden Spaces of Fashion Production', in Sandy Black et al., eds, *The Handbook of Fashion Studies* (London: A&C Black, 2014), 191.
48. Farrell-Beck and Parsons, *20th Century Dress*, 97.
49. Celanese, *Photoplay*, October 1934, 81.
50. 'Suggested Methods for Reducing Certain Types of Set Noises', *Technical Bulletin*, 19 May 1941, 4, MHL.
51. Higashi, *Stars, Fans, and Consumption*, 39.
52. See for example, Michael J. Lisicky, *Filene's: Boston's Great Specialty Store* (Charleston, SC: Arcadia Publishing, 2012), 41.
53. Eye, *Women's Wear Daily*, 28 March 1975, 63.
54. Robert A. DeLeon, 'Diahann Carroll's "Oscar" Diary', *Jet*, 24 April 1975, 15.
55. Eye, *Women's Wear Daily*, 28 March 1975, 63.
56. Alan Cartnal, 'Friedkin Runs the Show Exorcising Oscar's Image', *Los Angeles Times*, 28 March 1977, E1.
57. 'Fireworks Likely on Imports Issue: A National Survey', *Women's Wear Daily*, 20 July 1971, 4–5.
58. 'Work Stoppage Hits Dress Firms', *Women's Wear Daily*, 18 February 1976, 1.
59. See OC Archive, 'ILGWY-Emma.mov', *YouTube*, https://youtu.be/DsctsFOTQS8/
60. Robatsea2009, 'Look for the Union Label 1978 ILGWY ad', *YouTube*, https://youtu.be/7Lg4gGk53iY/
61. Ruffin won a Coty Award in 1972 and was the youngest fashion designer to do so. See Bruce Lambert, 'Clovis Ruffin, 46, A Fashion Designer for Women, is Dead', *The New York Times*, 9 April 1992.
62. 'Record 70 Million Watch Oscar Show on ABC-TV', *The Bulletin* 11 (Spring 1976), 1, MHL.

63. The documentary also appears as *TVTV Looks at the Academy Awards* in some contexts. This nomenclature correlates the documentary titles and information found at the Paley Center for Media.

64. Lee Margulies, 'TVTV to Go Commercial', *Los Angeles Times*, 22 December 1976, E19.

65. Cartnal, 'What They'll Wear Tonight', E1.

66. See Ellis Cashmore, *Elizabeth Taylor: A Private Life for Public Consumption* (London: Bloomsbury Academic, 2016).

67. See Dyer, *Stars*.

68. Jane Fonda, *My Life So Far* (New York, NY: Random House, 2010 [2005]), 279.

69. Ray Aghayan, interviewed by Karen Herman, 26 August 1998, Oral History, People, Archive of American Television.

70. Cartnal, 'Friedkin Runs the Show', E1. See also Cecil Smith, 'The Oscars: Hollywood's Night to Shine', *Los Angeles Times*, 27 March 1977, T2.

71. Theoni Aldredge would also be the show's costume designer in 1981, 1985 and 1987.

72. Cartnal, 'Friedkin Runs the Show', E1.

73. Ibid., E1.

74. George Kilday, 'Outtakes from an Oscarcast', *Los Angeles Times*, 30 March 1977, F1.

75. Bill Carter, 'The Academy Awards Production Was Very Smooth but Very Boring', *The Sun*, 30 March 1977, B3.

76. See Chart, Academy Awards Television Broadcast, Academy Awards Ceremony Files, MHL. Ratings in 1976: 35.5. Ratings in 1977: 31.1. Ratings in 1978: 36.3.

77. Alan Cartnal, 'What They'll Wear Tonight', E1.

78. Betijane Leving and Timothy Hawkins, 'Oscar: Puttin' on the Glitz', *Los Angeles Times*, 6 April 1979, G7.

79. Farrell-Beck and Parsons, *20th Century Dress*, 250.

80. English, *A Cultural History of Fashion*, 143.

81. Enid Neny, 'Behind Some Designer Labels, Fashion Conglomerates Prosper', *The New York Times*, 16 January 1971, 14.

82. 'Carole Little Set to Create and Design Oscar Show Costumes', Press Release, 8 March 1984, Academy Awards Ceremony Files, MHL.

83. Elaine Woo, 'Carole Little, Designer of Working Women's Fashion, dies at 80', *Los Angeles Times*, 26 September 2015.

84. Timothy Hawkins, 'All-out Glamour Is the Winning Look for Oscars', *Los Angeles Times*, 6 April 1984, H1.

85. Hawkins, 'All-out Glamour Is the Winning Look for Oscars', H1.

86. Liz Smith, 'People Talk', *Philadelphia Inquirer*, 9 April 1984, E2.

87. 'Non-Awards TV Special Another Academy First', *The Bulletin* 9 (Fall 1975): 1, MHL.

88. 'Academy Awards Pre-Show', Academy Awards Ceremony Files, MHL.

# 8

# The fashion revolution

On 9 November 1989, David Hasselhoff sang 'Looking for Freedom' on top of a crane to a crowd of an estimated 1 million people in Berlin.[1] It was the fall of the Berlin Wall and a stepping-stone towards the fall of the Iron Curtain in 1991. Henry Luce's vision of the American Century was made manifest; an emblem of communism was falling in the midst of a celebration coated with American popular culture. The event stands as a symbolic victory for capitalism, and a cultural, social, political and economic turning point in globalisation.

The consolidation of fashion conglomerates brought about a new perception of fashion, led by a branding mania towards the end of the 1980s. This model, resting on brand equity, is central to understanding how exposure at the Oscars became vital to high-end fashion brands during the fourth period. The new brand power gave birth to an industry that turned designer names into luxury brands listed in the stock market. Fashion brands became a product *per se*, independently of products.

The mediascape was rapidly shifting by the late 1980s and early 1990s. The advent of the internet brought about an influx of information and connectivity that changed the world's perception amid the uncertainty that surrounded its potential uses. Thinking retrospectively, the speed of technological development throughout the 1990s, as well as the economic, social and cultural adaptation this demanded, can only be described as hectic. Hollywood was now focusing on the global market.[2] The media industries that grew successfully through mergers and conglomerates in the previous decades had been restructured under oligopolies concentrating power through multimedia empires.[3] The multiplication of media outlets led to an increasing interest in celebrity culture that revived media gossip.[4] This demand for celebrity news opened up a spot for discussing what they were wearing. The proliferation of niche international cable networks and the internet replicated this worldwide.

The American economy began to grow from the recession in the mid-1990s, partly due to the boom of technology-based companies. The rapid expansion of the internet and the concomitant technological developments altered perceptions of space and distance, enabling the concept of a smaller world that directly affected the clothing industry. The new global economic configurations standardised offshore manufacturing in remote parts of the world, pushing down production wages while increasing profits.[5] Consumption witnessed a shift 'from "hard goods" to enjoying "experiences"' through a new approach to branding, as a way to compensate for the loss of consumer/brand identity carried by globalisation.[6]

During this period, the Academy launched a fashion comeback, promoting the ceremony as the biggest fashion show of the year, the world's largest fashion show and the greatest showcase of international fashion in its press releases. Emphasis was placed on how designers from all over the world helped make the show the perfect event to celebrate Hollywood glamour.[7] The media latched onto this sentiment. The focus on fashion brought back the idea of the Oscars as the most acclaimed fashion show worldwide, echoing Head's heyday. This chapter discusses the events that put fashion at the forefront during the 1990s and 2000s. It examines the return of the fashion representatives, the renewed strategies that set fashion as a promotional discourse for the show's build-up and the Academy's sudden interest in creating its own version of the red-carpet fashion pre-show.

## A fashionable expansion

Fashion had officially entered big business by the 1990s. Bernard Arnaud created the LVMH luxury conglomerates in 1987, and the Richemont conglomerate was formed in 1988. Others, like Kering, had existed since the 1960s, but shifted business practices towards the acquisition of luxury fashion brands in the 1990s. Profiting from brand equity was no longer limited to product consumption, but also derived from the economic revenues of stock trading. Fashion's entry into the stock market intensified branding; it was moving away from selling products and into selling an image of luxury that helped the growth of these corporations in the financescape.[8]

These luxury conglomerates permeated the media. Their global marketing strategies brought luxury brands into the mass market, sold in the context of lifestyle advertising. The cultural mediation of fashion through celebrities crystallised the role that Hollywood personalities had had in representing modern beauty ideals and class performance. It was an exacerbation of a mechanism of emulation exploited by consumer culture. These aspirational qualities had only been rehashed and magnified with each growing step of media and globalisation. The widespread circulation of American popular culture opened up the opportunities of reinforcing these Western beauty ideals endorsed by Hollywood celebrities.

The rapid global media growth increased advertising opportunities in a market that was ready for more complex branding practices. Under the wing of these corporations, fashion brands could pump large sums into advertising and marketing, challenging the fashion media's gatekeeping role by shifting power away towards fashion brands.[9] Such large investments and the advancement of technology aided the global growth of mainstream fashion magazines, leading to the launch of glocal versions of these glossy publications, multiplying the openings for fashion, cosmetics and jewellery advertisement.[10]

An expanding dialectic of fashion supply and demand began. Celebrities and supermodels rapidly replaced the predominantly anonymous faces on fashion magazine covers. Even at the Oscars, Claudia Schiffer and Naomi Campbell appeared on stage with Pierce Brosnan to present the award for Best Costume Design in 1996, with supermodels wearing the costumes in a runway show staged by fashion photographer Matthew Rolston. George Michael's 'Funky' and 'Freedom' videoclips, and even one-hit-wonder 'I'm Too Sexy' by Right Said Fred are testimonies of how the fashion world and its newly branded supermodels impinged on popular culture throughout the 1990s and 2000s. In 1997, cable channel FashionTV launched in France, rapidly expanding worldwide via satellite. Designer names flooded the mass media as brands and celebrities in their own right.[11]

To exploit mass production, fashion conglomerates needed to expand brand recognition among audiences. Product placement agencies began specialising in fashion products for films and television during the 1990s.[12] Scripts were soon filled with mentions of Hermès, Prada and Manolo. Movies like *Prêt-à-Porter* (Etalon/Miramax, 1994) offered glimpses into the world of fashion, fusing fiction and cameo roles. *Catwalk* (Robert Leacock, 1995) and *Unzipped* (Hachette Filippachi/Miramax, 1995) documented the lifestyle of supermodels and designers as glamorous, hectic and whimsical. *Sex and the City* (HBO, 1998–2004) arrived to instruct audiences in what to like or buy, perfecting what *Dynasty* (ABC, 1981–9) had started and putting names and price tags to fashion choices. The renewed liaison between the fashion and film industries turned the red-carpet into an official promotional platform to showcase fashion brands worldwide through Hollywood's intermedial reach. The unprecedented number of fashion media outlets turned the wheel of Oscars fashion vortextuality. The advent of Web 2.0 pushed the phenomenon further through amateur fashion blogs and, eventually, social media. The shift towards luxury revamped and exported cultural ideals of wealth through lifestyle advertising. In a sense, the climate of the 1990s reflected the overt phenomena of the 1950s that, in turn, were manifestations of phenomena that had emerged at the turn of the twentieth century, now exacerbated by new technologies and business models that oiled the global flow of cultural and economic capital.

## The fashion coordinator

Fashion returned to the Oscars with the appointment of Fred Hayman as fashion coordinator in 1989. Producer Allan Carr put Hayman in charge of curating gowns, accessories and footwear for the celebrities and stars to choose from. It was the first time a businessman, and more specifically a fashion retailer, instead of a costume designer had worked in this capacity. According to Carr, the goal was to have a fashion coordinator with 'unquestionable taste' and 'special care and regard for women'.[13] In Hayman's words, Carr's appointment was 'a campaign to articulate how important it is to look right on Oscars night, to encourage celebrities away from the disappointing "plain Jane" look too many had adopted'.[14] The Academy presented Hayman as one of the most celebrated figures in the fashion and fragrance world. His retail boutique, Giorgio Beverly Hills, specialised in high-end imports. Aside from managing the store, Hayman was trying to develop the local fashion scene in Rodeo Drive.

Fred Hayman started his career in the hospitality business working at the Waldorf Astoria and later moved to the Beverly Hilton, where he successfully established the banquet and catering department in his role as banquet manager. He turned the Beverly Hilton into a hub for celebrities and in 1961 began organising the Golden Globes ceremony there, consolidating his clout with the entertainment industry. That same year, he invested in a friend's boutique to save it from going under, receiving a 30 per cent share in return. In 1963, Hayman left his job and bought his partner out, becoming the sole owner of Giorgio Beverly Hills.[15] By the late 1960s, other big brands such as Gucci and Tiffany & Co. had moved into Rodeo Drive.[16] Working close to the rich and famous in the hospitality business helped Hayman's vision of how to run his store and he built a reliable network of influential celebrities. Giorgio Beverly Hills combined leisure and shopping, with a strong focus on service. The store had a bar and a pool table to entertain customers and appease those who had long waits. This combination of fashion and hospitality-inspired customer service attracted Hollywood clients such as Natalie Wood, Barbra Streisand, Zsa Zsa Gabor, Diana Ross and Lucille Ball. The store offered an assortment of national and international designer items that until that point could only be acquired on the East Coast or in Europe. Some designers even gave Hayman exclusive rights to sell some of their creations.[17] In the absence of a product line of his own, he launched a fragrance.

Hayman was the right man to mediate in product placement and endorsement practices. He had acted as an intermediary and provided gowns for celebrities to attend the Oscars since as far back as the 1970s. Articles reported how actresses rushed into Beverly Hills boutiques for the Oscars.[18] These media discourses may have been propelled by the creation of the Rodeo Drive Committee in 1971. The organisation, founded and presided over by Hayman, gathered local businesspeople together, intending to promote the area as a luxury shopping destination. In 1981, his store reported a peak of $6 million in sales.[19]

Giorgio Beverly Hills was sold to Avon Products in 1987 for $165 million, plus acquisition costs, mainly for exploiting the perfume.[20] Avon planned to open a dozen licensed boutiques around the US, but the project never prospered.[21] The fragrance had annual net sales of more than $100 million.[22] Avon received offers to sell the brand from 1989 onwards, but refused to due to the product's high revenues. It finally sold the licence to P&G for $150 million in 1994.[23] Hayman's contribution turned him into one of the first men to break the gender barrier when he became a member of the Fashion Group in 1988.[24] He also served on the board of trustees of the Fashion Institute of Technology. After the Avon deal, Hayman bought a bigger store on the corner of Rodeo Drive and rebranded it as Fred Hayman Beverly Hills in 1989.[25]

## King of Beverly Hills

Hayman's knack for promotion helped Beverly Hills become a fashion hub for luxury brands, but he needed to position his name as a new brand after selling Giorgio Beverly Hills. While he was an influential player in the fashion scene, it was the name 'Giorgio' that resonated among audiences and costumers. He took his position in the Oscars to heart, and created an Oscar fashion runway show to premiere red-carpet trends for the media in the Grand Lobby of the Academy's headquarters in Beverly Hills. These gatherings followed a press conference, where the invited journalists could interview Hayman and other members of the Oscars production team afterwards. The pseudo-event had the twofold purpose of, first, promoting the Oscarcast and positioning Hayman and Rodeo Drive as a fashion mecca where celebrities shopped, and, second, promoting fashion at large, bringing consumers to Rodeo Drive and, consequently, attracting more brands to elevate business in the area.

His work for the Oscars put his name all over the media on an unprecedented scale, a name that was already showcased on Rodeo Drive's most visible store. His free Oscars consultation reportedly included a call to each nominee, double-checking there would be no duplicate gowns and offering advice over the phone.[26] Business as usual since the days of Edith Head. Nominees and presenters were invited to borrow dresses from Fred Hayman's new boutique. Designers shipped dresses to be borrowed, avoiding designs that were 'too simple or not glamorous enough'.[27] Nominated actresses and presenters were invited to the store to choose their outfits. Actresses signed a letter of indemnification taking responsibility for the dress being lost, damaged or stolen.[28] Hayman also worked as a guide to Oscars fashion in the media during a two-week build-up publicity campaign, emulating Head's role while executing his public relations plan for his new brand and Rodeo Drive at large.

The first group of designers to officially work with the Oscars in 1989 were Giorgio Armani, Geoffrey Beene, Marc Bohan for Christian Dior, Perry Ellis, Luis Estevez, Carolina Herrera, Tommy Hilfiger, Jera, Donna Karan, Calvin Klein, Bob Mackie, Oscar de la Renta, Carolyne Roehm, Arnold Scaasi, Gail Simms, Yves Saint Laurent, Vicky Tiel, Bill Travilla and Stephen Yearick.[29] By 1990 these contributions were centralised and formally acknowledged as product placement, with designers including Loris Azzaro, Geoffrey Beene, Eva Chun, Victor Costa, Oscar de la Renta, Pamela Dennis, Giorgio di Sant' Angelo, Fabrice, Ann Lawrence, Bob Mackie, Mignon, Roland Nivelais, Carolyne Roehm, Arnold Scaasi, Gail Simms, Vicky Tiel, Bill Travilla and Stephen Yearick (see Table A.2 in the Appendix).[30] Giorgio Armani rapidly monopolised the production of the hosts' tuxedos and gowns, becoming the designer who, since then, has dressed most emcees.

In 1991, Hayman recruited fashion designer Patty Fox as an assistant.[31] She had been fashion director at Saks Fifth Avenue for a decade and helped launch the premiere collections of Christian Lacroix, Donna Karan, Isaac Mizrahi and Karl Lagerfeld.[32] After leaving her job at Saks, Fox opened a PR firm, offering opportunities to connect luxury clients with celebrities attending award ceremonies. Her prominent career as the spokesperson for Saks made her a media-savvy asset with a broad social capital to mediate these endorsement deals. Hayman and Fox's aim was to return to Hollywood glamour. Procuring gowns and jewellery for the fashion pre-shows was the main priority. They raided showrooms in New York, taking advantage of Hayman's reputation as the man behind the success of the fashion industry in Beverly Hills. The selection was shipped to Hayman for the Oscars collection; around thirty to forty garments arrived from New York and Milan yearly.

These fashion shows anticipated the year's trends through the selection of gowns curated by Hayman, but not all the dresses displayed were full-length or appropriate for a red-carpet gala. This premiere of general fashion trends translated into publicity, piquing the audience's interest in what the stars would wear. There was no overlap between the gowns in the pre-fashion show and those worn by celebrities on the red carpet. According to Hayman, the first designers to embrace the benefits of celebrity exposure were the Italians, led by Armani, Versace and Valentino. As the fashion shows gained popularity in the media, brands and stylists became increasingly interested in showcasing their creations and lending gowns for Hayman's promotional enterprise. While the increase in fashion media outlets offered free publicity, the coverage of the red-carpet required the fashion industry to accommodate the tight deadlines of the event and media logistics. Fox would coordinate and distribute information about the celebrities attending and what they would wear to the ceremony, in order to give a heads up to journalists covering the red-carpet.

Hayman received no remuneration for his work for the Academy. Neither was he assigned a budget to produce the shows or the promotional campaign around it. He financed these himself in full awareness of the power that this association with the Academy gave him through the Oscars' global reach. The role came along just as he was embarking on the process of rebranding himself. His new store required as much media coverage as possible to position his name, Fred Hayman, as a brand. Showmanship was central. Hayman kept the characteristic shade of yellow used for Giorgio Beverly Hills. Everything around him was yellow: the new store, staff uniforms, his tie and even the convertible Mercedes in which he arrived at interviews, with his German shepherd in the back seat, to make an on-camera grand entrance. The media attention afforded to Hayman in news coverage before the Oscars provided plenty of opportunities for building a corporate identity. He succeeded at turning the eyes of media and the luxury fashion industry towards the Oscars. The same popularity attained by these cross-promotional practices pushed him out of the game. The proliferation of stylists and the media's initiatives to produce their own fashion forecast pre-shows, among other Academy plans, may have encouraged him to step aside.

## Out of the Rodeo and into Hollywood

During Hayman's last year at the ceremony, in 1999, Saks Fifth Avenue Beverly Hills was added to the long list of brands collaborating with the Oscars. The retail giant's presence challenged the position of smaller boutiques. The incorporation of Saks Fifth Avenue also marked a hinge moment in which fashion took off and embraced the branded status of high-end ready-to-wear. The incorporation of a stylist to replace Hayman the following year is telling. His departure may be indicative of a conflict of interests between a new-found opportunity for turning Hollywood into an epicentre of luxury and his interest in using his position to promote Rodeo Drive. It is impossible to state with certainty that Hayman anticipated the potential consequences the arrival of this new competitor could bring. However, one might speculate that it was for these reasons that Hayman, being the savvy entrepreneur that he was, decided to sell his Rodeo Drive locale to the LVMH conglomerate in 1998 and retired from retail. The fashion scene no longer needed small boutiques importing goods. In the era of big business, department stores' purchasing power allowed them to put garments on sale seasonally while flagship stores opened in all fashion centres around the world to keep supplying the demands of the most exclusive clientele. A giant ad in *Variety* that read 'Louis Vuitton salutes the 70th Annual Academy Awards', followed by the LV logo, announced that the French fashion titan had disembarked in Rodeo.

On 7 May 2001, *Women's Wear Daily* reported that a new real estate development in Hollywood was geared towards being 'a major player on the retail front', and listed Tommy Hilfiger, Céline and Christian Dior among some of the big names planning to open their stores there.[33] The aspiration was to establish a new spot for luxury shopping that was, in a sense, a potential competitor to Rodeo Drive. The project began in 1997, when a group of investors embarked on a quest to build a new palace of modernity that would merge commerce and entertainment in the heart of Hollywood. This retail complex included a hotel, a cinema, a nightclub, restaurants, live performance spaces, luxury shops and a theatre, entirely conceived to meet the requirements of the Oscarcast. The cost of building and maintaining such an infrastructure was out of the Academy's reach, but it signed a ten-year initial lease with the owners, giving both parties the freedom to capitalise on the venture.[34]

The mall had the potential to attract local consumers as well as tourists, both from hosting the Oscars and from its proximity to iconic locations such as the Chinese Theatre, the Hollywood Walk of Fame, the Roosevelt Hotel and the view of the Hollywood sign. The complex would be showcased worldwide on live television and in countless media references, an ideal scenario for free publicity to attract tourists. The area was rundown and still considered dangerous. The investors sought to change this by establishing the site as the epicentre of Hollywood glamour. Up to 80 per cent of the complex was reportedly leased by international brands even before it was completed. Tommy Hilfiger, for example, signed a lease for a large unit after closing his flagship store in Rodeo Drive, hoping to attract younger customers. The DFS Gallerias, a high-end duty-free store from the LVMH conglomerate, planned to open a unit to retail Louis Vuitton, Christian Dior, Coach, Loewe, Céline and Ralph Lauren Polo, in addition to a duty-free section for tourists that included Hermès, Bulgari and Burberry.[35] Tourists were DFS's specific target customers. Counting on a substantial investment from LVMH to move into the new complex, DFS Gallerias also shuttered its Beverly Hills location in favour of a Hollywood future.

## Return to the promised land

In 2002, the ceremony returned to Hollywood after thirty-three years with the construction of the Kodak Theatre. Investors hoped to revive the area as the home of the Oscars. Attracting tourists would function as an incentive for companies to lease their premises, but the levels of criminality in that part of the city worried some Academy veterans. Hollywood was considered a remote location at that time. Despite the improvements made in the previous twenty years, Howard W. Koch explained that people were afraid to walk the streets.[36] So, even if the area would be self-contained for the ceremony, the success of this new venture was unpredictable. The extended four-year promotion resulting from the delay in construction unintentionally translated into a strategy to cleanse Hollywood.

The construction of the Kodak Theatre thus marked a Hollywood comeback through the neighbourhood's gentrification. Despite the grand plans, the complex opened in the middle of an economic crisis, marked by the burst of the internet bubble and the plummeting of the market following 9/11. After 9/11, bleacher seats were allocated on a reservation basis only and once an application had been submitted via the Academy's official website. Camping outside the venue was now strictly forbidden. For the first time, fans were subject to background checks and had to go through a metal detector wearing photo ID badges in order to access the bleachers.[37] The potential rivalry between Rodeo Drive and Hollywood for the high-end fashion scene had been deactivated just in time. The tourist-friendly nature of the new enterprise called for a mix of high-end and fast-fashion retail that would be distanced from the exclusive allure that Rodeo Drive cultivated through its association with Beverly Hills as a residential area for the rich and famous.

## Let the fashion games begin

The Academy produced its first red-carpet pre-show in 1999. By then, other networks were successfully exploiting the red-carpet arrivals and benefiting from the spectacle created by Hayman's fashioning of the event. This thirty-minute pre-show, called *Sunday at the Oscars* (ABC, 1999), promised red-carpet arrivals and behind-the-scenes segments with a total of nine cameras prepared to capture every angle of the celebrities. It was to feature Geena Davis as host and Jim Moret as the red-carpet correspondent.[38]

The Academy assembled a separate team for the pre-show, consisting of Gilbert Cates as the executive producer, Paul Miller as director, and Stephen Pouliot and Jon Macks as writers. The show combined pre-recorded footage with live broadcast.[39] It opened with a montage of arrivals, starting at the Pantages Theatre in the 1950s, with a voiceover presenting the Oscars as a decades-long tradition. Emphasis was placed on the glamour, the lavishness and, foremost, the exclusive backstage access that audiences would be treated to. Davis exits the limousine and greets the viewers with: 'Happy Oscar night everybody. Welcome to our special countdown, and it goes something like this'. She walks along the red carpet while giving the audience at home precise instructions: 'First of all, don't trip on your trail'. She describes the show as an opportunity to preview Oscar excitement, the nominees, the glamour, dazzle and surprises of Oscar fashion for the first time.[40] Then, she introduces the fans sitting in the bleachers and waves at them. As Davis walks the red carpet, home viewers can see Army Archerd interviewing some celebrities, continuing a tradition established decades before.

As the show develops, other pre-recorded segments include celebrity interviews backstage and a conversation with Archerd. Despite using fashion as the selling point, only two short pre-recorded segments addressed the subject. The first is a historical recap of Oscars fashion, briefly introducing what actresses wore to the ceremony, with expected references to Adrian and Edith Head. Throughout the feature, trends are described in a manner that ascribes a coherent fashion identity to the different decades, such as 'in the 70s, fashion simplicity ruled' and 'flamboyance was the benchmark of the 80s', finally arriving at the contemporary fashion phenomenon, with 'The 1990s opened the door to a who's who of international designers for Oscars fashion such as Armani, Versace, Valentino and Vera Wang. Today, all are competing to dress the stars for the greatest fashion show on earth'.[41] A note in the script read that to introduce this fashion segment, there should be 'some girl talk with female star(s) re. fashion', which consisted of an interview with Helen Hunt.[42] This pejorative denomination links the perception of fashion-related topics to commentary about Francis Scully's fashion coverage in the 1940s being a feminine affair, intolerable to men. In the final script, the interview focused primarily on Hunt's career achievements, closing with two fashion-related questions: 'You've been attending a lot of award shows – that's a lot of dresses. Do you work with a designer – ever enjoy a day of shopping by yourself?' and 'Do you get a kick out of watching what everybody's wearing to the Awards?'[43] This condescending attitude towards fashion resulted in a missed opportunity to plug the industry in a way that would appeal to advertisers. The second segment was an overview of an auction of Oscars dresses organised by Christies, presented as 'Memorable Fashion Moments'.

Moret asked no fashion-related questions on the red-carpet but invited the cameras to show the looks. Towards the third and final act, the show becomes fully live. It goes back and forth between Davis and Moret as he initially stands on the bleachers and later moves into the Governors Ballroom to show the preparations for the after-party, while she enters the theatre to find her seat.

*Sunday at the Oscars* differed from the informal tone set by other red-carpet coverage at the time. No other television outlets were allowed to broadcast live from the red carpet in 1999, but they returned in 2000.[44] Eventually, the Academy and ABC set a rule to exploit an advantage they had over other networks, granting ABC exclusivity during the last hour before the ceremony began.[45] During that hour, other networks were allowed to broadcast pre-recorded footage, discuss the event from the studio or schedule other programmes leading up to the ceremony.

The Academy simultaneously launched www.oscar.com, a website carrying live coverage of the event, promising 'a dynamic internet experience'.[46] Over the years, the website experimented with different ways to engage the fans through interactive contests, quizzes and other activities.[47] The now rebranded www.oscar.go.com has become a platform for enjoying full red-carpet live coverage and backstage interviews for fans around the world, while also serving as a historical repository of Oscars information and imagery with a special section dedicated to the red-carpet.

The name of the Academy's official pre-show on ABC changed throughout the years and many presenters took on the role but failed to make their mark as red-carpet host.[48] In 2000, *Countdown to Oscars 2000* featured supermodel Tyra Banks, together with *Variety* columnist Chris Connelly and talk-show host Meredith Vieira. Connelly continued to be part of the pre-shows until 2007. Other fashionable figures joined. *Vogue's* editor-at-large, André Leon Talley, was part of *Road to the Oscars 2007* while also working as the ceremony's fashion coordinator. American model Kathy Ireland participated in *Oscars Red Carpet 2010*. Tim Gunn, the designers' mentor in the television reality show *Project Runway* (Bravo/Lifetime Television, 2004–), was part of the coverage in 2009, 2011 and 2012. *Marie Claire's* fashion director Nina Garcia, who also worked with Gunn as a judge in the reality show, joined him for *Oscar Red Carpet* in 2012. The official red-carpet pre-show's ratings ranged between 10.9 (in 2006) and a peak of 20.6 (in 2000), staying almost steady at 15 since 2008. The duration of the pre-show has increased significantly in recent years.

## Unforgettable Auctions

By the end of the 1990s, the media were referring to the Academy Awards as the most important fashion show in the world. Hayman had successfully proved the importance of the Oscars to the fashion world. On 18 March 1999, *Vogue*'s editor-in-chief Anna Wintour, Christie's president Patricia Hambrecht and actress Natasha Richardson chaired an auction under the title 'Unforgettable: Fashion of the Oscars'. *Vogue* sponsored the event in support of amfAR (the American Foundation for AIDS Research). The auction featured more than fifty-five gowns, including Bob Mackie's gown for Cher in 1973, Jean-Paul Gaultier's outfit for Madonna in 1998, Mariano Fortuny's dress for Lauren Bacall in 1979 and Edith Head's gown for Elizabeth Taylor in 1970.[49] The dress designed by Head for Janet Leigh in 1960 and used for the promotional campaign for the first fashion pre-show, was one of the many featured in the auction. Despite being the most central piece in the Academy Awards red-carpet fashion history, the item went entirely unacknowledged in the media. Kate McEnroe, former president of television channel American Movie Classics, bought the dress for $40,000.

## A tale of fragrances and copycats

According to Giorgio Armani, the Oscars gowns are the first in his collections to sell out.[50] Not everyone, of course, can afford these dresses however. One of the biggest money-makers among mass consumers in the high-end sector are licensed products such as perfumes. Red-carpet creations also spark parallel businesses. Just as department stores reproduced Parisian couture to sell affordable versions in the US mass market, companies today copycat Oscars dresses. The fashion industry continues to discuss and wrangle over copyrights and the boundaries of design plagiarism.

Counterfeits of red-carpet looks are not frequently discussed, but they proliferate. These copies target a broad market of consumers looking for ballgowns for proms, *quinceañeras* and weddings. In 2000, West Coast brand Allen B. Schwartz (ABS) and designer Victor Costa worked round the clock to produce their version of Randolph Duke's brown strapless dress for Hillary Swank. Designers like Costa sell these gowns to department stores such as Saks Fifth Avenue as soon as a month after the event, taking advantage of the window during which the audience will still have a clear memory of them. ABS's copy of Gwyneth Paltrow's pink Ralph Lauren dress sold 15,000 copies at $300 each in 1999.[51] Some dresses that landed on the worst-dressed list can, interestingly, transition into being best-sellers. ABS's copy of Donna Karan's dress for Susan Sarandon in 1997 became a top-selling item despite the unfavourable reviews.[52] Schwartz correctly made the point that these copies represent only 5 per cent of the brand's catalogue, but translate into 5,000 per cent of the brand's publicity.[53]

Manhattan-based store Faviana has been selling reproductions of celebrity gowns since the early 1990s. The price of their replicas can range from $300 to $700. With the boom in online shopping and globalisation, websites with questionable provenance also entered the competition.[54] In 2014, Faviana's CEO denounced Chinese websites who were using their trademark and photos and claiming to sell their gowns.[55] The US District Court of New Jersey intervened to block more than 1,000 suspicious retailers from China, freezing all payments going through American systems. Allegedly, this accounted for $1 million in counterfeit money in PayPal alone.[56] In sum, the Chinese counterfeiters were prosecuted for counterfeiting American counterfeiters.

## The reign of the fashionistas

With the advent of the new millennium, Hayman's role as fashion coordinator was replaced by a 'style designer' in 2000. At first, the Academy contacted Wanda McDaniel, the woman behind the success of Giorgio Armani's red-carpet endorsement deals, but her commitment to the brand impeded her from taking on the job. Instead, they hired stylist L'Wren Scott.[57] Scott secured only four brands to dress presenters and nominees: Timothy Everest, Donna Karan New York, Giorgio Armani and Stella McCartney for Chloé. Five companies provided shoes for actors and one – Jimmy Choo – for actresses. With the embracing of branding and licencing practices, celebrities appeared on the red-carpet wearing sunglasses and hats through a product placement deal with Cutler & Gross and Stephen Jones. Sunglasses companies led product placement practices in film and television. Scott's position lasted for just one year.

In 2001, Patty Fox brought the fashion coordinator position back and, with it, the fashion forecasts runway shows. Fox used her connection with Saks Fifth Avenue and continued with Hayman's old ritual of visiting showrooms in New York City to select gowns.[58] She described her position as devoted to couture and guided by the premise 'one gown for one body for one night', a paradoxical concept to define the era that virtually erased couture in favour of mass production.[59]

## A celebration of Oscar fashion

*Vogue*'s editor-at-large, André Leon Talley, replaced Fox in 2007, albeit for one year only. He organised a retrospective runway show in association with *Vogue*, featuring memorable Oscar looks under the title 'A Celebration of Oscar Fashion'. Oscarcast producer Laura Ziskin encouraged people to contact the Academy's publicity department with any leads about where to find gowns worn at previous Oscar ceremonies.

> We are still looking for some of the greatest dresses that were auctioned, like one of Mia Farrow's disco-era outfits, Julie Andrews' 1965 Oscar dress, one of Natalie Wood's dresses, or an exquisite gown that we haven't even thought of and that André may hope to include.[60]

Talley selected forty dresses for the event. Among these was Janet Leigh's 1960 gown, which went unnoticed once again in all press releases relating to the event. Instead, gowns worn by Cher, Annette Bening, Ingrid Bergman, Halle Berry, Cate Blanchett, Geena Davis, Edith Head, Angelina Jolie, Keira Knightley, Sophia Loren, Barbra Streisand, Elizabeth Taylor and Charlize Theron were promoted and made headlines.[61]

**Figure 8.1** 'A Celebration of Oscar Fashion' – the retrospective organised by André Leon Talley in association with *Vogue* as an Oscar fashion preview on 30 January 2007 in the lobby of the Academy headquarters. Photographer: Michael Buckner/Getty Images Entertainment Collection via Getty Images.

Talley took every chance to be on camera. He visited Rodeo Drive to interview designer Monique Lhuillier and anticipate the red-carpet parade. The voiceover described:

> I am right here in the middle of Rodeo Drive in Beverly Hills. It's no secret that top designers look at the Oscars as a time to show off their hottest looks, and the whole world tunes into the Oscars to see who is wearing what, who's gonna be on the best-dressed list and who is gonna be the best of the worst.[62]

Talley joined Allyson Waterman for that year's red-carpet pre-show, *Road to the Oscars 2007*, as a fashion commentator.[63] The show also featured Chris Connelly and Lisa Ling.

During the broadcast, fashion inserts showcased Talley and the show's preparations. He reviewed past gown choices with clips from *Vogue's* fashion pre-show and went shopping with actress Jennifer Hudson for an Academy Awards look. Hudson was nominated that night for Best Actress in a Supporting Role for *Dreamgirls* (Dreamworks/Paramount Pictures, 2006). In their makeover spree, they picked a brown draped dress by Oscar de la Renta and shoes from Manolo Blahnik.[64] For the red-carpet, Hudson topped the look with a gold python bolero, as instructed by Talley. Hudson won an Oscar that night, but the look spurred much criticism. She alllegedly disliked the dress and had intended to wear a Roberto Cavalli custom-made gown in gold, arranged for her by stylist Jessica Paster.[65] Motivated by an argument with an infuriated Talley, she wore the chosen dress for the ceremony and Cavalli's creation for the after-party. Whether the discussion actually took place or if it was the result of media gossip, Hudson's last-minute change of gown would have disrupted the production of the red-carpet pre-show, not to mention Talley's fashion credibility. No deals were made with fashion designers to provide dresses that year. Talley was dismissed after this brief *Vogue*scapade, and Patty Fox returned in 2008.

## Behind the dress

Another promotional build-up to replace Hayman's fashion shows was the 'Oscars Designer Challenge', featuring a group of young designers competing to create an Oscars look that would appear on the red carpet in 2009. The contest resulted in a short special for www.star.com, hosted by fashion designer Nick Verreos, former *Project Runway* participant and mentor. Patty Fox appears in her role as fashion coordinator for the event. The show did not have the same dynamic as a full design reality show. It consisted instead of a recap of the design process and the casting of the Awards escort who would parade the winning gown on the red carpet. Fox and the telecast producers were in charge of the pre-selection of the seven designers; the audience got to vote for the winning look through an online ballot.[66] The contest was held again in 2010. The reality web series documenting the competition, *Oscars Designer Challenge: Behind the Dress*, was released daily between 3 March and 8 March at www.oscar.com.[67] The winners were announced live on the red carpet, and the model escorting the Oscar statuette wore the winning gown.

Patty Fox remained the fashion coordinator until 2011, the last year the Oscars appointed someone to oversee the event's fashion. From then on, the show only featured costume designers, mirroring the 1970s. The reason behind the sudden discontinuation of the role is unclear. Arguably, the proliferation of stylists, red-carpet events and the direct endorsement contracts marked an instrumental shift in the business of fashion at the Oscars.

## Landing

The 1990s brought fashion discourses of the 1950s back in a new wave of globalisation that integrated the participation of international designers in the show. The association of fashion and the Oscars has historically been dialectic, benefiting all parties. The Oscars used fashion as a promotional tool for the media event in the 1950s. The 1990s consolidated the ceremony's role as a display window to the world through new technologies, generating brand equity. The global circulation of fashion-related content, by way of fashion's expansion in popular culture, enabled product placement practices. Celebrities turned into visible billboards, not least due to the vortextuality they generated through their participation in the show. In 2010, *Chicago Tribune* estimated that the fashion endorsement of one gown at the Oscarcast was worth $1 million in publicity for designers.[68] Audiences around the world became increasingly receptive and knowledgeable about fashion brands and their standing as symbols of prestige. This exposure served to create brand awareness, to position designer names and to establish local luxury hubs. The Oscars were up for big fashion business. By 2011, the LVMH conglomerate had accumulated more than sixty prestigious brands in its portfolio and expanded its retail network to more than 2,500 stores with 80,000 employees worldwide.[69] This consolidation of fashion conglomerates vis-à-vis the forces of globalisation gave the Oscars and the fashion industry unprecedented exposure. For the fashion industry, the new era had shifted business elsewhere – into the stock market, where the profits made surpassed those of any Oscar dresses they could sell.

# Notes

1. Olivia B. Waxman, "'I Was Just a Man Who Sang a Song About Freedom': 30 Years Later, David Hasselhoff Looks Back on His Surprising Role in the Fall of the Berlin Wall', *Time*, 7 November 2019.
2. For more about 1990s mergers and globalisation, see Tino Balio, "'A Major Presence in All the World Markets": The Globalization of Hollywood in the 1990s', in Steve Neale and Murray Smith, eds, *Contemporary Hollywood Cinema* (London: Routledge, 1998), 58–73.
3. Chris Holmlund, Introduction to *American Cinema of the 1990s: Themes and Variations* (New Brunswick, NJ: Rutgers University Press, 2008), 1–23. Holmlund mentions the new oligopoly of 'The Big Six', consisting of Disney, Warner Bros., Sony, Twentieth Century Fox, Universal and Paramount.
4. Desjardins, "'Marion Never Looked Lovelier", 434.
5. Farrell-Beck and Parsons, *20th Century Dress in the United States*, 241.
6. Regina Lee Blaszczyk, *American Consumer Society, 1865–2005* (Wheeling, IL: Harlan Davidson, Inc., 2005), 194.
7. 'Fred Hayman Named Fashion Coordinator for 62nd Oscar Show', Press Release, 7 March 1990, Academy Awards Ceremony Files, MHL; 'Fred Hayman Named Fashion Coordinator for 64th Oscar Show', Press Release, 21 January 1992, Academy Awards Ceremony Files, MHL; 'Fred Hayman Named Fashion Coordinator for 65th Oscar Show', Press Release, 27 January 1993, Academy Awards Ceremony Files, MHL; 'Fred Hayman Named Oscar Show Fashion Coordinator for Seventh Time', Press Release, 9 February 1995, Academy Awards Ceremony Files, MHL; 'Fred Hayman Named Oscar Show Fashion Coordinator for Eighth Time', Press Release, 26 January 1996, Academy Awards Ceremony Files, MHL; 'Hayman is Oscar Show Fashion Coordinator for Ninth Year', Press Release, 23 January 1997, Academy Awards Ceremony Files, MHL.
8. Appadurai, *Modernity at Large*, 49–50, 167.
9. Nelson Best, *The History of Fashion Journalism*, 201.
10. Ibid., 190.
11. Ibid., 200.
12. See Pamela Church Gibson, *Fashion and Celebrity Culture* (London: Berg, 2012), 83–102.
13. 'Fred Hayman Named 61st Oscar Show Fashion Coordinator', Press Release, 27 February 1989, Academy Awards Ceremony Files, MHL.
14. Rose Apodaca, *Fred Hayman, The Extraordinary Difference: The Story of Rodeo Drive, Hollywood Glamour and the Showman Who Sold It All* (Venice, CA: A+R Projects, 2011), 341.
15. Rachel Brown, 'Fred Hayman Recounts Wild Ride on Rodeo Drive', *Woman's Wear Daily*, 28 December 2011, 11.
16. Tamara Abraham, 'The Man Who Made Rodeo Drive: Giorgio Beverly Hills Founder Fred Hayman Joins Fashion Greats on Walk of Style', *Mailonline*, 2 June 2011, http://www.dailymail.co.uk/femail/article-1393332/The-man-Rodeo-Drive-Giorgio-Beverly-Hills-founder-Fred-Hayman-joins-fashion-greats-Walk-Of-Style.html/
17. Martha Groves, 'Giorgio Beverly Hills is Reestablished – Symbolically', *Los Angeles Times*, 2 May 2009, http://articles.latimes.com/2009/may/02/local/me-rodeodrive2/
18. Eye, 'Oscar Togs', *Women's Wear Daily*, 2 April 1974, 12.
19. Brown, 'Fred Hayman Recounts Wild Ride on Rodeo Drive', 11.

20. 'Avon Annual Report 1987', avon_annual_reports_1980s_00081, f. HD9970.5.T.654A45, Published Collections Department, Hagley Museum and Library. See also Steve Ginsberg, 'Giorgio's Michael Gould – Now It's His Turn', *Women's Wear Daily*, 17 July 1987, 7; 'Hear Revlon Eyes Giorgio, Beverly Hills', *Women's Wear Daily*, 20 December 1989, 2; Steve Ginsberg, 'Court Tells Hayman to Rewrite His Ad', *Women's Wear Daily*, 20 March 1989, 11.

21. 'Beverly Hills Giorgio Store has Good Start', *Women's Wear Daily*, 6 October 1989, 13.

22. 'Avon Annual Report 1989', avon_annual_reports_1980s_00001, f. HD9970.5.T654A45, Published Collections Department, Hagley Museum and Library.

23. Company Reports, 'Avon to Sell its Giorgio Unit for $150 Million to P&G', *The New York Times*, 27 July 1994; Bruce Horovitz, 'P&G to Buy Giorgio for $150 Million: Fragrances: The Purchase from Avon will Make Procter & Gamble a Leader in the Prestige Perfume Market', *Los Angeles Times*, 27 July 1994.

24. 'Listen: 9 Men and 7,000 Women', *Los Angeles Times*, 22 April 1988, G6.

25. Steve Ginsberg, 'Fred Hayman, from a Name to a Number', *Women's Wear Daily*, 28 November 1988, 16; Steve Ginsberg, 'Giorgio Planning Return to Rodeo Drive in Sept.', *Women's Wear Daily*, 27 June 1989, 10.

26. Jane Galbraith, 'A Look Inside Hollywood and the Movies. THE FASHION GAME Don't Read This One Either', *Los Angeles Times*, 21 March 1993, 18.

27. Maureen Sajbel, 'The Best Dress Competition: Fashion: The Academy Awards Make for TV's Most Glamorous Night', *Los Angeles Times*, 25 May 1990, E1.

28. Ibid., E1.

29. Academy Awards Program, 1988 (61st) Academy Awards, Academy Awards Collection, MHL.

30. Academy Awards Program, 62nd Annual Academy Awards 1990, Award Ephemera, CEYRL.

31. References to these runway shows date back to 1993, but some media outlets place their beginning as early as 1991. See Marcy Medina, 'Obituary, Patty Fox, Oscars' Fashion Coordinator', *Women's Wear Daily*, 28 September 2010, 11; 'Pre-Dawn Nominations Announcement Kicks Off Five Weeks of Activities and Photo-Ops . . .', *Academy Report* 5.1 (Spring 1993): 4, Academy History Archive, MHL.

32. 'Patty Fox Returns as Oscar Fashion Coordinator', Press Release, 14 January 2003, Academy Awards Ceremony Files, MHL.

33. Kristin Young, 'Stores Flock to Hollywood Venue', *Women's Wear Daily*, 7 May 2001, 22.

34. An Oral History of Howard W. Koch interviewed by Douglas Bell, 118, 1999, W1308787, Oral History Collection, MHL.

35. Ibid.

36. Ibid.

37. Lorenza Muñoz, 'The New Bleacher Features', *Los Angeles Times*, 4 February 2002.

38. Pre-Show Camera Plot, Series 1, Box 2, f. Awards 71st Annual Academy Awards Pre-Show 1999 Technical Information, Stephen L. Pouliot Collection, Raynor Memorial Libraries, Marquette University, Department of Special Collections and University Archives (hereafter Marquette University).

39. 'Sunday at the Oscars' – Pre-show One-Page Rundown Series 1, Box 2, f. 16 Awards 71st Annual Academy Awards Pre-Show 1999 Press, Stephen L. Pouliot Collection, Marquette University.

40. Sunday at the Oscars Pre-Show final Draft, Box 2, f. 18 Awards, 71st Annual Academy Awards Pre-Show 1999 script, Stephen L. Pouliot Collection, Marquette University.

41. Sunday at the Oscars – 71st Annual Academy Awards pre-show, W062315, Pickford Center, AMPAS.
42. Oscars Countdown Show Routine Revised as of 2/19/99, and Sunday at the Oscars pre-show Rundown, 31 March 1999, Series 1, Box 2, f. 17 Awards 71st Annual Academy Awards Pre-Show 1999 Rundowns, Stephen L. Pouliot Collection, Marquette University.
43. Sunday at the Oscars Pre-Show Final Draft, Box 2, f. 18 Awards, 71st Annual Academy Awards Pre-Show 1999 Script, Stephen L. Pouliot Collection, Marquette University.
44. 'Academy Awards Pre-Show' file, Academy Awards Collection, MHL. The show changed names in the following years to *Countdown to the Oscars, Oscar Countdown, On the Red Carpet, Road to the Oscars* and *Oscars' Red Carpet Live,* among others. See also 'Fred Hayman to Coordinate Fashions for the 1998 Oscars', 20 January 1999, Press Releases, Academy Awards Collection, MHL.
45. Brian Stelter, 'The Quirky Oscar Red Carpet Rule That Helps ABC', *CNN* Business, 22 February 2015, https://money.cnn.com/2015/02/22/media/oscars-red-carpet-tv-rules/
46. 'Fred Hayman to Coordinate Fashions for the 1998 Oscars', 20 January 1999, Press Releases, Academy Awards Collection, MHL.
47. Ibid.
48. Among the many hosts are Robin Roberts, Jess Cagle, Lara Spencer, Kelly Rowland, Louise Roe, Krista Smith, Maria Menounos, Sherri Shepherd, Regis Philbin, Samantha Harris, Shaun Robinson, Lisa Ling, Allyson Waterman, Vanessa Minillo, Cynthia Garrett and Billy Bush.
49. 'Unforgettable: Fashion of the Oscars', Christie's catalogue, Thursday 18 March 1999. New York Sponsored by *VOGUE,* f. 17, Janet Leigh Papers, MHL. For footage of the auction see 'USA: New York: Oscars Charity Dress Auction', AP from APTN, no. 112609, 19 March 1999, AP Archive.
50. 'On with Show Business', *Women's Wear Daily,* 12 March 1999, 29.
51. 'Picking the Trends from Oscar Night', *Women's Wear Daily,* 29 March 2000, 13.
52. 'On with Show Business', 30.
53. Eric Wilson, 'The Culture of Copycats', *Women's Wear Daily,* 2 November 1999, 10.
54. The Celebrity Dresses, 2008–20, https://www.thecelebritydresses.com/catalogsearch/result/?q=oscars
55. Kathleen Caulderwood, 'Businesses That Copy Oscar Dresses Face Counterfeiting from Chinese Websites', *International Business Times,* 28 February 2014.
56. Ibid.
57. 'Stylist L'Wren Scott to Coordinate Oscar Night Attire', Press Release, 24 February 2000, Academy Awards Ceremony Files, MHL.
58. 'Academy Hosts the 2001 Fashion Preview', Press Release, 8 March 2001, Academy Awards Ceremony Files, MHL.
59. Marcy Medina, 'Couture According to Fox', *Women's Wear Daily,* 26 February 2001, 17.
60. 'AMPAS Seeks Memorable Oscar Fashions', Press Release, 9 January 2007, Academy Awards Ceremony Files, MHL.
61. 'Talley Brings Glamour Back from Past Academy Awards', Press Release, 30 January 2007, Academy Awards Ceremony Files, MHL.
62. W089036 79th Academy Awards Oscar.com video content compilation, Pickford Center, AMPAS.

63. 'André Leon Talley Named Oscar Pre-Show Host', Press Release, 30 January 2007, Academy Awards Ceremony Files, MHL.

64. W087851 Road to the Oscars 2007 pulled blacks, Pickford Center, AMPAS.

65. Wendy Donahue, 'The Truth About Hudson's Oscar Gown', *Chicago Tribune*, 4 March 2007.

66. See 'Academy Announces Oscars Designer Challenge', Press Release, 10 February 2009, Academy Awards Collection, MHL.

67. 'Academy Announces Oscars Designer Challenge', Press Release, in email correspondence, 23 February 2010, Series 1, Box 5, f. 5 Awards 82nd Annual Academy Awards Correspondence 2010 Technical Information, Stephen L. Pouliot Collection, Marquette University.

68. Julie Neigher, 'Dressing for Oscar: Actresses-Designer Collaborations Have a Dazzling Back Story – Before Kidman and Galliano, There Was Dietrich and Dior', *Chicago Tribune*, 4 March 2010, 4.

69. English, *A Cultural History of Fashion*, 143.

# 9

# Twilight of the idols

On 26 February 2014, CBS news anticipated the Academy Awards ceremony with a photo gallery entitled 'Hollywood Royalty at the Oscars' comprising eight pictures taken between 1955 and 1978.[1] Unintentionally, these images captured the historical transition whereby Hollywood stars were turned into royalty by the power of celebrity culture. The Oscars red-carpet has become a much anticipated annual parade for this ruling elite of entertainment's kings and queens of the American Century and its aftermath. Modernity's advent of mass production has impinged on exclusive realms, seemingly democratising them. Such is also the case with mass-produced and ephemeral celebrities. Fashion endorsement of high-end brands on the red-carpet, and the representation of celebrities as Hollywood royalty, are manifestations of an aspirational and seemingly transformative nature of commodity consumption, in which pecuniary emulation creates the illusion of social prestige.

Democratisation is relative. Every elite structure requires exclusion to sustain its status. There is no equal redistribution of wealth, power or prestige, only a vortex that keeps the centre further away as more are included and, subsequently, excluded. These elite systems propel an industry that profits from desire, disguised beneath a veneer of social mobility and possible social inclusion. Instead of celebrating the presumed democratising nature of celebrity culture, it is time to start questioning this worshipping attitude towards this new privileged elite of strangers. This chapter critically addresses the dichotomies and disparities between discourses and actions, while problematising the role of celebrities in culture at large. It provides an overview of different scenarios of political empowerment that have arisen in recent years. In doing so, it provides a glimpse into the red carpet's symbolic standing in contemporary culture while underlining the reasons why we should be questioning our fascination with it.

## The red-carpet: a space of spectacle, a space of reflection, a celebrity

Red-carpet events are the new catwalks of the twenty-first century.[2] Among these, the Academy Awards stands at the apex of all red-carpet events, closing the awards season. Fans have even built a tradition out of following what celebrities wear in this build-up towards Oscars night, with the Golden Globes being a sneak peek into which promising celebrity may transcend during the final red-carpet stroll.

In recent years, media outlets around the globe have replicated articles following the entire trajectory of the actual fabric that constitutes the carpet, recording every stage of the journey from the moment it arrives in trucks to its unrolling, cleaning and staging, turning the carpet itself into a celebrity. The Academy's official YouTube channel released *Inside the Oscars*, a series of short behind-the-scenes footage addressing different aspects of the ceremony, including the red-carpet pre-show set-up. The host promises to take the viewer on 'a stroll down the most fashionable walkway in Hollywood [and to] give a sneak peek on how all the magic happens, [to give] a sense of what is actually like to walk the red carpet on Oscar Sunday'.[3] Different staff members reflect upon it, with descriptions from the technical and practical aspects of the experience.[4] The expressions used to describe exiting the arrival tent and stepping on to the red-carpet are 'amazing', 'electric', 'loud', 'crowded', 'intimidating' and 'controlled chaos'.

As the clip approaches the end, the non-diegetic music reaches an emotional crescendo. Neil Meron, producer of the 86th Academy Awards ceremony, narrates the epic experience of being on the red carpet for the viewers:

> Walking down the Oscars red carpet is unlike anything that anybody has ever experienced. It is like ascending to Mount Olympus, it's like balahala [sic]. You are with the movie gods. It's like some dream-like experience cos you are at the height of glamour; you are at the height of the business. Just to get to the Oscars is the aspirational dream of anybody that is associated to film. So, that carpet takes on so much more than actually walking it.[5]

The reference to celebrities as 'gods of Mount Olympus' establishes them as superiors, not only from a perspective of capital (social, economic or cultural) but also due to their ascribed godlike qualities. The cult of celebrities is presented as a new religion. The essence of the red-carpet event was to see how the stars 'really were', how they behaved and dressed 'out of character'. In these equally constructed performances, they are now presented as gods.

In 2014, a *Vanity Fair* photographer wrote an article entitled 'What's it *Really* Like to Be on the Oscars Red Carpet?' in which he described his ten years' experience covering the event.[6] He sets 'the carpet' as a protagonist, enhancing the transformative qualities of entering the physical space as though inhabiting this heterotopia automatically ascribed status and prestige. But then again, what is prestige? As with 'glamour', the etymology of prestige carries entirely negative connotations. Prestige originally meant deceit and illusion.[7] Prestigious meant deceitful or illusory. Neither of these words connoted sophistication or luxury.

The magnitude of the red-carpet pre-show demands an entire production team of its own, at least since the Academy joined efforts with ABC in 1999. While red-carpet interviews are perceived as spontaneous, leading to the bashing of reporters for asking the wrong questions, the red-carpet broadcast is a much more choreographed venture. It includes not only a pre-selection of those who will appear in the press line but also a script with a reservoir of potential questions. Even the opening montage of images is carefully scripted. The red-carpet is not conceived as a space of dialogue, as many would hope. The producers meticulously schedule the stops along the promenade to keep up with the flow of celebrities along the press line. The format itself does not invite an in-depth conversation of the type that could emerge in the intimate setting of *Inside the Actors Studio* (Bravo, 1994–2018). In an era where celebrities open up through social media, it is pertinent to question this constructed façade of pageantry and glamour.

## A space of protest

Photographic records outside theatres in Chicago and Washington DC registered anti-racist protests against *Gone with the Wind* (MGM) in 1940.[8] That year, Hattie McDaniel became the first black winner of an Academy Award for her performance in the film.[9] McDaniel sat at the banquet that night only after David O. Selznick intervened, and was segregated from her fellow nominees at a corner table.[10] Fay Bainter warmly introduced McDaniel with a highly political speech, referring to the award as a door opener that moved back the walls to embrace America as a whole, paying tribute to their best regardless of creed, race or colour. Bainter's speech can be judged for erasing the contemporary problem with racism in the US, or it can, if given context, be understood as a wishful expression with an underlying political note of how inclusion and diversity could be at the core of American values. By then, the Nazi regime's actions had led to the outbreak of World War II. The racist basis for the war touched the roots of Hollywood's community closely.[11] That year, the Academy and Warner Bros. took a radical political stand when including Bainter's presentation and McDaniel's speech in the short film *Cavalcade of Academy Awards*, screening a scene of integration across the country despite the potential controversies.

The ceremony's mediatisation and reach turned it into a stage for political exposure. After all, the red carpet has a line-up of international journalists ready to reproduce news events. In 1978, the Jewish Defence League opposed Vanessa Redgrave's nomination for Best Supporting Actress in *Julia* (20th Century Fox, 1977) after she produced a pro-Palestine documentary.[12] In 1979, members of the Vietnam Veterans Against the War organisation were arrested when protesting *The Deer Hunter* (Universal Pictures, 1978) for its racist presentation of Vietnamese people.[13] That same year, Susan Power hit the red-carpet wearing a 100-year-old Sioux heirloom, after appearing in *The Divided Trail: A Native American Odyssey* (Jerry Aronson, 1977), a nominated documentary that shed light on the segregation of Native Americans. In 1987, fans carried signs to raise awareness of the rapidly rising numbers of homeless people in the US. Celebrities wore the AIDS red ribbon to raise awareness of HIV in 1992.[14] Outside, the activist group Queer Nation protested against the number of homicidal queer characters and the lack of any positive representation on screen.[15] The following year, the president of Black Entertainment Television requested that African-American entertainers wear a purple ribbon to draw attention to urban violence.[16] In 1999, people spontaneously mobilised when the Academy honoured Elia Kazan with a Lifetime Achievement Academy Award.[17] Kazan testified before the HUAC in 1952, helping persecute and blacklist his colleagues during McCarthyism. Crowds also protested Jerry Lewis's Humanitarian Award in 2009, alleging that the comedian had built a career out of being funny at the expense of disability.[18]

With the eyes of the world watching and forty-five uncensored seconds guaranteed, the ceremony's stage also became an opportunity for political intervention. In 1973, Howard W. Koch allegedly threatened to arrest Sacheen Littlefeather if she went on stage to accept the Oscar on behalf of Marlon Brando.[19] In her speech, she addressed the film industry's mistreatment of Native Americans and invited journalists to the press area for further discussions. In 1993, Susan Sarandon and Tim Robbins called out Washington for the criminalisation of HIV and Richard Gere pleaded for Tibetan independence. Michael Moore questioned President George W. Bush's Middle East interventionist agenda in 2003, and Jared Leto acknowledged the political tensions in Ukraine and Venezuela in 2014.

**Figure 9.1** Susan Power wearing a 100-year-old Sioux heirloom for the 51st Academy Awards ceremony in 1979. She was featured in the nominated documentary *The Divided Trail: A Native American Odyssey* (Jerry Aronson, 1977). Photographer Chris Gulker, *Los Angeles Herald Examiner* Photo Collection. Courtesy of Los Angeles Public Library.

These events showcase the potential of public exposure and invite reflection on the possibility of shifting these spaces of distraction into spaces of con-scientisation. The risk is that the same glamour that surrounds them casts a shadow of banality over problematics that affect millions of people beyond the film industry. Social media hashtags have provided new mechanisms to propagate these messages, but how empowering are these for those in vulnerable situations? Are there networks of contention set up for them, or does the searchlight of celebrity discourse blind public opinion, leaving only a sensation of accomplishment?

## #AskHerMore

In 2014, Jennifer Siebel Newsom launched the #AskHerMore campaign, urging reporters to ask women about their professions instead of their looks. The hashtag gained momentum in 2015, when Reese Witherspoon turned it into a Twitter campaign. Witherspoon explained that the movement drove attention to actresses as 'more than just the dresses', stressing how hard it is to be a woman in any industry. Witherspoon sparked the conversation, tackling the historical representation of actresses' bodies as vessels for consumption – and for the promotion of commodity consumption – that goes back to the days of silent cinema. It also shed light on the residual conception of women as sole consumers of so-called trivial feminine topics, a stereotype created in tandem with the emergence of the beauty industry, photography and other modern phenomena that became visible through the growth of advertising and the printed press. These discourses were disseminated throughout the country and exported around the globe, moulding and enforcing gender stereotypes and resulting in a questionable tradition of scrutinising the female body as a site of spectacle.

Giorgio Armani described the fashion frenzy surrounding the Oscars as 'disturbing' in 1999, describing how '[w]hen a star on Oscar night is quizzed first about her jewels and dress, it marginalises the substance of the occasion'.[20] Change cannot rely merely on discourse. Commodification is intrinsic to consumer culture. Does Witherspoon's legitimate complaint lose credibility as actresses continue to profit from fashion endorsement? After all, promoting these designers if they are wearing their gowns is also part of the job, if they have entered into a deal to do so. Witherspoon wore a Tom Ford dress to the Oscars during the #AskHerMore campaign and posted photos on social media. An angry Ford jumped into the controversy, alleging that the designer's name had to be at the centre of conversations because red-carpet events force designers to work for months, making five different dresses for

reesewitherspoon ⊚ • Follow   ⋯

reesewitherspoon ⊚ Show time! 💜
#Oscars (dress @TomFord; jewels
@TiffanyAndCo; styling @lesliefremar;
hair by @hairbyadir; glow @mrsbymrs )

284w

⊕

♡ ◯ ▽                          ◁

**174,061 likes**

FEBRUARY 23, 2015

Add a comment...

**Figure 9.2**  Reese Witherspoon promoting her Oscar look on Instagram for the 87th Academy Awards ceremony in 2015. (@reesewitherspoon)

each actress and spending hundreds of thousands of dollars, not to mention those that paid celebrities for their endorsement.[21] From this perspective, the red-carpet conversation should be seen as a business platform and not only as a cultural performance. Actresses accept these conditions when they sign an endorsement contract. On reflection, #AskHerMore can also be understood as a privileged problem, placing actresses who engage in these practices as functional to a network of oppression that filters down into society and culture.

This discussion needs to acknowledge the origins of the red-carpet as a fashion-related phenomenon to help the promotion of films, actresses and actors and the event itself. Fashion and glamour were brought to the forefront to satisfy the audiences' thirst for Hollywood splendour. Much has changed since, so it is pertinent to ask if this illusory approach to red-carpet events should continue to exist at all.

## Not naming names

In 2003, producers toned down the spectacle in the context of the Iraq war. All fashion-related questions vanished from interviews.[22] Discussions were sparked among fashion and jewellery designers who wondered if it was worth the investment and effort without any subsequent mentions. Understanding the force majeure context, Carolina Herrera found this decision pertinent given the circumstances and Calvin Klein did not think the absence of a mention would impact sales.[23] Many celebrities opted for simpler wardrobe choices, while others wore millions of dollars' worth in jewellery yet remained reluctant to plug designers. The pre-show caviar and champagne VIP treatment in hotel suites continued behind closed doors.[24] This dichotomy between discourse and action evokes the importance of Boorstin's critical understanding of 'the image', insofar as the image of reality that coats these public appearances has become more valuable than actual change, making it crucial to question what real action and change mean.

Social media and endorsement contracts are ways around this name-dropping demand. As brand ambassadors, celebrities work for brands all year round, appearing in advertising campaigns for perfumes and cosmetics. The presence of brand ambassadors on red carpets is growing. In 2018, Emma Stone landed a $10 million contract as ambassador for Louis Vuitton, becoming the centre of fashion conversations as the specialist media waits to see what the brand will design for each new red-carpet appearance.[25] Louis Vuitton also signed Alicia Vikander, Gucci recruited Dakota Johnson, Zoe Kravitz signed with Saint Laurent, Chanel has Margot Robbie under contract, while Dior lists Natalie Portman, Charlize Theron and Jennifer Lawrence.

### Do you ask these questions to the guys?

The scrutinising eye of fashion critics has been indisputably tyrannical when discussing women's appearances on the red-carpet. Jennifer Lawrence expressed her discomfort about how certain shows, such as E!'s *Fashion Police* (2002– ), encouraged mean critiques about women's bodies instead of the dresses.[26] During E!'s 1993 red-carpet coverage, *Glamour* magazine journalist Charla Krupp asked her co-host, *Star* magazine journalist Janet Charlton, about a potential bias when putting men and women under the fashion scanner. Are we being too hard on all the women and letting the men off the hook, Krupp pondered.[27] 'We'd never do that', replied Charlton. 'All a man has to do to be ready for the Oscars is put on a tuxedo, shave and jump into a limo.'[28]

Red-carpet questions negotiate industries' demands and viewers' expectations. It is naive to think that these come from the anchors' creative minds. All ABC's red-carpet interviewees are pre-selected, notified and confirmed, and pre-show scriptwriters prepare customised questionnaires for them that are meticulously revised and rehearsed.[29] As a general rule, the interviewees are presenters and nominees for that night. It is true that more women than men are asked about their fashion choices, but this does not imply that there are no fashion questions scripted for men. The industry has pushed to include men's fashion discourses. This was particularly evident in the 1990s, when the high-end menswear market expanded. Fred Hayman encouraged variations on the tuxedo, and the Academy included Tom Julian, a menswear expert, for their online coverage of the red-carpet that year.[30]

With reporters unusually interested in menswear during the 1990s, Fred Hayman encouraged designers to follow in the footsteps of Armani, Versace, Gucci, Hugo Boss, Richard Tyler, Ermenegildo Zegna, Donna Karan and Cerruti in introducing variations to lead the trends.[31] These discourses experienced a revival in 2007, with Italian designer Domenico Vacca forecasting an increase in male fashion-related discussion as actors enter similar endorser agreements.

## #MeToo and Time's Up

The year 2017 marked a hinge moment for sexism in the film industry when several actresses accused Harvey Weinstein of sexual harassment and assault. Alyssa Milano's #MeToo tweet started a conversation, but the original MeToo had emerged a decade earlier, when activist Tarana Burke began working with survivors of sex crimes. Milano contacted her to suggest they join forces. The traction of Hollywood exposure put Burke under the spotlight. Contrasting the eleven years that passed between the emergence of this group and its immediate acknowledgment after Milano's tweet unravels the same system of injustice that marginalised those vulnerable women in the first place. Under the #MeToo hashtag, Hollywood celebrities and millions of anonymous women were united in the same suffering. As noble as that sounds, the need to have these powerful women affected in order to address these issues in the first place calls for an intersectional perspective to this debate.

Allegations against other Hollywood personalities increased after the overwhelming number of victims who came forward led to Weinstein's trial and incarceration, and other powerful men in the industry were exposed when Hollywood actresses launched the 'Time's Up' initiative.[32] In 2018, #MeToo and Time's Up hit the Golden Globes red-carpet with an unofficial dress code of all black. The intention behind wearing only black was to deflect attention away from the dresses.[33] Uniformity created a collective impact, while repetition allowed nothing to stand out, working as a powerful statement to gatekeep any digressions.

Feminist groups criticised the Golden Globes parade. Actress Rose McGowan called out the strategy, suggesting that 'a real silent protest' would have been refusing to attend, arguing that 'they'd care if the women refuse to make money for them'.[34] Journalist Jenny McCartney questioned the authenticity of red-carpet feminism by outing a double standard, stating that the event would 'be yet another example of female grooming taken to insane levels of time, effort and money'.[35] Far from disregarding the actresses' struggle and their valid claim for equal rights, particularly at an early stage of their career when many lack the clout to stand up for themselves, she pointed out how established actresses continue to be functional to an industry that has historically fostered women's insecurities. While the point is not to bring any more pressure on women regarding how they should transit their feminist awakening, shedding light on the contradictions that continue to emerge in a world that is transversally crossed by the residuals of patriarchal ideologies is essential.

There was no black dress code for the 90th anniversary of the Oscars. Jennifer Todd, one of the ceremony's producers, explained that they wanted to keep the focus on the films and not on 'the cultural moment around them', making it 'as entertaining as possible – reverential and respectful'.[36] ABC's president explained that they wanted to give air space to the Time's Up movement, but in an organised way that would not 'overshadow the artists and films being honoured'.[37] The movement secured a slot to speak on stage and encouraged actresses to invite activists as their guests to the event.[38] Burke gave several interviews on the red-carpet that night, expressing her concern about the attention drawn to Hollywood. 'I think focus has to shift from Hollywood at this point, because there are millions of people around the world asking for help'.[39]

### Kept Seacrest

Ryan Seacrest's former stylist publicly accused him of sexual misconduct days before the ceremony, alleging years of abuse endured in fear of losing her job while a single mother.[40] Seacrest denied the allegations. E! stood by him; they fired her and conducted an internal investigation that concluded there was 'insufficient evidence'. Nominated actresses refused to talk to Seacrest on the red carpet and E! avoided #MeToo altogether that night. The network bounced back to dresses and designers, focusing on their GlamBot, a robotic high-speed camera that takes a succession of photographs to create a slow-motion clip. Celebrities usually flip their gown this way and that to enhance the camera's glamorous effect.[41] The general pre-show was described as awkward, 'as hosts attempted to mention politics without getting too political'.[42]

## Blurring the gender code

Gender diversity has never seen such a vibrant moment of mainstream discussion. In 2019, Billy Porter made worldwide news after wearing a Christian Siriano tuxedo-gown, described by *Vogue* as 'a play on masculinity and femininity'.[43] Porter declared that his goal was to be a walking piece of political art to challenge expectations.[44] Plenty of women had already challenged the rigid dress code. Back in the mid-1960s, Edith Head was as scandalised about mini-skirts as she was about women wearing trousers. Barbra Streisand's 1969 Scaasi ensemble was scandalously revealing. Jane Fonda's black Yves Saint Laurent trouser suit sobriety in 1972 and Bob Mackie's silver satin suit excess for Diana Ross in 1973 are two juxtaposing examples of women in so-called menswear. Other examples are Ellen Burstyn's 1977 black tuxedo, Diane Keaton's white suits in 1976, 1997 and 2004, Celine Dion in 1999, Angelina Jolie in 2001 and Emma Stone's Louis Vuitton pantsuit in 2019. Porter wore a gown again in 2020, but the establishment had now incorporated his fashion statement into the usual pool of red-carpet critique.

### Your money where your mouth is

Natalie Portman appeared on the red-carpet wearing a black cape embroidered with the names of women directors in 2020. The Dior ensemble made it on to countless best-dressed lists. Social media users called Portman out on her 'performative white feminism', accusing her of being a hypocrite for not hiring any female directors in her production company.[45] Rose McGowan unapologetically labelled Portman's attitude of 'acting the part of someone who cares' as 'deeply offensive'.[46] McGowan's peripheral critique underlines the double standard of an industry that continues to reject blunt criticism, but performatively supports enough controversy to appease minimum social demands.

## The future of fashion on the red carpet

As seen throughout this book, the red-carpet dynamics are a response to the synergies between the fashion and film industries. Questions of sustainability are knocking hard on the fashion industry's door amid climate change. For a business that relies on fast-paced trends, bridging discourse and action has become the foremost challenge. Can the fashion industry solve the equation of sustainability and profit margins? Or will sustainability remain a PR discourse of corporate commitment?

## Sustainability

In 2013, nominee Helen Hunt wore a strapless dress in midnight blue silk satin by H&M. The dress was an eco-friendly design to launch their Conscious Collection through a liaison with the environmentalist group Global Green.[47]

The selection of an affordable brand is also a statement of inclusion, standing against the hierarchies exacerbated by discourses of privilege. The dress's estimated retail price of $650 would have supposedly made the unaffordable luxury of red-carpet gowns accessible to a broader audience. The media attacked the seemingly inferior quality of the dress, but the eco-friendly angle put the conversation to the forefront. Discourses of sustainability contradict the consumption cycle that fast-fashion retailers encourage and therefore should be put under a magnifying glass. The H&M initiative did not prosper, but discussions about sustainability remained.

'Red Carpet Green Dress' entered into an association with the Oscars in 2020, seeking 'to draw attention to the importance of more sustainable practices in fashion'.[48] The organisation was formed in 2009 and focuses on eco-practices and developing biodegradable textiles for sustainable products. They have also engaged fashion brands in using previous collections for endorsement purposes. In 2017, for example, Emma Roberts endorsed them by wearing an Armani Privé dress from 2005.

Adding to this recycling trend, actress Rita Moreno captured everyone's attention when, for the 2018 red-carpet, she wore a modified version of the gown she had worn in 1962. At the age of eighty-seven, Moreno's vintage chic climbed the 'best-dressed' lists, revitalising her career for a new generation. Moreno expressed her support for current political movements, reflecting on the difficulties she had faced when working in Hollywood as a Latina.[49] Los Angeles has countless high-end vintage stores. These gowns, however, may not offer the opportunity to cash in on the economic benefits of endorsement contracts, unless the dress belongs to the brand's 'heritage' collection.

## Heritage and the return of couture

Vintage dresses can bridge endorsement and sustainability, offering branding opportunities while reflecting positively on corporate image. Even though real sustainability rests on minimising consumption in order to decrease production, this is an idea no brand would embrace. Heritage has become the industry's buzzword in recent years. Unlike vintage, the word 'heritage' connotes a certain flair with regard to the cultural products, ascribing a symbolic value that makes them worth preserving. Heritage enhances these pieces from clothes to museum-worthy artefacts.

Italian designer Valentino is a precursor of putting dresses from what he calls 'the Valentino Archives' on the red-carpet.[50] As far back as 2001, Julia Roberts received her Oscar wearing a vintage Valentino dress from 1992. More brands

**Figure 9.3** Above: Rita Moreno at the 34th Academy Awards Ceremony in 1962, when she won the statuette for Best Supporting Actress for *West Side Story* (The Mirisch Corporation, 1961). Below: Moreno wearing a modified version of her Oscar-winning dress at the 2018 Oscars. The gown was made in the Philippines using a Japanese obi for the skirt. Academy Awards Collection. Courtesy of ©A.M.P.A.S.®

are now following this lead. In 2020, Margot Robbie wore a Chanel gown from 1994. For these brands, having their ambassadors wearing vintage gowns continues to create brand equity, improves their image in terms of corporate responsibility and saves them time and money that goes into creating a new Oscar look.

In recent years, brands like Louis Vuitton and Dior have returned to the custom-made tradition for dressing their brand ambassadors. These brands that originally emerged as couture houses now have to present their gowns through a sub-branding strategy that adds the word 'couture' to the brand name (Dior Couture Collection). In revisiting couture, they are positioning themselves within a discourse of the atelier's mystique. This allure of sophistication as a nod to the fashion industry before the age of mass production has led to the resurgence of emblematic names that built Hollywood glamour during the 1930s. Elsa Schiaparelli closed her atelier in the late 1950s, unable to compete with the ready-to-wear sector, and died in 1973. The brand, however, returned to the fashion scene in 2014.[51] Emily Blunt walked the red carpet in 2018 with an ice-blue gown of layered tulle and lace, putting Schiaparelli back into the best-dressed lists. In 2017, *The Hollywood Reporter* announced that the 'architect of classic Hollywood glamour', Adrian, was about 'to get a second life'.[52] Adrian Original is the relaunch of Gilbert Adrian's heritage in a fashion present that is looking to profit from the past. This rebranding arrived on the Oscars red-carpet in 2019 but went unnoticed. It remains to be seen if this Hollywood comeback will succeed, with retail prices starting at $1,900 for an evening gown.

## The eternal return of the same

Discussions about returning to 'the real Hollywood' continue to clash with ideas about modernising the event. In 2016, scriptwriter Buz Kohan described how every new producer believes their innovative vision will improve the show. Kohan describes the Oscars as 'a dinosaur. If you paint it green, it's a green dinosaur. If you paint it red, it's a red dinosaur. But still, it's a dinosaur'.[53] His observation tackles the core of this endless quest to find a new identity for an event inspired by the emulation of rigid ceremonial traditions. These nostalgic discourses evidence how the studio system's mythical image has been carved in stone in popular culture. The idea of a 'real Hollywood style' at the Oscars dating back to the 1930s remains anchored in the idealisation of on-screen looks that did not translate into what the stars wore to the event at the time. The closest to this ideal of grandiose elegance was the style that Edith

**Figure 9.4** Emily Blunt crowning the return of Schiaparelli to the Oscars red-carpet at the 90th Academy Awards ceremony in 2017. Photographer: Michael Baker. *Academy Awards Collection*. Courtesy of ©A.M.P.A.S.®

Head helped construct and promote during the 1950s, fuelled by the vibrant fashion landscape of the postwar era.

Throughout all periods of fashion at the Academy Awards, actresses, if not wearing their own clothes, have been dressed either by costume designers or fashion designers. It is the way fashion at the Academy Awards has been mediated concomitantly with the changes happening in the fashion and film industries that has changed the dynamics and our perception of fashion at the Oscars. The tables turned in the 1990s when the red-carpet became functional to the fashion industry and not the other way round. Endorsement demands today inevitably shift power towards the fashion brands as contractors. As problematic and controversial as this commodification appears, celebrities embellish the showcased gowns in this contemporary dynamic. While endorsement contracts objectify actresses' bodies as they are rented to display a gown, there is no coercion of actresses' agency since they no longer work under the studio system's laborious conditions.

The red-carpet enables the possibility of using fashion as a political statement. It also allows fashion not to be used at all, instead acting as a statement to focus on the actresses' work. The plural mediascape has given voice to anonymous users around the globe to function as decoders in a deconstruction of discourses until they finally – hopefully – become actions. Yet to be seen is an honest rebellion against the entire status quo of red-carpet events, one that tackles not only gender discussions about the oppressive nature of discourses that reinforce acceptable patterns of femininity, but also the exacerbation of privilege and the performance of class values and class identity based on the emulation of Western monarchic traditions.

At this point it is redundant to say that the fashion industry has predominantly perpetuated a beauty canon that rehashes the Gibson Girl: feminine, white, slender and young. In fact, the best-known luxury brand ambassadors fit this *physique du rôle*. After her appearance on the red carpet in 2014, Lupita Nyong'o became the first black brand ambassador for Lancôme.[54] Amid the #OscarsSoWhite campaign, Rihanna became the first black ambassador for Dior in 2015, as did Willow Smith for Chanel in 2016.[55] Nyong'o has committed to a more profound cause, authoring the children's book *Sulwe* and entering into discussions in the media about how colourism affected her.[56] Nyong'o's noble initiative reminds us that real conversation surpasses a small group of privileged celebrities and the veneer of change with the purpose of increasing aspirational consumption.

## Awakening

In 2002, the Academy Awards ceremony returned to Hollywood, in a theatre built specifically to cater to its needs. Oscar found in the former Kodak

Theatre a place to call home. During the days leading up to the ceremony, traffic is rerouted down Highland Avenue to set up the bleachers and the tent and to lay out the red carpet for the event. The juxtaposition of urban life along Hollywood Boulevard and the red carpet staging synthesise this heterotopia's illusory construction as a space created annually to represent a Hollywood kingdom. The corner of Highland marks the boundary between urban life and this symbolic space. Limousines stop briefly on Highland for celebrities and stars to step out onto the asphalt and walk the few steps leading to this socially ranked space. The tent's exit leads to the red carpet, to the heterotopic space that Hollywood has created as a harbinger of glamour. In the car park, some limousine drivers 'get into heavy poker games while waiting for their "loads" [customers]'.[57] Back on Highland, the public buses continue with urban life's routine, signalling how the symbolic distance is broader than the geographical one. Once the ceremony is over and the structures have been rapidly dismantled, the thousands of tourists and character impersonators that populate the walk of fame daily return to step on the same pavement that Hollywood elites inhabited only hours before. By then, the shopping mall has lost its special power to ascribe social status to those entering the Dolby Theatre.

## Notes

1. 'Hollywood Royalty at the Oscars', *CBS News*, https://www.cbsnews.com/pictures/hollywood-royalty-at-the-oscars/
2. Church Gibson, *Fashion and Celebrity Culture*, 53.
3. Oscars, 'Inside the Oscars: The Red Carpet Show', *YouTube*, https://www.youtube.com/watch?v=6u7gLSUedkQ/
4. 'Oscar Awards Swept by "West Side Story"', *Los Angeles Times*, 10 April 1962, 1.
5. Oscars, 'Inside the Oscars', *YouTube*. He may be referring to Valhalla, the place inhabited by the gods in Nordic mythology.
6. Julie Miller, 'What's It *Really* Like to Be on the Red Carpet? One Expert Tells All', *Vanity Fair*, February 2017, http://www.vanityfair.com/style/2017/02/oscars-red-carpet-expert/
7. Boorstin, *The Image*, 246.
8. Photographic records can be found on the Getty Images and Flickr websites. See item #107420252 in Getty Images, https://www.gettyimages.co.uk, and the 'Washington Area Spark' collection in Flickr, https://www.flickr.com/photos/washington_area_spark/sets/72157647077464017/
9. It took eight years for the second African American, James Baskett, to win an (honorary) Oscar for his portrayal of Uncle Remus in *Song of the South* (Walt Disney, 1946). Frederick Gooding, Jr. argues that these roles perpetuated and normalised the servile and passive behaviour of black people towards the white. Gooding, Jr., *Black Oscars*, 48–9.
10. Smithsonian Channel, 'The Horrific Bigotry Endured by This "Gone with the Wind" Star', *YouTube*, https://www.youtube.com/watch?v=in_xAcNZYRw/

11. The history of Hollywood and Nazism is complex. See Steven J. Ross, *Hitler in Los Angeles: How Jews Foiled Nazi Plots Against Hollywood and America* (New York, NY: Bloomsbury, 2017).

12. Murray Zuckoff, 'Demonstrations at Oscar Ceremonies Scheduled Over Redgrave Nomination', *Jewish Telegraphic Agency Daily News Bulletin*, 30 March 1978, 4.

13. Aljean Harmetz, 'Oscar-Winning "Deer Hunter" is Under Attack as "Racist" Film', *The New York Times*, 26 April 1979, C15.

14. Jesse Green, 'The Year of the Ribbon', *The New York Times*, 3 May 1992, section 9, 7.

15. Bernard Weinraub, 'A Day to Demonstrate Affection for the Stars and Some Dismay', *The New York Times*, 31 March 1992, C13.

16. Clarence Page, 'A Purple Ribbon for Urban Violence? It Could Be a Start', *Chicago Tribune*, 7 April 1993, https://www.chicagotribune.com/news/ct-xpm-1993-04-07-9304070054-story.html/

17. 'Hollywood: Reaction to Honorary Oscar for Kazan', Story no. 113292, *AP Archive*, 22 March 1999, http://www.aparchive.com/metadata/youtube/6865fa43e18f37c50251a9dddd97a595/

18. 'US Oscar Protest', Story no. 596783, *AP Archive*, 22 February 2009, http://www.aparchive.com/metadata/youtube/8582352157e5b499787bf0c5216d7c82/

19. Marlon Brando Biography by Turner Classic Movies, *YouTube*, https://www.youtube.com/watch?v=4O2xT2XLhIM

20. 'On with Show Business', *Women's Wear Daily*, 12 March 1999, 29.

21. Emma Akbareian, 'Tom Ford Hits Back at #Askhermore Red Carpet Dress Controversy', *The Independent*, 2 March 2015.

22. Oscar Pre Show Memo, 16 March 2003, Series 1, Box 3, f. 17 Awards 75rd Annual Academy Awards Pre-Show 2003 Correspondence, Stephen L. Pouliot Collection, Marquette University; Untitled questionnaire for interviews, 19 March 2003, Series 1, Box 3, f. 22 Awards 75rd Annual Academy Awards Pre-Show 2003 Miscellaneous, Stephen L. Pouliot Collection, Marquette University.

23. 'Red Carpet's Big Bust: Fashion Counts Costs of Hype-Less Oscars – Losing the Name Game', *WWW Thursday*, 25 March 2003, 6.

24. Ibid., 18.

25. Elizabeth Logan, 'Emma Stone Scores a Major Fashion Campaign as the New Face of Louis Vuitton', *W Magazine*, 7 October 2017, https://www.wmagazine.com/story/emma-stone-louis-vuitton-fashion-contract/

26. ET Canada, 'Kelly Ripa Addresses Ryan Seacrest Allegations', *YouTube*, https://www.youtube.com/watch?v=foaRKm6ZBL4/

27. W065234 66th Academy Awards AMPAS FASHION SHOW TV coverage E!, 1993, Pickford Center, AMPAS.

28. Ibid.

29. Generic Questions and Dress Questions, Series 1, Box 3, f. 34 Awards 77rd Annual Academy Awards Pre-Show 2005 Miscellaneous, Stephen L. Pouliot Collection, Marquette University.

30. W072315 Main Floor/Academy Awards Fashions: Setting the Trends, 69th Annual Academy Awards, Episode #325, 1996, Pickford Center, AMPAS.

31. Ibid.

32. The goals of the movement have since expanded, and now it 'aims to create a society free of gender-based discrimination in the workplace and beyond', https://timesupnow.org/about/

33. 'The 2018 Golden Globes: The Message Behind the BLACK Dress Code', *Furinsider*, 6 January 2018, https://www.furinsider.com/2018-golden-globes-message-behind-black-dress-code/

34. Brooke Bobb, 'What Jane Fonda's 1972 Oscar Suit Can Teach Us About #MeToo at the Golden Globes', *Vogue*, 5 January 2018, https://www.vogue.com/article/fashion-runway-golden-globe-awards-2017-metoo-black-dress-code/

35. Jenny McCartney, 'Is This Feminism', *The Spectator*, 3 March 2018, https://www.spectator.co.uk/article/is-this-feminism-/

36. Lisa Amstrong, 'Why the Oscars Called TimesUp on the Black Dress Code', *Stuff*, 5 March 2018, https://www.stuff.co.nz/life-style/fashion/101968008/why-the-oscars-called-timesup-on-the-black-dress-code/

37. Emma Dibdin, 'Will Celebrities Wear Black on the Oscars', *Cosmopolitan*, 23 February 2018, https://www.cosmopolitan.com/entertainment/movies/a18698575/will-celebrities-wear-black-to-oscars-red-carpet/

38. Ibid.

39. Cara Buckley, 'We Asked Oscar Stars About #MeToo. Here's What They Said', *The New York Times*, 4 March 2018, https://www.nytimes.com/2018/03/04/movies/oscars-metoo-response-red-carpet.html/

40. Jocelyn Noveck, 'No Dress Code, But Plenty of References to #MeToo at Oscars', *The Denver Post*, 4 March 2018, https://www.denverpost.com/2018/03/04/metoo-references-2018-oscars/

41. Jenna Ross, '#MeToo Takes Muted Tone on Oscars Red Carpet', *Star Tribune*, 4 March 2018, https://www.startribune.com/metoo-takes-muted-tone-on-oscars-red-carpet/475787403/

42. Anna North, '#MeToo at the 2018 Oscars: The Good, The Bad, and The in Between', *Vox*, 5 March 2018, https://www.vox.com/2018/3/5/17079702/2018-oscars-me-too-times-up-frances-mcdormand-jimmy-kimmel/

43. Christian Allaire, *Vogue*, 24 February 2019, https://www.vogue.com/article/billy-porter-oscars-red-carpet-gown-christian-siriano/

44. Ibid.

45. Jacob Sarkisian, 'People are Calling Natalie Portman a Hypocrite for her Snubbed Female Directors Dress as her Own Production Company Only Features one Female Director – Herself', *Insider*, 10 February 2020, https://www.insider.com/oscars-natalie-portman-labelled-hypocrite-for-snubbed-female-directors-dress-2020-2/

46. Lindsey Ellefson, 'Rose McGowan Dismisses Natalie Portman's Oscar Outfit Honouring Female Directors as "Deeply Offensive"', *The Wrap*, 12 February 2020, https://www.thewrap.com/rose-mcgowan-dismisses-natalie-portman-oscars-outfit/

47. Charlotte Cowles, 'Was Helen Hunt Paid to Wear H&M at the Oscars?' *The Cut*, 25 February 2013, https://www.thecut.com/2013/02/was-helen-hunt-paid-to-wear-hm-at-the-oscars.html

48. 'About', Red Carpet Green Dress, https://www.rcgdglobal.com

49. Cynthia Littleton, 'Sharing Stories of Sexual Harassment in Hollywood', *Variety*, 12 October 2017, https://variety.com/2017/biz/news/rita-moreno-sexual-harassment-fox-1950s-studio-1202589012/

50. W095532 AFA Compilation 81st Annual Academy Awards pre-show and show, Pickford Center, AMPAS.

51. CPP Luxury, 'The House of Elsa Schiaparelli Makes Controversial Come-Back with Collection Not For Sale', 2 July 2014, https://cpp-luxury.com/the-house-of-elsa-schiaparelli-makes-controversial-come-back-with-collection-not-for-sale/

52. 'Resurrection of an Iconic Costume Designer', *The Hollywood Reporter*, 4 October 2017, 72.

53. Buz Kohan, 'Oscars Flashback: When the Academy Awards "Had to Deal with Reagan's Assassination Attempt"', *The Hollywood Reporter*, 4 March 2016, https://www.hollywoodreporter.com/news/oscars-flashback-academy-awards-had-867991/

54. AP, 'Lancome Taps Lupita Nyong'o as First Black Ambassador', *Business of Fashion*, 4 April 2014, https://www.businessoffashion.com/articles/news-analysis/lancome-taps-lupita-nyongo-first-black-ambassador/

55. Tre'vell Anderson, 'Rihanna Makes History as Dior's First Black Star', *Los Angeles Times*, 18 March 2015, https://www.latimes.com/fashion/alltherage/la-ar-rihanna-history-dior-first-black-star-20150318-story.html; Marjon Carlos, 'Willow Smith is Chanel's New Ambassador', *Vogue*, 8 March 2016, https://www.vogue.com/article/willow-smith-chanel-karl-lagerfeld-paris-fashion-week/

56. Lupita Nyong'o, *Sulwe* (New York: Simon & Schuster, 2019).

57. Grant, 'Limousines: Drive, They Said, on Oscar Night', *Los Angeles Times*, 28 March 1982, L30.

# Appendix

**Table A.1** List of fashion-related roles at the Academy Awards ceremony, 1953–2016

| Year | Ceremony | Name | Role |
|------|----------|------|------|
| 1953 | 25th | Edith Head | Fashion consultant |
| 1954 | 26th | Edith Head | Fashion consultant |
| 1955 | 27th | Edith Head | Fashion consultant |
| 1956 | 28th | Edith Head | Fashion consultant |
| 1957 | 29th | Edith Head | Fashion consultant |
| 1958 | 30th | Edith Head | Fashion consultant |
| | | Helen Rose, Jean Louis, Howard Shoup, Charles LeMaire, Renie Conley, Edward Stevenson and Gwen Wakeling, Bill Thomas. | Uncredited collaborators |
| 1959 | 31th | Edith Head | Fashion consultant |
| | | Donfeld | Special coordinator |
| 1960 | 32nd | Edith Head | Fashion consultant |
| | | Donfeld | Special coordinator |
| 1961 | 33rd | Edith Head | Fashion consultant |
| | | Donfeld | Costume coordinator |
| 1962 | 34th | Edith Head | Fashion consultant |
| | | Donfeld | Assistant to producer Arthur Freed |
| 1963 | 35th | Edith Head | Fashion consultant |
| 1964 | 36th | Edith Head | Fashion consultant |
| 1965 | 37th | Edith Head | Costume supervisor |
| | | Michael Travis | Costume designer |
| 1966 | 38th | Edith Head | Costume supervisor |
| | | Michael Travis | Costume designer |

| 1967 | 39th | Edith Head | Costume supervisor |
|------|------|------------|--------------------|
|      |      | Michael Travis | Costume designer |
| 1968 | 40th | Edith Head | Costume supervisor |
|      |      | Michael Travis | Costume designer |
| 1969 | 41st | Ray Aghayan | Costume designer/consultant |
| 1970 | 42nd | Edith Head | Costume consultant |
|      |      | Moss Mabry | Costume coordinator |
| 1971 | 43rd | Edith Head | Costume consultant |
|      |      | Bob Mackie | Costume designer |
| 1972 | 44th | Ray Aghayan | Costume designer |
|      |      | Bob Mackie | Costume designer |
| 1973 | 45th | Ray Aghayan | Costume designer |
|      |      | Bob Mackie | Costume designer |
| 1974 | 46th | Michael Travis | Costume designer |
|      |      | Waldo Angelo | Costume designer |
| 1975 | 47th | Walt Hoffman | Costumes |
| 1976 | 48th | Ray Aghayan | Costumes |
|      |      | Bob Mackie | Costumes |
|      |      | Ret Turner | Costumes |
| 1977 | 49th | Ray Aghayan | Costumes |
|      |      | Theoni Aldredge | Costume designer |
|      |      | Bob Mackie | Costumes |
| 1978 | 50th | Moss Mabry | Costume designer |
|      |      | Theoni Aldredge | Costume designer |
| 1979 | 51st | Ron Talsky | Costume designer |
| 1980 | 52nd | Bob Mackie | Costume designer |
| 1981 | 53rd | Theoni Aldredge | Costume designer |
| 1982 | 54th | Bob Mackie | Costume designer |
|      |      | Elizabeth Courtney | Costume designer |
| 1983 | 55th | Ray Aghayan | Costume designer |
| 1984 | 56th | Ron Talsky | Costume designer |
| 1985 | 57th | Theoni Aldredge | Costume designer |
| 1986 | 58th | Nolan Miler | Costume designer |
| 1987 | 59th | Theoni Aldredge | Costume designer |

| 1988 | 60th | Bob Mackie | Costume designer |
|------|------|------------|------------------|
| | | Ray Aghayan | Costume designer |
| 1989 | 61st | Fred Hayman | Fashion coordinator |
| | | Pete Menefee | Costume design |
| 1990 | 62nd | Fred Hayman | Fashion coordinator |
| | | Ray Aghayan | Costume designer |
| 1991 | 63rd | Fred Hayman | Fashion coordinator |
| | | Ray Aghayan | Costume designer |
| 1992 | 64th | Fred Hayman | Fashion coordinator |
| | | Ray Aghayan | Costume designer |
| 1993 | 65th | Fred Hayman | Fashion coordinator |
| | | Ray Aghayan | Costume designer |
| 1994 | 66th | Fred Hayman | Fashion coordinator |
| | | Ray Aghayan | Costume designer |
| 1995 | 67th | Fred Hayman | Fashion coordinator |
| 1996 | 68th | Fred Hayman | Fashion coordinator |
| | | Matthew Rolston | |
| 1997 | 69th | Fred Hayman | Fashion coordinator |
| 1998 | 70th | Fred Hayman | Fashion coordinator |
| 1999 | 71st | Fred Hayman | Fashion coordinator |
| | | Ray Aghayan | Costume designer |
| 2000 | 72nd | L'Wren Scott | Stylist |
| 2001 | 73rd | Patty Fox | Fashion coordinator |
| | | Ray Aghayan | Costume designer |
| 2002 | 74th | Patty Fox | Fashion coordinator |
| | | Ann Roth | Costume designer |
| 2003 | 75th | Patty Fox | Fashion coordinator |
| 2004 | 76th | Patty Fox | Fashion coordinator |
| | | Ret Turner | Costume designer |
| 2005 | 77th | Patty Fox | Fashion coordinator |
| 2006 | 78th | Patty Fox | Fashion coordinator |
| 2007 | 79th | André Leon Talley | |
| 2008 | 80th | Patty Fox | Fashion coordinator |
| | | Katja Cahill | Costume coordinator |

| 2009 | 81st | Patty Fox | Fashion coordinator |
|------|------|-----------|---------------------|
|      |      | Katja Cahill | Costume supervisor |
| 2010 | 82nd | Patty Fox | Fashion coordinator |
|      |      | Toni Pickett (stylist) | Assistant fashion coordinator |
|      |      | Rita Ryack | Costume designer |
| 2011 | 83rd | Toni Pickett (stylist) | Fashion coordinator |
|      |      | Paula Elins | Costume designer |
| 2012 | 84th | Paula Elins | Costume designer |
| 2013 | 85th | Julie Weiss | Co-costume designer |
|      |      | Bruce Pask | Co-costume designer |
| 2014 | 86th | Julie Weiss | Co-costume designer |
|      |      | Bruce Pask | Co-costume designer |
|      |      | Christine Cover Ferro | Assistant costume designer |
| 2015 | 87th | Julie Weiss | Costume designer |
|      |      | Hope Slepak | Costume supervisor |
|      |      | Christine Cover Ferro | Assistant costume designer |
| 2016 | 88th | Daria Hines | Costume designer |
|      |      | Jilian Atun | Costume coordinator |

**Table A.2** Fashion brands officially credited as contributors to the Academy Awards ceremony, 1989–2017

| Year | Ceremony | Fashion brands |
|------|----------|----------------|
| 1989 | 61st (1988) | Giorgio Armani, Geoffrey Beene, Marc Bohan for Christian Dior, Perry Ellis, Luis Estevez, Carolina Herrera, Tommy Hilfiger, Jera, Donna Karan, Calvin Klein, Bob Mackie, Oscar de la Renta, Carolyne Roehm, Arnold Scaasi, Gail Simms, Yves Saint Laurent, Vicky Tiel, Bill Travilla and Stephen Yearick |
| 1990 | 62nd (1989) | Loris Azzaro, Geoffrey Beene, Eva Chun, Victor Costa, Oscar de la Renta, Pamela Dennis, Giorgio di Sant Angelo, Fabrice, Ann Lawrence, Bob Mackie, Mignon, Roland Nivelais, Carolyne Roehm, Arnold Scaasi, Gail Simms, Vicky Tiel, Bill Travilla and Stephen Yearick |
| 1991 | 63rd (1990) | Geoffrey Beene, Bill Blass, Chanel, Oscar de la Renta, Pamela Dennis, Dior, Giorgio di Sant'Angelo, Fabrice, Fred Hayman Beverly Hills, Genny, Albert Capraro, Ann Lawrence, Bob Mackie, Mary McFadden, Carolyne Roehm, Arnold Scaasi, Stephen Yearick, Eva Chun, Mignon, Van Cleef & Arpels, Valentino, Versace, Vicky Tiel and Harry Winston |
| 1992 | 64th (1991) | Giorgio Armani (Billy Crystal's tuxedo)<br>Giorgio Armani, Bill Blass, Marc Bouwer, Eva Chun, Pamela Dennis, Christian Dior, Giorgio di Sant' Angelo, Fred Hayman Beverly Hills, Karl Lagerfeld, Karl Lagerfeld for Chanel, Bob Mackie, Mary McFadden, Zandra Rhodes, Scaasi, Ungaro, Van Cleef & Arpels, Versace, Harry Winston and Zang Toi |

| 1993 | 65th (1992) | Giorgio Armani (Billy Crystal's tuxedo)<br>Donna Karan (Liza Minnelli's gown)<br>Anna Sui, Badgley Mischka, Bob Mackie, Carolina Herrera, Christian Lacroix, Donna Karan, Eva Chun, Genny, Geoffrey Beene, Gianni Versace, Giorgio Armani, Givenchy, House of Harry Winston, Karl Lagerfeld, Krizia, Mary McFadden, Pamela Dennis, Todd Oldham, Van Cleef & Arpels, Vicky Tiel, Yves Saint Laurent, Zandra Rhodes and Zang Toi |
|---|---|---|
| 1994 | 66th (1993) | Giorgio Armani (Whoopi Goldberg's wardrobe)<br>Alaïa, Badgely Meschka, Carolina Herrera, Cerruti Tux, Christian Dior, Christian Lacroix, Eric Gaskins, Escada, Alberta Ferretti, Genny, Gianfranco Ferré, Gianfranco Ferré Tux, Hic, Hubert Franco, Kathryn Dianos, Karl Lagerfeld, Krizia, Laura Biagiotti, Mary McFadden, Moschino, Nina Perenna, Pamela Dennis, Robert Danes, Scaasi, Thierry Mugler, Todd Oldham, Ungaro, Vera Wang, Vicky Tiel and Yves Saint Laurent |
| 1995 | 67th (1994) | Anna Sui, Badgely Mischka, Bradley Bayou, Bryon Lars, Calvin Klein by Scott Hill, Carmen Mark Valvo, Carolina Herrera, Chloé, Escada, Fernando Sanchez, Fred Hayman Beverly Hills, Genny, Gianfranco Ferré, Giorgio Armani, Isaac Mizrahi, Jeanette Kastenberg, John Galliano, Karl Lagerfeld, Krizia, Nicole Miller, Pamela Barrish, Pamela Dennis, Rena Lange, Robert Massimo Freda, Todd Oldham, Ungaro, Vera Wang, Vicky Tiel, Yves Saint Laurent, Whiting & Davis and Zang Toi |
| 1996 | 68th (1995) | Andre Van Pier, Anna Sui, Badgley Mischka, Balenciaga, Bill Kaiserman for Sami Dinar, Byblios, Byron Lars, Carlos Marquez LTD, Carmen Marc Valvo, Carolina Herrera, Chanel, Chloé, Christian Dior, Claude Montana, Debra Moises, Diego Dellvalle, Donna Karan, Emmanuel Ungaro, Escada, Finale Gloves, Fred Hayman Beverly Hills, Gaspar Saldanha, Genny, Gianfranco Ferré, Issey Miyake, Jackie Rogers, Jeannette Kastenberg, John Anthony, Karl Lagerfeld, Lawrence Steele, L.A. Eyeworks, Luxxotica, Manolo Blahnik, Mark Bouwer, Matsuda, New Republic, Nolan Miller, Paco Rabanne, Pamela Barrish, Todd Oldham, Thierry Mugler, Tomasz Starzewski, Vera Wang, Vicky Tiel, Zandra Rhodes, Zang Toi, Manaudieres provided by Judith Leiber |
| 1997 | 69th (1996) | Giorgio Armani (Billy Crystal's tuxedo)<br>Alberto Ferretti, Angel Sanchez, Anna Sui, Badgley Mischka, Balenciaga, Bob Mackie, CD Greene, Carlos Marquez, Carmen Marc Valvo, Chloé, Debra Moises, Emanuel Ungaro, Eric Gaskins, Escada, Galanos, Gianfranco Ferré, Giorgio Armani, Holly Harp, Isabelle Kristensen, J.P. Todd, Jackie Rodgers, Jean-Louis Scherrer, Jean-Paul Gaultier, Jeannette Kastenberg, Lanvin, Manolo Blahnik, Marc Bouwer, Maria Dionyssiou, Maria Grachvogel, Mary McFadden, Moschino, New Republic, Paco Rabanne, Pamela Barrish, Pamela Dennis, Rifat Ozbek, Scott Hill for Donna Karan, Sophie Garel, Stephen Yearick, Todd Oldham, Vera Wang, Vestimenta, Vicky Tiel, Vivienne Tam and Zang Tot |
| 1998 | 70th (1997) | Giorgio Armani (Billy Crystal's tuxedo)<br>Adrienne Landau, Angel Sanchez, Badgley Mischka, Balenciaga, Bill Blass, Bob Mackie, Christian Dior, Debra Moises, Emanuel Ungaro, Gianfranco Ferré, Guy Laroche, Halston, Han Feng, Isabell, Kristensen, Issey Miyake, Jacques Azagury, Jaanette Kastenberg, John Galliano for Fred Hayman Beverly Hills, Marc Bouwer, Maria Dionyssiou, Mary McFadden, Moschino, Paco Rabanne, Pamela Dennis, Sophie Sitbon, Thierry Mugler, Vicky Tiel, Vivienne Tam, Zandra Rhodes, Giorgio Armani, Scott Hill for Donna Karan, Tommy Hilfiger and Fred Hayman Beverly Hills |

| 1999 | 71st (1998) | Amsale, Angel Sanchez, Badgley Mischka, Betsey Johnson, Bill Blass, Bob Mackie, CD Greene, Carmen Marc Valvo, Chado-Ralph Rucci, Chloé by Stella McCartney, Christian Dior by John Galliano, Cynthia Rowley, Debra Moises, Dolce & Gabbana, Elizabeth Galindo, Emmanuel Ungaro, Gianfranco Ferre, Giorgio Armani, Guy Laroche, Issey Miyake, Jacques Azagury, Jeanette Kastenberg, Jessica McClintock, Junko Koshino, Kenth Andersson, Lane Davis, Lanvin, Lee Young Hee, Manolo, Marc Bouvier, Mary McFadden, Maurizio Galante, Michelle Lacy, Mila Schon, Oliver & Company, Pamela Dennis, Pamela McMahon, Randolph Duke, Shangum Tang, Tommy Hilfiger, Tuleh, Vera Wang, Vicky Tiel, Vivienne Westwood and Zandra Rhodes<br>Special acknowledgements: Saks Fifth Avenue, Beverly Hills<br>Shoes: Donald J. Pliner, Figueroa, Jimmy Choo, Manolo Blahnik, Saks Fifth Avenue, Salvatore Ferragamo, Stuart Weitzman, Vanessa Noel, Yves Saint Laurent<br>Bags: Absolute Necessities, Daniel, Swarovski, Judith Lieber, Katherine Baumann, Lana Marks, Lily<br>Eyewear by Morgenthal Frederics<br>Additional accessories by Emporio Armani, Frederic Fekkai, Tarina Tarantino |
|------|------------|------------------------------------------------------------------------------------------------------------------------------------------------------------------------------------------------------------------------------------------|
| 2000 | 72nd (1999) | Timothy Everest, Donna Karan New York, Chloé by Stella McCartney, Giorgio Armani<br>Eyewear: Cutler & Gross<br>Hats: Stephen Jones<br>Ladies' shoes: Jimmy Choo<br>Men's shoes: Oliver Sweeney, Michael Sharkey, Barney's NY, John Hayles, Robert Farrell |
| 2001 | 73rd (2000) | Anne Klein, Badgley Mischka, Bill Blass, Bob Mackie, Carolina Herrera, Chanel, Christian Dior, Dolce & Gabbana, Donald Deal, Donna Karan, Halston, Jimmy Choo, Joanna Mastroianni, John Galliano, Marc Jacobs, Marc Bouwer, Michael Kors, Oscar de la Renta, Pamela Dennis, Reem Akra, Richard Tyler, Saks Fifth Avenue, Vera Wang |
| 2002 | 74th (2001) | No mention of a direct collaboration with designers. Only contributions except for gift bags |
| 2003 | 75th (2002) | Giorgio Armani (Steve Martin's tuxedo)<br>Angel Sanchez, Arnold Scaasi, B Michael, Bob Mackie, Bradley Bayou, Brioni, Christian Dior, Council of Fashion Designers of America, David Cardona, Elie Saab, Ermenegildo Zegna, Escada, Gemma Kahng, Gianfranco Ferré, Herve Leger, Hugo Boss, Hylan Booker, Jackie Rogers, Joan Vass, John Anthony, Kay Unger, Kevan Hall, Lloyd Klein, Monique Lhuillier, Reem Acra, Richard Tyler, Saks Fifth Avenue, Stephen Borrows, Sully Bonnelly, Tom & Linda Platt, Valentino, Yeohlee, Zandra Rhodes and Zang Toi<br>Accessories: Carolina Amato, Kate Spade, Lana Marks, Nancy Giest, Robin Piccone, Sigerson Morrison, Stuart Weitzman and Vanessa Noel |
| 2004 | 76th (2003) | Giorgio Armani (Billy Crystal's tuxedo)<br>Angel Sanchez, Bill Blass, Christian Dior, Donald J. Pliner, Elie Tahari, Gianfranco Ferré, Halston, Herve Leger, Hugo Boss, Jackie Rogers, Jhane Barnes, John Varvatos, Kay Unger, Kevan Hall, Luca Luca, Monique Lhuillier, Morgane Le Fay, Nicole Miller, Reem Acra, Richard Tyler, Rikke Gudnitz, Saks Fifth Avenue, Stuart Weitzman, Sully Bonnelly, Sylvia Heisel, Valentino and Zang Toi |
| 2005 | 77th (2004) | Giorgio Armani (Chris Rock's tuxedo)<br>Afshin Feiz, Angel Sanchez, Badgley Mischka, Bill Blass, Bradley Bayou for Halston, Brian Cook, Christian Dior, Chrome Hearts, Colleen Quen, David Meister, David Rodriguez, Dolce & Gabbana, Douglas Hannant, Gianfranco Ferré, Isaac Mizrahi, Jennifer Nicholson, Jeremy Scott, Jhane Barnes, Kay Unger, Kevan Hall, Krizia, Luca Luca, Marc Bouwer, Monique Lhuillier, Ralph Lauren, Reem Acra, Richard Tyler, Sully Bonnelly, Sunny Choi, Sylvia Heisel, Tom & Linda Platt, Valentino and Zegna |

| 2006 | 78th (2005) | Ralph Lauren Black Label (Jon Stewart's tuxedo) Badgley Mischka, Bill Blass, Carolina Herrera, CD Greene, Christian Dior, Colleen Quen, David Rodriguez, Douglas Hannant, Elie Saab, Escada, Georges Chakra, Gianfranco Ferré, Halston, Isaac Mizrahi, Jennifer Nicholson, Josef Statkus Couture, Junko Yoshioka, Kai Milla, Kay Unger, Kevan Hall, Krizia, Lanvin, Lily et Cie, Marc Bouwer, Monique Lhuillier, Olga Simonov, Pamella Rolland, Randolph Duke, Reem Acra, Richard Tyler, Scott & Co., Sylvia Heisel, Tom & Linda Platt, Valentino and T&Kei |
|------|------------|----------------------------------------------------------------------------------------------------------------|
| 2007 | 79th (2006) | No mention of a direct collaboration with designers |
| 2008 | 80th (2007) | Giorgio Armani (Jon Stewart's tuxedo) Reem Acra, Giorgio Armani, Oscar de la Renta, Pamela Dennis, Randolph Duke, Kevan Hall, Lloyd Klein, Marchesa, Isaac Mizrahi, Zuhair Murad, Lorenzo Riva, Pamella Roland, Elie Saab, Angel Sanchez, Valentino and Ella Zahlan |
| 2009 | 81st (2008) | No mention of a direct collaboration with designers |
| 2010 | 82nd (2009) | No mention of a direct collaboration with designers |
| 2011 | 83rd (2010) | No mention of a direct collaboration with designers |
| 2012 | 84th (2011) | Giorgio Armani (Billy Crystal's tuxedos) |
| 2013 | 85th (2012) | Gucci (Seth MacFarlane's tuxedos) |
| 2014 | 86th (2013) | No mention of a direct collaboration with designers |
| 2015 | 87th (2014) | No mention of a direct collaboration with designers |
| 2016 | 88th (2015) | No mention of a direct collaboration with designers |
| 2017 | 89th (2016) | No mention of a direct collaboration with designers |

# Archives

Anna-Maria and Stephen Kellen Design Archives, the Parsons New School for Design.
Archives of American Television, Television Academy Foundation.
Avenir Museum of Design and Merchandising, Colorado State University.
Billy Rose Theatre Division, The New York Public Library for the Performing Arts, Dorothy and Lewis B. Cullman Center.
Charles E. Young Research Library, University of California, Los Angeles.
David M. Rubenstein Rare Book & Manuscript Library, Duke University.
Delta Flight Museum Digital Archive.
Doheny Memorial Library, University of Southern California.
FDR Presidential Library & Museum.
Gladys Marcus Library Special Collections & College Archives, Fashion Institute of Technology.
Hagley Museum and Library.
Harry Ransom Centre, The University of Texas at Austin.
Los Angeles Public Library.
Manuscripts and Archives Division, The New York Public Library.
Margaret Herrick Library, Academy of Motion Picture Arts and Sciences.
MCNY Archive, Museum of the City of New York.
Moving Image Research Collections, University of South Carolina.
National Museum of American History, Smithsonian Institution Archives.
New York Historical Society Library.
Pickford Center for Motion Picture Research, Academy of Motion Picture Arts and Sciences
Raynor Memorial Libraries, Marquette University.
Special Collections and College Archives, Fashion Institute of Technology.
The British Library Sound Archive.
The Brooke Russell Astor Reading Room for Rare Books and Manuscripts, New York Public Library.
The Paley Center for Media.
Thomas J. Watson Library, The Metropolitan Museum of Art.
UCLA Film & Television Archive, University of California, Los Angeles.
Wisconsin Center for Film and Theater Research, Wisconsin Historical Society.

# Bibliography

Abel, Richard. *Menus for Movieland: Newspapers and the Emergence of American Film Culture 1913–1916*. Oakland, CA: University of California Press, 2015.

Amory, Cleveland. *Who Killed Society?* Whitefish, MT: Literary Licensing, LLC, 2012 [New York, NY: Harpers & Brothers Publishers, 1960].

Amory, Cleveland, Earl Blackwell and Sidney Wolfe Cohen. *International Celebrity Register*. New York, NY: Celebrity Register, LTD, 1959.

Anderson, Christopher. *Hollywood TV: The Studio System in the Fifties*. Austin, TX: University of Texas Press, 1994.

Anselmo-Sequeira, Diana. 'Apparitional Girlhood: Material Ephemerality and the Historiography of Female Adolescence in Early American Film'. *Spectator* (2013), http://works.bepress.com/diana_anselmo-sequeira/2/

Apodaca, Rose. *Fred Hayman, The Extraordinary Difference: The Story of Rodeo Drive, Hollywood Glamour and the Showman Who Sold It All*. Venice, CA: A+R Projects, 2011.

Appadurai, Arjun. *Modernity at Large: Cultural Dimensions of Globalization*. Minneapolis, MN: University of Minnesota Press, 1996.

Arnold, Rebecca. *The American Look: Fashion, Sportswear and the Image of Women in 1930s and 1940s New York*. New York, NY: I.B. Tauris, 2009.

Balio, Tino, ed. *Grand Design: Hollywood as a Modern Business Enterprise, 1930–1939*. Berkeley, CA: University of California Press, 1995.

Barbas, Samantha. *Movie Crazy: Fans, Stars, and the Cult of Celebrity*. New York, NY: Palgrave, 2001.

Barbas, Samantha. *First Lady of Hollywood: A Biography of Louella Parsons*. Oakland, CA: University of California Press, 2005.

Barbas, Samantha. *Laws of Image: Privacy and Publicity in America*. Stanford, CA: Stanford University Press, 2015.

Barnouw, Erik. *The Sponsor: Notes on a Modern Potentate*. Oxford: Oxford University Press, 1979.

Baughman, James L. *Same Time, Same Station: Creating American Television, 1948–1961*. Baltimore, MD: Johns Hopkins University Press, 2007.

Beardsley, Charles. *Hollywood's Master Showman: The Legendary Sid Grauman*. New York, NY: Cornwall Books, 1983.

Bender, Marylin. *The Beautiful People*. New York, NY: Coward-McCann, Inc., 1967.

Benstock, Shari and Susanne Ferriss, eds. *On Fashion*. New Brunswick, NJ: Rutgers University Press, 1994.

Berard, Jeanette M. and Klaudia Englund. *Radio Series Scripts, 1930–2001: A Catalog of the American Radio Archives Collection.* Jefferson, NC: McFarland, 2006.

Bernays, Edward. *Crystallizing Public Opinion.* New York, NY: Ig Publishing, 2011 [1923].

Berry, Sarah. *Screen Style: Fashion and Femininity in 1930s Hollywood.* Minneapolis MN: University of Minnesota Press, 2000.

Black, Sandy, Joanne Entwistle, Agnes Rocamora, Amy De La Haye and Helen Thomas, eds. *The Handbook of Fashion Studies.* London: A&C Black, 2014.

Blackwell, Richard. *From Rags to Bitches.* Los Angeles, CA: General Publishing Group, Inc., 1995.

Blaszczyk, Regina Lee, ed. *Producing Fashion: Commerce, Culture, and Consumers.* Philadelphia, PA: University of Pennsylvania Press, 2008.

Blaszczyk, Regina Lee. *American Consumer Society, 1865–2005.* Wheeling, IL: Harlan Davidson, Inc., 2005.

Boddy, William. *Fifties Television: The Industry and Its Critics.* Champaign, IL: University of Illinois Press, 1993.

Bolton, Kingsley and Jan Olsson. *Media, Popular Culture, and the American Century.* Stockholm: National Library of Sweden, 2010.

Boorstin, Daniel J. *The Image: A Guide to Pseudo-Events in America.* New York, NY: Vintage, 1992 [1962].

Bordwell, David, Janet Staiger and Kristin Thompson. *The Classical Hollywood Cinema: Film Style and Mode of Production to 1960.* London: Routledge, 1985.

Bourdieu, Pierre. *Distinction: A Social Critique of the Judgement of Taste.* New York, NY: Routledge, 2013 [1979].

Braudy, Leo. *The Frenzy of Renown: Fame and Its History.* New York, NY: Vintage Books, 1997 [1986].

Brown, Judith. *Glamour in Six Dimensions: Modernism and the Radiance of Form.* Ithaca, NY: Cornell University Press, 2009.

Calistro, Paddy and Edith Head. *Edith Head's Hollywood.* Santa Monica, CA: Angel City Press, 2008.

Cashmore, Ellis. *Celebrity Culture.* New York, NY: Routledge, 2014 [2006].

Cashmore, Ellis. *Elizabeth Taylor: A Private Life for Public Consumption.* London: Bloomsbury Academic, 2016.

Castaldo Lundén, Elizabeth. 'Oscar Night in Hollywood: Fashioning the Red-Carpet from the Roosevelt Hotel to International Media'. PhD diss., Stockholm University, 2018.

Church Gibson, Pamela. *Fashion and Celebrity Culture.* London, Berg, 2012.

Clifford, Marie. 'Working with Fashion: The Role of Art, Taste, and Consumerism in Women's Professional Culture, 1920–1940'. *American Studies* 44, no. 1/2 (2003): 59–84.

Cohen, Lizabeth. *A Consumers' Republic: The Politics of Mass Consumption in Post-war America.* New York: Vintage Books, 2003.

Collins, Sue. 'Star Testimonial and Trailers: Mobilizing During World War I'. *Cinema Journal* 57, no. 1 (Fall 2017): 46–70.

Cosgrave, Bronwyn. *Made For Each Other: Fashion and the Academy Awards.* London: Bloomsbury Publishing, 2008.

Crafton, Donald. *The Talkies: American Cinema's Transition to Sound 1926–1931.* Berkeley, CA: University of California Press, 1999.

Critchlow, Donald T. *When Hollywood was Right: How Movie Stars, Studio Moguls, and Big Business Remade American Politics.* New York, NY: Cambridge University Press, 2013.

Cruikshank, Jeffrey and Arthur W. Schultz. *The Man Who Sold America: The Amazing but True Story of Albert D. Lasker and the Creation of the Advertising Century*. Brighton, MA: Harvard Business Press, 2010.

Curran, James, David Morley and Valerie Walkerdine, eds. *Cultural Studies and Communication*. London: Bloomsbury, 1996.

Dayan, Daniel and Elihu Katz. *Media Events: The Live Broadcasting of History*. Cambridge, MA: Harvard University Press, 1992.

Decherney, Peter. *Hollywood and the Culture Elite: How the Movies Became American*. New York, NY: Columbia University Press, 2005.

deCordova, Richard. *Picture Personalities: The Emergence of the Star System in America*. Champaign, IL: University of Illinois Press, 2001 [1990].

de Grazia, Victoria. *Irresistible Empire: America's Advance Through 20th-Century Europe*. Cambridge, MA: Harvard University Press, 2006.

DeJean, Joan. *The Essence of Style*. New York: Free Press, 2005.

Delis Hill, Daniel. *Fashion: From Victoria to the New Millennium*. London: Pearson, 2012.

Desjardins, Mary. '"Marion Never Looked Lovelier": Hedda Hopper's Hollywood and the Negotiation of Glamour in Post-war Hollywood'. *Quarterly Review on Film and Video* 13, no. 3–4 (2009): 421–37, DOI: 10.1080/10509209709361474/.

Desjardins, Mary. *Recycled Stars: Female Film Stardom in the Age of Television and Video*. Durham, NC: Duke University Press, 2015.

Doherty, Thomas Patrick. *Pre-code Hollywood: Sex, Immorality, and Insurrection in American Cinema, 1930–1934*. New York, NY: Columbia University Press, 1999.

Dyer, Richard. *Stars*. London: BFI, 1998 [1975].

Endres, Kathleen L. and Therese L. Lueck, eds. *Women's Periodicals in the United States: Consumer Magazines*. Santa Barbara, CA: Greenwood Publishing Group, 1995.

Engel, Jeffrey A. *The Four Freedoms: Franklin D. Roosevelt and the Evaluation of an American Idea*. Oxford: Oxford University Press, 2016.

English, Bonnie. *A Cultural History of Fashion in the 20th and 21st Centuries: From Catwalk to Sidewalk*, 2nd edn. London: Bloomsbury, 2013.

English, James F. *The Economy of Prestige: Prizes, Awards, and the Articulation of Cultural Value*. Cambridge, MA: Harvard University Press, 2005.

Evans, Caroline. 'The Enchanted Spectacle'. *Fashion Theory: The Journal of Dress, Body & Culture* 5, no. 3 (2001): 271–310.

Faggella, Chiara. 'Not So Simple: Reassessing 1951, G.B. Giorgini and the Launch of Italian Fashion'. PhD diss., Stockholm University, 2019.

Farnan Leipzig, Sheryl, Jean L. Parsons and Jane Farrell-Beck. 'It is a Profession that is New, Unlimited, and Rich: Promotion of the American Designer in the 1930s'. *Dress* 35 (2008–9): 29–47.

Farrell-Beck, Jane and Jean Parsons. *20th Century Dress in the United States*. New York, NY: Fairchild Publication, Inc., 2007.

Feeley, Kathleen A. and Jennifer Frost, eds. *When Private Talk Goes Public: Gossip in American History*. New York, NY: Palgrave Macmillan, 2014.

Fine Collins, Amy. *The International Best-Dressed List: The Official Story*. New York: Rizzoli, 2019.

Fishback, Price, ed. *Government and American Economy: A New History*. Chicago, IL: University of Chicago Press, 2008.

Fonda, Jane. *My Life So Far*. New York, IL: Random House, 2010 [2005].

Foucault, Michel. 'Of Other Spaces'. Jay Miskowiec, trans. *Diacritics* 16, no. 1 (1986): 22–7. DOI: 10.2307/464648/

Fox, Stephen R. *The Mirror Makers: A History of American Advertising and its Creators.* Champaign, IL: University of Illinois Press, 1997 [1984].

Frost, Jennifer. *Hedda Hopper's Hollywood: Celebrity Gossip and American Conservatism.* New York, NY: New York University Press, 2011.

Fuller, Kathryn H. *At the Picture Show: Small-Town Audiences and the Creation of Movie Fan Culture.* Washington, DC: Smithsonian Institution Press, 1997.

Gabler, Neal. *An Empire of Their Own: How the Jews Invented Hollywood.* New York, NY: Anchor Books, 1988.

Gabler, Neal. *Winchell: Gossip, Power and the Culture of Celebrity.* New York, NY: Vintage Books, 1994.

Gaines, Jane and Charlotte Herzog, eds. *Fabrications: Costume and the Female Body.* New York, NY: Routledge, 1990.

Gamman, Lorraine and Margaret Marshment, eds. *The Female Gaze: Women as Viewers of Popular Culture.* London: The Women's Press Ltd, 1988.

Givhan, Robin. *The Battle of Versailles: The Night American Fashion Stumbled into the Spotlight and Made History.* New York, NY: Flatiron Books, 2016.

Golub, Philip S. *Power, Profit & Prestige: A History of American Imperial Expansion.* New York, NY: Pluto Press, 2010.

Gooding, Fredrick, Jr. *Black Oscars: From Mammy to Minny, What the Academy Awards Tells Us About African Americans.* London: Rowman & Littlefield, 2020.

Gregory, Paul M. 'An Economic Interpretation of Women's Fashions'. *Southern Economic Journal* 14, no. 2 (1947): 148–62, DOI: 10.2307/1052931/.

Greig, Hannah. *The Beau Monde: Fashionable Society in Georgian London.* Oxford: Oxford University Press, 2013.

Gundle, Stephen. *Glamour: A History.* Oxford: Oxford University Press, 2008 [2001].

Harrison Martin, Richard. *Charles James.* New York, NY: Universe/Vendome, 1999.

Haven Blake, David. *Liking Ike: Eisenhower, Advertising, and the Rise of Celebrity Politics.* Oxford: Oxford University Press, 2016.

Herman, Edward S. and Noam Chomsky. *Manufacturing Consent: The Political Economy of the Mass Media.* New York, NY: Pantheon Books, 2002 [1988].

Higashi, Sumiko. *Stars, Fans, and Consumption in the 1950s: Reading Photoplay.* New York, NY: Palgrave Macmillan, 2014.

Holmlund, Chris, ed. *American Cinema of the 1990s: Themes and Variations.* New Brunswick, NJ: Rutgers University Press, 2008.

Homberger, Eric. *Mrs. Astor's New York: Money and Social Power in a Gilded Age.* New Haven, CT: Yale University Press, 2004.

Jacobs, Lea. *The Wages of Sin: Censorship and the Fallen Woman Film, 1928–1942.* Berkeley, CA: University of California Press, 1997.

Jenkins, Henry and David Thornurn, eds. *Democracy and New Media.* Cambridge, MA: MIT Press, 2003.

Jones, Geoffrey. 'Globalization and Beauty: A Historical and Firm Perspective'. *EurAmerica* 41, no. 4 (December 2011): 885–916.

Jorgensen, Jay. *Edith Head: The Fifty-Year Career of Hollywood's Greatest Costume Designer.* Philadelphia, PA: Running Press, 2010.

Jorgensen, Jay and Donald L. Scoggins. *Creating the Illusion: A Fashionable History of Hollywood Costume Designers.* Philadelphia, PA: Running Press, 2015.

Kazin, Michael and Joseph A. McCartin, eds. *Americanism: New Perspectives on the History of an Ideal*. Chapel Hill, NC: University of North Carolina Press, 2006.

Khavar Fahlstedt, Kim. 'Chinatown Film Culture: The Appearance of Cinema in San Francisco's Chinese Neighborhood'. PhD diss., Stockholm University, 2016.

Kitch, Carolyn. *The Girl on the Magazine Cover: The Origins of Visual Stereotypes in American Mass Media*. Chapel Hill, NC: University of North Carolina Press, 2001.

Klinger, Barbara. 'Digressions at the Cinema: Reception and Mass Culture'. *Cinema Journal* 28, no. 4 (Summer 1989): 3–19. DOI: 10.2307/1225392/.

Lambert, Eleanor and Bettina Zilkha. *Ultimate Style: The Best of the Best Dressed List*. New York, NY: Assouline, 2004.

Leach, William. *Land of Desire: Merchants, Power, and the Rise of a New American Culture*. New York, NY: Random House, 1993.

Leese, Elizabeth. *Costume Design in the Movies: An Illustrated Guide to the Work of 157 Great Designers*. New York, NY: Dover Publication, Inc., 1991.

Lev, Peter. *The Fifties: Transforming the Screen 1950–1959*. Berkeley, CA: University of California Press, 2003.

Lippmann, Walter. *Public Opinion*. Miami, FL: BN Publishing, 2010 [1922].

Lisicky, Michael J. *Filene's: Boston's Great Specialty Store*. Charleston, SC: Arcadia Publishing, 2012.

Luther Mott, Frank. *American Journalism: A History 1690–1960*, 3rd edn. London: Macmillan, 1962.

McCracken, Grant. 'Culture and Consumption: A Theoretical Account of the Structure and Movement of the Cultural Meaning of Consumer Goods'. *Journal of Consumer Research* 13 (June 1986): 71–89.

McCracken, Grant. 'Who is the Celebrity Endorser? Cultural Foundations of the Endorsement Process'. *Journal of Consumer Research* 16 (December 1989): 310–21, DOI: 10.1086/209217

McCraw, Thomas K. *American Business Since 1920: How it Worked*. Wheeling, IL: Harlan Davidson, 2009 [2000].

McDonald, Paul. *Hollywood Stardom*. Oxford: Wiley-Blackwell, 2013.

McGovern, Charles F. *Sold American: Consumption and Citizenship, 1890–1945*. Chapel Hill, NC: University of North Carolina Press, 2006.

McLean, Adrienne and David Cook. *Headline Hollywood*. New Brunswick, NJ: Rutgers University Press, 2001.

McLuhan, Marshall. *Understanding Media: The Extensions of Man*. London: Routledge, 2001 [1964].

Marketti, Sara B. and Jean L. Parsons. 'American Fashions for American Women: Early Twentieth Century Efforts to Develop and American Fashion Identity'. *Dress* 34, no. 1 (2007): 79–95.

Marshall, P. David and Joanne Morreale. *Advertising and Promotional Culture*. London: Palgrave, 2018.

Mendes, Valerie D. and Amy De La Haye. *Lucile Ltd: London, Paris, New York and Chicago, 1890s–1930s*. London: V&A Publishing, 2009.

Mitchell, George. 'The Movies and Münsterberg'. *Jump Cut* 27 (July 1982): 57–60, http://www.ejumpcut.org/archive/onlinessays/JC27folder/Munsterberg.html

Monaco, Paul. *The Sixties, 1960–1969*. New York: Charles Scribner's Sons, 2001.

Morin, Edgar. *The Stars: An Account of the Star-System in Motion Pictures*, trans. Richard Howard. Minneapolis, MN: University of Minnesota Press, 2005 [1960].

Mower, Jennifer M. and Elaine L. Pedersen. '"Pretty and Patriotic": Women's Consumption of Apparel During World War II'. *Dress* 29, no. 1 (2013): 37–57, https://doi.org/10.1179/0 361211213Z.0000000010

Murray, Susan. *Hitch Your Antenna to the Stars: Early Television and Broadcast Stardom*. New York, NY: Routledge, 2005.

Neale, Steve and Murray Smith, eds. *Contemporary Hollywood Cinema*. London: Routledge, 1998.

Nelson Best, Kate. *The History of Fashion Journalism*. New York, NY: Bloomsbury, 2017.

Nyong'o, Lupita. *Sulwe*. New York: Simon & Schuster, 2019.

Olsson, Jan. 'Screen Bodies and Busybodies: Corporeal Constellations in the Era of Anonymity'. *Film History* 25, no. 1–2 (April 2013): 188–204.

Olsson, Jan. *Hitchcock a la Carte*. Durham, NC: Duke University Press, 2015.

Packard, Vance. *The Hidden Persuaders*. New York, NY: Ig Publishing, 2007 [1957].

Packard, Vance. *The Status Seekers: An Exploration of Class Behavior in America and the Hidden Barriers that Affect You, Your Community, Your Future*. Philadelphia, PA: David McKay Company, Inc., 1958.

Paulicelli, Eugenia. 'Fashion: The Cultural Economy of *Made in Italy*'. *Fashion Practice* 6, no. 2 (2015): 155–74.

Pawlak, Debra Ann. *Bringing Up Oscar: The Story of the Men and Women Who Founded the Academy*. New York, NY: Pegasus Books, 2001.

Peiss, Kathy. *Hope in a Jar: The Making of America's Beauty Culture*. Philadelphia, PA: University of Pennsylvania Press, 2011.

Ponce de Leon, Charles L. *Self-Exposure: Human-Interest Journalism and the Emergence of Celebrity in America, 1890–1940*. Chapel Hill, NC: University of North Carolina Press, 2002.

Pouillard, Véronique. 'Design Piracy in the Fashion Industries of Paris and New York in the Interwar Years'. *Business History Review* 85, no. 2 (2011): 319–44.

Pouillard, Véronique, 'Managing Fashion Creativity: The History of the Chambre Syndicale de la Couture Parisienne During the Interwar Period'. *Economic History Research* 12, no. 2 (June 2016): 76–89, http://dx.doi.org/10.1016/j.ihe.2015.05.002/.

Radosh, Ronald and Allis Radosh. *Red Star Over Hollywood: The Film Colony's Long Romance with the Left*. San Francisco, CA: Encounter Books, 2004.

Rein, Irving, Philip Kotler, Michael Hamlin and Martin Stoller. *High Visibility: Transforming Your Personal and Professional Brand*. New York, NY: McGraw-Hill, 2006.

Resor, Stanley. 'Personalities and the Public: Some Aspects of Testimonial Advertising'. *The J. Walter Thompson News Bulletin* 138 (April 1929).

Ribke, Nahuel. *A Genre Approach to Celebrity Politics: Global Patterns of Passage from Media to Politics*. New York, NY: Palgrave Macmillan, 2015.

Riley, Sam G. *Biographical Dictionary of American Newspaper Columnists*. Santa Barbara, CA: Greenwood Publishing Group, 1995.

Roberts, Sam. *Grand Central: How a Train Station Transformed America*. New York, NY: Grand Central Publishing, 2017.

Ross, Steven J. *Hitler in Los Angeles: How Jews Foiled Nazi Plots Against Hollywood and America*. New York, NY: Bloomsbury, 2017.

Samuel, Lawrence R. *Brought to You By: Postwar Television Advertising and the American Dream*. Austin, TX: University of Texas Press, 2003.

Sandler, Monica. 'PR and Politics at Hollywood's Biggest Night: The Academy Awards and Unionization (1929–1939)'. *Media Industries* 2, no. 2 (2015), DOI: http://dx.doi.org/10.3998/mij.15031809.0002.201/

Schatz, Thomas. *Boom and Bust: American Cinema in the 1940s.* Berkeley, CA: University of California Press, 1999.

Schneirov, Matthew. *The Dream of a New Social Order: Popular Magazines in America 1893–1914.* New York, NY: Columbia University Press, 1994.

Schweitzer, Marlis. 'Patriotic Acts of Consumption: Lucile (Lady Duff Gordon) and the Vaudeville Fashion Show Craze'. *Theatre Journal* 60, no. 4 (December 2008): 585–608.

Schweitzer, Marlis. *When Broadway Was the Runway: Theater, Fashion, and American Culture.* Philadelphia, PA: University of Pennsylvania Press, 2009.

Seebohm, Caroline. *The Man Who Was Vogue: The Life and Times of Condé Nast.* New York, NY: The Viking Press, 1982.

Segrave, Kerry. *Endorsements in Advertising: A Social History.* Jefferson, NC: McFarland & Company, Inc., 2005.

Shields, David. *Still: American Silent Motion Picture Photography.* Chicago, IL: University of Chicago Press, 2013.

Sivulka, Juliann. *Ad Women: How They Impact What We Need, Want, and Buy.* New York, NY: Prometheus Book, 2009.

Spanabel Emery, Joy. *A History of the Paper Pattern Industry: The Home Dressmaking Fashion Revolution.* London: Bloomsbury Academic, 2014.

Spigel, Lynn. *Make Room for TV: Television and the Family Ideal in Postwar America.* Chicago, IL: University of Chicago Press, 1992.

Stacey, Jackie. *Star Gazing: Hollywood Cinema and Female Spectatorship.* New York, NY: Routledge, 1994.

Stadiem, William. *Jet Set: The People, the Planes, the Glamour, and the Romance in Aviation's Glory Years.* New York, NY: Random House, 2014.

Staiger, Janet. 'Announcing Wares, Winning Patrons, Voicing Ideals: Thinking about the History and Theory of Film Advertising'. *Cinema Journal* 29, no. 3 (1990): 3–31.

Staiger, Janet. 'Seeing Stars'. *The Velvet Trap* 20 (Summer 1983): 10–14.

Steele, Valerie. 'Anti-Fashion: The 1970s'. *Fashion Theory* 1, no. 3 (1997): 280–1.

Steele, Valerie. *Paris Fashion: A Cultural History.* London: Bloomsbury, 2017 [1988].

Sumner, David E. *The Magazine Century: American Magazines since 1900.* New York, NY: Peter Lang Publishing, 2010.

Sutton, Denise H. *Globalizing Ideal Beauty: How Female Copywriters of the J. Walter Thompson Advertising Agency Redefined Beauty for the Twentieth Century.* New York, NY: Palgrave Macmillan, 2009.

Tolini Finamore, Michelle. *Hollywood Before Glamour: Fashion in American Silent Film.* New York, NY: Palgrave Macmillan, 2013.

Tortora, Phyllis G., ed. *Berg Encyclopedia of World Dress and Fashion: The United States and Canada.* Oxford: Bloomsbury Academic, 2010, http://dx.doi.org/10.2752/BEWDF/EDch3811/

Turim, Maureen. 'Fashion Shapes: Film, the Fashion Industry, and the Image of Women'. *Socialist Review* 71 (1983): 78–96.

Vanderbilt, Arthur T. *Fortune's Children: The Fall of the House of Vanderbilt.* New York, NY: William Morrow, 2001.

Veillon, Dominique. *Fashion Under the Occupation.* New York: Berg Publishers, 2002.

Weinstein, David. *The Forgotten Network: DuMont and the Birth of American Television.* Philadelphia, PA: Temple University Press, 2006.

Welter, Barbara. 'The Cult of True Womanhood: 1820–1860'. *American Quarterly* 18, no. 2 (1966): 151–74.

Welters, Linda and Patricia A. Cunningham, eds. *Twentieth-Century American Fashion*. Oxford: Berg, 2005.

Whannel, Garry. 'News, Celebrity, and Vortextuality: A Study of the Media Coverage of the Michael Jackson Verdict'. *Cultural Politics* 6, no. 1 (2010): 65–84, DOI: http://doi.org/10.2752/175174310X12549254318782/

Whitaker, Jan. *Service and Style: How the American Department Store Fashioned the Middle Class*. New York: St. Martin's Press, 2006.

Willey, Mason, Damien Bona and Gail MacColl. *Inside Oscar: The Unofficial History of the Academy Awards*. Bromley: Columbus Books, 1986.

Williams, Raymond. *Marxism and Literature*. Oxford: Oxford University Press, 1977.

Williams, Raymond. *The Sociology of Culture*. Chicago, IL: University of Chicago Press, 1995 [1981].

Williams, Raymond. *Television: Technology and Cultural Form*. New York: Routledge, 2003 [1974].

Williams Rutherford, Janice. *Selling Mrs. Consumer: Christine Frederick and the Rise of Household Efficiency*. Athens, GA: The University of Georgia Press, 2003.

Wilson, Elizabeth. 'A Note on Glamour'. *Fashion Theory* 11, no. 1 (2007): 95–108.

Woolman Chase, Edna and Ilka Chase. *Always in Vogue*. New York, NY: Doubleday & Company, Inc., 1954.

# Index

All illustrations are shown by a page reference in *italics*.

CPSIA information can be obtained
at www.ICGtesting.com
Printed in the USA
JSHW061540190723
45045JS00003B/31